THE HISTORY OF CONSUMER CREDIT

The History of Consumer Credit

Doctrines and Practices

Rosa-Maria Gelpi
Vice-President, Cetelem
Professor of Economics
Université Libre de Lille
France

and

François Julien-Labruyère
International CEO, member of the Board of Cetelem

Translated by Mn Liam Gavin

First published in English in Great Britain 2000 by
MACMILLAN PRESS LTD
Houndmills, Basingstoke, Hampshire RG21 6XS and London
Companies and representatives throughout the world

A catalogue record for this book is available from the British Library.

ISBN 0–333–77897–9

 First published in English in the United States of America 2000 by
ST. MARTIN'S PRESS, INC.,
Scholarly and Reference Division,
175 Fifth Avenue, New York, N.Y. 10010

ISBN 0–312–22415–X

Library of Congress Cataloging-in-Publication Data
Gelpi, Rosa-Maria.
[Histoire du crédit à la consommation. English]
The history of consumer credit : doctrines and practices / Rosa
-Maria Gelpi and François Julien-Labruyère.
p.   cm.
Includes bibliographical references and index.
ISBN 0–312–22415–X (cloth)
1. Consumer credit—History.   I. Julien-Labruyère, François.
II. Title.
HG3755.G413   1999
332.7'43—dc21

99–35381
CIP

This book is printed on paper suitable for recycling and made from fully managed and sustained forest sources.

10   9   8   7   6   5   4   3   2   1
09   08   07   06   05   04   03   02   01   00

Printed and bound in Great Britain by
Antony Rowe Ltd, Chippenham, Wiltshire

Contents

List of Plates

Preface

The recent focus of public attention on consumer credit can be seen as a veritable surge of media interest. Some claim it is an indication of shrewd orchestration, while others see it as no more than a fashionable trend. The elaboration and discussion of laws and European Directives is constantly placing consumer credit before the public eye, thus making it a subject of everyday popular interest. In the United States, public attention peaked in 1984 with the revision of the laws governing personal bankruptcy. Japanese methods of debt collecting came under public scrutiny at about the same time, while in Europe the debate about consumer credit began to take hold. Then, kindled by the recession, attention peaked in Great Britain in the 1990s, and in France it culminated in the passing of the Neiertz law on 31 December 1989.

However, whereas the Americans, and to a lesser degree the British, prepared the way for the debate and revision of laws in a climate of in-depth reflection, having recourse to University studies on the economic effect of consumer credit and its social role, nothing of the sort happened in France which, like Belgium, Spain and Italy, was also redefining its laws. The same holds true at the European level: the preparation of Directives (so important for national legislation) is conducted without sufficient research. The information considered is usually no more than a distant observation of the market, without any real back-up in the form of socio-economic reflection.

In a setting of American excess and against a backdrop of ancient usury, for a long time fiction has been cranking out the image that too much borrowing engulfs the low-income household in a downward spiral of moral and material bankruptcy. Arthur Miller's *Death of a Salesman* closes with the payment of a final monthly instalment which is as liberating as it is incongruous, given that it comes just after the head of the family has committed suicide. The same idea can be found reflected in Elsa Triolet's *Roses à Crédit* which shows us the devastating and – here again – deadly effect of an unbridled desire for household appliances which can no longer be paid for.

Miller's play and Triolet's novel are the two best known recent works in which credit is presented as a protagonist in everyday life. The fact that both were written during the 1950s, that is right in the middle of the post-war boom which introduced so much profound social change, is not without significance. A few rungs down the ladder of literary merit, credit was coming into its own in so far as train station literature is representative of dominant attitudes. Here, as if to foreshadow revolving accounts, revolver stories were making credit respectable. The most popular hero of Californian pulp fiction in those years was none other than the collector working for the credit establishments. This literary genre has since disappeared, in all likelihood because the foot-slogging collector has been replaced by telephones and computers!

This seedy literature stressed the apparent effects of collecting payments and not the internal anxiety experienced by many clients when faced with the 'dark tunnel' of successive monthly payments. This sentiment, so perfectly captured in Miller's play, is confirmed by all quality studies of the subject. The highlighting of the effect of credit leads to the idea of social pressure, which is often linked with the act of debt collecting, and often blamed for the excesses to which it may give rise.

Curiously, and in direct contrast with reality, both in macro-economic terms in relation to the amount of the payment and in micro-economic terms in relation to its influence on household budgets, consumer credit has suffered more than any other form of credit from this negative social image. Housing loans, on the other hand, are dignified by the wholesome utility of dwellings. Consumer purchases are seen as superfluous expenditure. A car is considered as part of the equipment of a company therefore as a morally valid investment; but not of a household. Property loans are the only loans which are spared this moral stigma.

Without fail, America provides the most flagrant caricature of this mentality. A suburban house is part of the status quo of middle-America. Even the Sunday preacher aspires to credit-assisted ownership. The mobile home, however, vehicle *par excellence* of the new frontiersmen, is considered as the very epitome of an all-absorbing credit. But credit companies know that there are more cases of personal bankruptcy among house-dwellers than among mobile home dwellers, for the simple reason that there are more houses and more unemployment in zones which are being reconverted, and more mobile homes and job creation in newly developing zones.

One is mobile and the other immovable. In France this distinction has been an integral part of the cliché since the *Code Civil* came into force: with regard to movables, possession and therefore credit, gives a poor image. This constitutes one of the dominant themes in relation to a product whose very name, *crédit à la consummation, credito al consumo, Konsum Kredit*, locates it morally in the zone of excess, whereas property credit – or better still – a mortgage loan, reassures by the rootedness of the term, with its moral connotation of moderation. This opposition constitutes one of the bases for the incomprehension surrounding consumer credit. It is particularly in evidence in judicial and administrative supervision, as well as in the media and consumer movements. The Anglo-Saxons, being more pragmatic, introduced a slight nuance: the term 'consumer credit' does not contain the idea of credit for consumption, as the other terms do, rather it is credit for the consumer.

This credit, which can lead to over indebtedness and cause the debtor to lose social status, never fails to evoke the old fantasies about usury. Consumer credit seems to evoke usury by virtue of the fact that its interest rates are higher, and the sums involved are smaller than in property loans. In the archetypes of today, too much credit, that is over indebtedness, takes over from the idea of excessive interest rates habitually and even officially associated with the social plague of usury. Excessive interest nevertheless continues to be a tacit and insidious justification of the traditional moral standpoint. How could it be otherwise? For centuries the theme of usury has made its way into every nook and cranny of the collective unconscious, particularly in the Christian Occident.

Jacques Le Goff was the first to point out the extraordinary conjunction, at the beginning of the Middle Ages, of the ban on loans at interest (the theft of time), the invention of Purgatory, and the first shoots of the spirit of capitalist enterprise. This triptych was fundamental in the forming of Western mentalities. The technique of credit lay at a midway point between, on the one hand, the sublimation of earthly life through enterprise and, on the other, punishment in the afterlife in the context of the myth of redemption. This gives an idea of the almost totemic influence of anything related to credit. Beginning with the Bible, libraries are overflowing with sermons and analyses condemning it. It is absent from no painting of the last judgement. Even Giotto created the whole cycle of frescos of the famous Scrovegni Chapel in Padua to prevent his sponsor from erring towards the infernal path of usury.

From the very beginning of the Middle Ages, however, this philosophical domination began to be eroded by economic reality. The first to come to an arrangement with the bans was none other than Saint Thomas Aquinas. Next to open the breach was Saint Antonin, archbishop of Florence, under whose archbishopric the city emerged as a centre for banking. A century later, and with the same desire to increase economic liberty, the theologians of Salamanca were already preparing the way for the blow which Protestant preachers were to deliver to the ban on loans at interest.

In spite of this slow process of maturation we can still find the old attitudes prevailing today: traditionally Protestant regions have a more relaxed and easy attitude to personal loans, whereas attitudes to credit in traditionally Catholic areas tend to be more rigid and guilt-associated. The typical attitude of credit professionals in mixed religion areas of Germany, Switzerland or Holland can be summed up as: commercially speaking, life is more difficult in the Protestant cantons, doubtless because of the banks' hold on the market; and in the Catholic cantons there is greater risk.

This awareness of working at the heart of one of the most fecund love–hate knots of the Western mind gives the directors of consumer credit companies a deliberately Genevan attitude, after the fashion of the most famous of them all, Kaminsky of the KKB in East Prussia in the 1920s. Initially financing only bicycles, in the 1950s, Kaminsky transformed the KKB into the first private bank in Europe and in 1959 he was the pioneer of Eurofinas, whose vocation to this day is to advocate a highly moral code of professional ethics for credit granters.

It would take the Catholic Church more than seven centuries to undo the knot. It was not until Vatican II that the dogma of Purgatory was transformed and stripped of all connotations associated with borrowing. In the meantime, or concomitantly with history, the principal movements claiming a socialist affiliation carried out their own *aggiornamento* of the spirit of enterprise and the values associated with credit. Today, the head of household no longer has a philosophical handicap preventing him or her from being seen, not as 'the adventurer of modern times' but, as the entrepreneur of the basic social cell.

It is clear, however, that between a doctrinal evolution on such a scale and the popular archetype, there will obviously be hangovers. Such hangovers constitute the greatest ferment for the rejection of the idea of the family as an enterprise, thus the ferment for the idea that as soon as there is credit, there is danger. Here again we find the old syndrome of social parasitism in the form of usury.

European literature has kept up a steady stream of images maintaining the archetype. From Dante to Zola, from Shakespeare to Dickens, or from Galdos to Balzac, the usurer forms part of the cohort of characters in the collective unconscious. The portraits are always the same, Shylock and Gobseck, pale, spiteful and greedy, constituting the most famous of all.

The most recent reiteration is to be found in the would-be prophetic tones of the *Cantos* of Ezra Pound, who considered them as a sort of poetic concentration or repository of all Western civilization. Two whole cantos of exceptional violence are devoted to the subject: Usura killing the child at the breast, and the dead feasting at a signal from Usura. In

Pound's view, Usura is the mother of nothing, no trade, no activity, no artistic endeavour. It is the chief sin, the only sin against nature because it steals time, the very substance of nature. This nevertheless magnificent text brings together the torrent of popular images and theological arguments which form one of the best known aspects of our mentality: credit is usury and usury is evil.

The religious and social bans also run through language, for example, the Italian word for a moneylender, 'lo strozzino', is derived from the verb to strangle. We can also find physical and even racial connotations, recently in the form of the Jew Süss, giving expression to Europe's guilt complex. It is no wonder at all that any discourse on the subject of consumer credit, however empirical, should be dressed and subtly directed by this intellectual and moral fabric handed down by history. It usually operates in the form of a mute yet active unconscious. It is rare today to find it dressed up as a theoretical standpoint.

This Christian train of thought has its roots in traditional practices and is no doubt best exemplified in the German language which uses one and the same word 'die Schuld' to express the ideas of debt and of fault. It is obvious that as long as a loan is contracted as a standby in order to permit a precise and temporary consumption dictated by time and place and guaranteed by a pledge of equipment – which is durable – it has no possible moral justification and its social role is highly ambiguous. In spite of an early attempt at moralization in the classical period of the *monts-de-piété*, the imbalance of the pledge in relation to an ephemeral consumption deformed the system as a whole by condoning behaviour which advocated blackmail as a rule of sociability. Such was the norm in former societies.

The situation still occurs today in under-developed countries, either in the form of rural customs or, unfortunately, and with increasing frequency, in an urban, often illegal, form. But we would be blinkered in our methods, or politically hypocritical, if we were to consider these archaic practices as credit, plain and simple, and to put them in the same category as market practices in the developed world. The simple fact that the repayments on this so-called credit are carried out for the most part in the form of some more or less open favour, profoundly transforms the nature of such loans.

Since the end of the nineteenth century, a new function of credit as promoting social integration has come to the fore. This is in direct opposition to the traditional village sociability which mixed salary, debt and assistance. The appearance of an industrial wage earning class had its necessary corollary in the management of a purely monetary household budget, initially on a weekly, then two-weekly and finally on a monthly basis.

Thus credit progressively became the commonest form of anticipating the household income. The old slogans praising credit, sometimes naively, as 'the modern form of saving' have been borne out by the in-depth studies of economists and sociologists. If we look at society as a whole, credit operates remarkably well to facilitate social integration. On a more private level it constitutes the first phase of a life cycle, that of equipping the household. Over a period of 40 or 50 years this equipping phase is progressively transformed into a saving phase in preparation for retirement and the transmission of the family inheritance.

Consumer credit obviously has a place in this cycle, less distinctly perhaps than property credit because of the depreciation of the goods bought, but with exactly the same virtue of planned increased wealth through the acquisition of goods. This constitutes the most widely accepted, because also the most obvious, form of social status. Thus consumer credit contributes to that self-actualization which is symbolically expressed by an improved standard of living.

What is perfectly clear and understandable for any household investing in equipment, or for the youngest employee in a credit establishment, is summed up in an extremely simple socio-economic observation. In order for the household to become richer, therefore a better risk for the creditor, the old common sense rule must be respected, that is the repayment period on a loan should never exceed the life-span of the object acquired. If there were only one rule in studying a credit file, it should be that, for it introduces balance and reason in terms of self projection in a life cycle.

Things seem to become more complicated when it comes to personal loans, and even more so when we speak of credit cards. There is no longer any sure and objective link with some item(s) of equipment. The credit card can even feed the enthusiasm for the futile, ephemeral or useless. All that has negative aspects in terms of increasing wealth.

The historical coincidence between the development of these products, firstly in the United States and later in Europe, and the appearance of a new method of evaluation based on a personal score, that is an assessment of probable behaviour, corresponds exactly with this change of point of view. The appreciation of enrichment is no longer related to the object but to the supposed capacity of the applicant to manage a budget. This was an essential development, the full consequences of which we have hardly begun to experience. Sociologically speaking, it means that households have greater autonomy in decision-making, therefore automatically greater awareness of their function as a micro-economic cell in quest of greater fulfilment.

But, some will say, what about impulse buying, easily influenced households, not to mention the famous American 'hard-selling' manuals? And there still remains the question for having the physical capacity for making repayments, and of course the spectre of overindebtedness. All true, although of marginal market importance. All of these problems continue to exist, regardless of so-called consumer protection legislation and the prudence of lending establishments. For the latter, relaxed checking of clients or insufficient authorization procedures always give the same result: increased risk. In other words, there is decreased profitability if they wish to remain competitive, or else they are marginalized on the market because of excessive rates.

We can learn much from the Anglo-Saxon model. It combines both a higher level of financial awareness on the part of householders than in Latin countries, and the availability of multiple financial products which are increasingly dissociated from investment goods, and more and more linked with optimized management of the life cycle. Concepts such as consumption, liquidity, investment, saving and contingency funds are beginning to be better and better understood by the households which the banks, and other increasingly specialist establishments, are serving. Against that, a type of pledged consolidation of the whole of these claims is developing as a sort of safety net in case of unforeseeable incidents. Some households in Great Britain and the United States take out a second mortgage as a lifebuoy. It is easy to see the ambiguity of this practice, with its moral soundness – 'as safe as houses' – while still evoking the old practice of the bridging loan.

We know that the implementation of these mortgages is rare because of the obvious expense for all concerned. Most people will agree that when the social risk of a product depends on its usefulness in avoiding backsliding in the life cycle, then it is preferable to have that product rather than the temporary exclusion from society which results from civil bankruptcy as practised in the United States. Unfortunately, in times of economic crisis, the life line proves to be insufficient, as happened in Great Britain in recent years.

By way of contrast, these examples help outline the principal role of consumer credit that is that of social actualization. To clarify this role, we should first underline the fact that a sizeable proportion of clients has always been made up of young couples and wage earners, often newly arrived immigrants in the cities. Corresponding to the Auvergnats arriving in Paris at the end of the nineteenth century and equipping their households thanks to the famous Dufayel vouchers; today we have Calabrian workers arriving in Turin, or Turks in the Ruhr, or even the children of first generation immigrants setting up home in the suburbs. Depending on the country and the society, these people constitute up to 30 per cent of credit files. They also constitute one of the main challenges for the system.

Following the example of the old leagues of temperance, consumer associations see the desire of these people to be integrated, therefore to consume, as the major danger of overindebtedness, therefore of marginalization. Inversely, but with the same desire to put an end to it, leftists of all shades have taken up Baudrillart's old refrain that consumer credit is the single most powerful integrating force in Western capitalist society. The most Utopian universalists are willing to countenance the right to credit as a by-product of non-discrimination taken to its limit.

Credit professionals obviously know from measuring it on a day-to-day basis that this clientele constitutes a greater risk than others. They also know that this is not a sufficient reason to introduce discriminatory subjectivism into their criteria of refusal. They are well aware that this clientele, more than others, is seeking social status through household durables and that social integration constitutes the first step towards self-actualization.

True professionals continue on their pragmatic way, more interested in the individual cases they meet and in statistical observations drawn from them than in often ambiguous theories. Finally, it is of little importance whether or not they are philosophically conscious of their role and its social utility. Indeed, any abuse on their part will automatically come back on them: overindulgence of a new client and their risk will increase; if they are at fault in collecting, their image will suffer. At the end of the day, they would eliminate themselves in accordance with the principle that a bad customer turns away a good one. If the risk is too high, interest rates rise; if market image is poor, market share will be lost.

However we look at it, consumer credit contains its own internal counterweights. The market has known this for a long time, basing its daily actions on it. Unfortunately, the fact remains unknown to the regulatory authorities who never stop imposing external counterweights which usually end up making procedures and therefore working accounts more unwieldy, so raising the cost of credit.

Just like its lack of socio-economic utility, the cost of credit comes back constantly. The professionals mention it to justify one or another of their policies; their denigrators use it in support of any and every argument. Credit is expensive, credit is inflationary, credit disturbs the commercial balance, the cost of credit is anti-economical, anti-social, anti-national, anti-moral ... There is an extraordinary convergence of reproach despite details varying with the period and the speaker. Plagues develop, but there is always a plague in society and, moreover, we all make our own plagues for our own reasons! Whether they be on the right or on the left, plagues generally cancel each other out, except in the case of consumer credit where they all build up merrily in the greatest incoherence.

Faced with this current of opinion which overflows into the private lives of thousands of wage earners in specialist establishments all over Europe, in the form of a sort of latent family reproach, credit providers are often tempted either to argue their way out of the quagmire they have been dragged into, or else to prettify their profession with considerations as specious as those used by their adversaries. To the charge that consumer credit upsets the commercial balance, they traditionally point out their support for French processing industries. Neither argument really sustains further analysis. They are nevertheless part of the polemic that has long been nourished by the historic unconscious which forms a screen between the reality of consumer credit and a dispassionate evaluation of the subject.

The aim of this book is to contribute to removing that screen. By no means does it claim to be a defence and illustration, nor an exhaustive analysis, any more than it claims to be a white paper to convince a decisionmaker. It is simply a stroll through history, undertaken by two colleagues in an establishment specializing in personal loans. Tired of feeling a diffuse opprobrium for their activity, they set out in quest of their professional identity by going back to the sources of their trade. The journey consists of trying to find in the depths of Western ideological traditions the reasons for the negative image of consumer credit, then tracing the true history of these practices.

The first part will thus deal with ancient times, when opposing theologies were developed, while techniques of credit were taking shape. The second part will analyze recent history where the development of consumer credit, as such, is confused with the traditional image of the old bans. Because the Reformation left such a strong and lasting effect on attitudes, and because the differences it gave rise to in the history of economic development are still so prevalent, the principal countries under study will be the United States and Great Britain on the one hand, and France on the other.

Consumer credit is situated at the heart of modern life, though suffering from archaic attitudes handed down through centuries of bans and shame. It is neither more nor less responsible than any other economic sector for fluctuations and the erring ways of society itself. Of course it has its role to play in society, as a factor of social integration and as a factor of economic growth. Its role is on a scale with itself i.e. without excess and at the normal rate of development in our society. For the very simple reason that excess kills consumer credit. There has been a veritable transition in the use of credit in household budgeting, just as there has been a demographic transition. This transition is quite simply the proof that countries going through these changes are adapting to the modern world. In short, consumer credit is one of the best indications of the state of advancement of a society.

REFERENCES

LE GOFF, D. *The Birth of Purgatory*, Chicago: University of Chicago Press, 1989.

Acknowledgements

We were assisted in the writing of this book by the comments and experience of many credit professionals. It would be impossible to name them all. We wish, however, to mention those who helped us most often: M. Baërt, P. Campaioli, P. Defourny, B. Drot, F. Félix, B. Müller, C. Nasse, G. d'Ottaviano, Y. Sato, E. Speranza, M. Van Lierde, P. Vaiter, J.-P. Vassal, C. Weiss, Ms C. Zingaro.

We also wish to thank Professor R.N. Cooper who facilitated our access to the wealth of American literature on the subject, and H. Francotte who shared with us some of his studies on ancient Greece.

L. Bertran and S. Tessier gathered and elaborated statistical data. Ms S. Gatti was in charge of typing the manuscript, as well as library research, gathering statistics, elaboration of numerical series and illustrations.

We sincerely thank them all.

Part I
Credit from Ancient to Modern Times: Dogma Versus Practice

Lending on interest, known quite simply as usury until the end of the sixteenth century, was one of the first economic manifestations of life in society and an essential driving force in its development. It is considered to date back to the period of agricultural settling in the neolithic age. It is thus older than industry, banking and the striking of coins.

The reason it seems to have been an established practice is precisely because it helps to satisfy certain fundamental needs such as survival, enhanced well-being and the development of economic life. It very soon began to be both desired and detested, since the borrower, in order to enjoy its benefits, undertook the obligation to return and pay for the favour granted. Moreover, this system of lending left the way open for forms of abuse: non-return of the loan by the borrower, and the demand for exorbitant repayments or excessive penalties by the lenders in cases of non-payment. Consequently, lending quickly drew the attention of legislators, the censure of moralists and later the consideration of theologians and philosophers.

Some societies were content to regulate the practice while others, sheltering behind the mantle of divine revelation, forbade interest-based loans. The ban lived on across the centuries, causing numerous tensions and difficulties. But divine revelation becomes concrete only in texts which reflect the socio-political preoccupations of the men who transmit it. Without doubt these laws responded to the needs of particular historical contexts. But because they were included in a theological corpus of work they became sacred and were thus imposed for centuries.

As part of theological dogma they were rigid, though applied to developing societies. Thus they became further and further removed from the very reality which they were supposed to regulate. Hence the necessity, which society felt very early on, of circumventing, reinterpreting and finally discarding them. The first part of this study traces these changes, which are essentially ideological, though in constant relation to the economic necessities of the time, as a kind of moral counterpoint to the development of merchant society. We shall be concentrating essentially on European history for it is only there that we find a religion based so exclusively on written revelation, and also the gradual development of capitalism. What heated discussions this question of borrowing and lending gave rise to! Simply because the Christian West felt the need to develop an elaborate system of doctrines in order to bring practice into harmony with faith.

The ideological stance transmitted by means of these controversies left its traces long after the debates had disappeared, and it still continues to have a certain influence on contemporary attitudes to borrowing and lending.

1 Usury in the Ancient World

Regulation of interest-based loans is at the very heart of the earliest legal texts dating from antiquity. For this reason, some historians have come to believe that the practice may well be of much earlier origin and may date from the period of agricultural settling in the neolithic age.

THE CODE OF HAMMURABI

The Code of Hammurabi is one of the earliest and best preserved general codes. The code was decreed in Mesopotamia by Hammurabi who reigned in Babylon from 1792 to 1750 BC. It consists of a collection of decrees partly concerning litigation between borrowers and lenders. The code is engraved on a black stele more than two metres tall and can be seen in the Louvre museum. It contains 282 paragraphs, about 260 of which have been preserved (*Lois de l'Ancien Orient* 1986). Thanks to the code, the royal pronouncements of the period acquire a universal range through time and space. In essence it concerns city dwellers and merchants, but it also devotes some clauses to peasants and, in particular, it stipulates conditions granting them ease of payment of debts.

At the time when the code was drawn up, Mesopotamia was a well-irrigated, agriculturally rich area with its own intense economic life and flourishing trade. Borrowing and lending were common practice, negotiated in one of the two currencies, that is barley or silver. All lending operations, whether interest-based or not, had to be recorded in a written contract and stamped by an official. The maximum interest rate for cereal loans, repayable in kind, was fixed at $33\frac{1}{3}$ per cent per year. The rate for silver currency was only 20 per cent (Homer 1963).

Article 71 of the Code of Hammurabi is the first known law governing usury. It punishes creditors who exceed the fixed interest rate by depriving them of their debt. Similarly, articles 48 to 52 come to the assistance of peasants in debt. In years of drought or flooding they were not obliged to pay back the capital, nor even the interest. If they had neither barley nor silver they could acquit their debt by giving up their agricultural produce to their creditor. They could also pay back a silver loan in cereal currency. In an attempt to moralize practices, article 113 forbids the creditor to pay himself by taking possession of the debtor's barley, under pain of returning the barley and cancellation of the debt.

Land and other items could be offered as pledge of payment, as well as the person of the debtor himself, his wife, concubine, children or slaves. A kind of shared family responsibility allowed the creditor to take possession of the debtor, his wife and his children. However, personal enslavement for non-payment of debts was limited to three years. Article 116 proscribed bad treatment which could cause the death of a man enslaved for non-payment of debts (*Lois de l'Ancien Orient* 1986).

The Code of Hammurabi is therefore a coherent system of laws defining the different forms of credit, interest rates, its legal basis, modes of repayment, guarantees and recovery. There are no moral prohibitions in the Code. Thus we find that credit, at the heart of life in society, constitutes one of its essential driving forces. The Code of Hammurabi affords us the first historical example of something which we shall often find in the course of this study, that is the conjunction of an advanced civilization and the widespread practice of credit.

CREDIT AND SERFDOM IN ANCIENT GREECE

The laws which had the greatest effect on the history of ancient Greece were decreed during the period of social upheaval which resulted from the transformations marking the passage from the archaic to the classical period. Credit, which was widely practised by the temples, and which represented a considerable share of their revenue, was to become one of the main issues of public debate and legislation within the Greek cities.

When the Hellenic tribes settled in Greece at the beginning of the first millennium BC they divided the land between the different families making up the tribes. Family property in this primitive society was declared indivisible and inalienable. Consequently, the descendants of each family had no choice but to share the cultivation of their ancestors' property. The banished, foreigners or bastards, had no right to land ownership. Confronted with a system linking property ownership to family line, those who found themselves excluded for whatever reason, including personal ambition, had no option but to colonize and conquer external territories. In fewer than 300 years the Mediterranean became a semi-Greek sea. When a group of colonists left the motherland and founded a new city, they had every interest in maintaining a good relationship with their parent city, in order to facilitate the creation of wealth through exchange and to foster trade (Hatzfield 1969).

The economic environment and the social structure changed at the same time that the colonial experiences enlarged the country. Some of the original large family domains split up. Furthermore, a legal and economic reform transfered the ownership, first of property and later of land, from the family to the individual. On behalf of that reform, properties were often divided after the death of the head of the family.

The development of cities changed the primitive situation in which every family was living in a large estate, mainly autarkical. Besides, with the growth of trade that also encouraged industry, agriculture was no longer the only way of creating wealth. Technical progress and increase in trade had major social repercussions. Power was no longer based exclusively on ownership of a large domain; merchant society was creating fortunes in movable properties, and the use of currency was making it easier to manipulate them. Families acquired large incomes through such exchanges and were thus able to play an important role in their cities.

In contrast with this gradual break up of the clans and the rise of social individualization, the situation of the lowly deteriorated considerably. While enormous incomes were being earned through trade and by the large domains, the poor peasant, with precarious tenure of ownership subject to bitter trials of succession and boundary disputes, eked out a living on a patch of land which was barely enough to support his family. If afflicted by illness, or victim of a poor harvest, a peasant could borrow in order to survive the winter, but by borrowing jeopardized the land. The first mortgages date from this early period. Of course the borrower had the option of redeeming the property if his fortune improved. But if, on the settlement date, the loan could not be paid back, the land could be forfeited. Beyond that date his own person, or his wife and children came under the control of the creditor, who could sell them into slavery. If the creditor chose to leave them to work the land the great majority of the proceeds went to him. Thus, unpaid debts led to servitude (Gaudemet 1982).

Of course these economic conditions relating to credit in the eighth century BC were not the only cause of serfdom. They nonetheless favoured its spread, and highlighted its oppressive nature. Serfdom was unknown to the Hellenic tribes and is mentioned by neither Homer nor Hesiod. The social demands of the financially ruined, abolition of debts and redistribution of land, accentuated the tensions created by the struggle for power between the eupatrid aristocrats and the new commercial bourgeoisie. Credit was only one of many far-reaching, transforming influences which shook society as a whole. It was nonetheless credit which, a few centuries later, became the prime target of the philosphers. In their attacks they claim to believe that the abolition of interest-based credit would bring about a return of the golden age. This was one of the first times in history when credit became the scapegoat for the confusion brought about by changes in society.

THE GREAT LEGAL REFORMS OF SOLON

The legal reforms of Draco, around 621 BC, introduced considerable progress on the evolution of the Greek society. Under these reforms the ancient law, based on the shared responsibility of the family as a unit, gave way to a more modern concept whereby the individual became responsible before the State. This reform proved to be insufficient, as it was no remedy for the social and political crises of the time. Power remained in the hands of a few landowners of noble stock who owned practically all the land in Attica. Before them, artisans, shopkeepers, landowners in debt or evicted from their property, were totally powerless. A deep current of discontent was feeding the spirit of revolt.

Between 594 and 591 BC, Solon, a widely-travelled nobleman who had made his fortune in trade, and who was also a Statesman and a poet, introduced far-reaching reforms. He refused to allow the division of land, but deprived creditors of the right to enslave an insolvent debtor, or any member of his family. Dispossessed landowners who had lost their property by falling into debt, were restored to ownership. Solon increased both the freedom of the citizen and of his land (Finley 1985; Glotz 1986).

The principles of justice in the Homeric age, like Oriental law, were dictated as if by divine imposition. Solon was the ideal contemporary of the first philosophers. Under their influence, law was secularized and became more objective. It became the product of reason and of human endeavour. In nothing less than a cultural revolution, law and religion were dissociated. Order was no longer seen as something which was pleasing to the Gods; it was now an essential element of life in society. Hesiod's belief that transgression of the law was followed by catastrophes of divine origin – such as war, flooding or famine – was no longer held. For Solon, a breach of the law gave rise to problems of a social nature, or to civil war, both direct consequences of secular disorder and nothing to do with divine retribution. Solon's method of restoring order and peace to the cities was to introduce new legislation.

In spite of the political troubles which affected a large number of Greek cities throughout the sixth century BC, commercial and industrial progress favoured the growth of fortunes. Commercial loans developed and, from the fifth century onwards, became one of the factors contributing to the economic prosperity of the country. Increases in wealth and the use of currency paved the way for investment. Greater market activity created the need for loans, which were usually contracted in written form, drawn up by the lender in the presence of the borrower, the agreement being interest-based. The Greek cities were particularly prosperous during this period and interest-based loans were looked on with favour. Even the State did not hesitate to borrow in order to meet pressing needs, such as those resulting from wars (Bernard *DTC*).

Limits to interest rates were not laid down by law. In spite of this, they did not exceed 18 per cent per annum in times of prosperity, except in the case of certain maritime loans, the risk of shipwreck being extremely high at the time. There was even a degree of competition between the different temples, part of their reputation being due to low rates; the famous example of 10 per cent in the temple of Appolo at Delos. The rates in Greater Greece, however, and later throughout the Alexandrian world, were closer to 24 per cent, the maximum fixed by Ptolemy Philadelphia in the third century BC (for details of rates, see Homer 1963)

THE FIRST PHILOSOPHICAL CONDEMNATIONS OF INTEREST-BEARING LOANS: PLATO AND ARISTOTLE

The fact that credit was widely accepted by both the population and the authorities, and played a positive role in the fifth and sixth centuries BC, did not deter such eminent philosophers as Plato and Aristotle from condemning it. It is important to examine their condemnations, for they were widely used by theologians in the Middle Ages to elaborate their doctrine of usury, which still influences our attitudes to credit today.

For Plato, the main purpose of legislation was to promote moral values over brute force. He was instrumental in giving credence to the concepts of natural right and natural law, which were to become fundamental in Western legal thinking. The idea of a legal order that is above and beyond the limited thinking of the legislator was to carry on across the centuries.

Generally speaking, Plato was hardly in favour of economic development: the rich could not be virtuous. Citizens were thus forbidden to work in 'productive' occupations, which he considered to be degrading. Instead, they should devote themselves entirely to the affairs of the city. In such a *Republic*, trade is of little importance and markets are rare. In his Utopian city, from which he banned gold and silver, he also, quite logically, banned lending. However, this decision is dictated, not so much by ethical consid-erations as by a natural aversion for lowly trades, and by a 'nationalism' which was exacerbated in Athenian politics by the repeated interruptions of cosmopolitan finance (Bernard *DTC*; Taveneaux 1977).

Aristotle also was trying to re-establish harmony between law and nature. For him, nature followed a rational order. The natural law was common to all, based on universal reason which all men share. Similarly, he speaks of a natural justice which is the highest form of virtue. Side by side with the natural law which, because of its universal nature was too general, positive human laws regulate social organization.

Thus, Aristotle condemns usury because he considers that it is incom-patible with the very nature of money. Money is only a convention, the principal purpose of which is to facilitate exchange and which, he admits, may also be used as a store of value. This reasoning leads him to make a distinction between natural things and conventional things. Only the for-mer can reproduce. The latter have no real existence, other than that accorded to them by men. Since money is a convention, it cannot repro-duce. Besides, of all social occupations, that of money-lender is the low-est, because he attempts to extract profit from money which is naturally sterile and which has no properties or uses other than that of serving as a common measure for the exchange of goods. In Aristotle's opinion, it is perfectly right to detest lending at interest. Because of such loans, money itself becomes productive, and is diverted from its principal function which is that of facilitating exchange. Moreover, interest multiplies money, hence the term 'offspring' which it received in Greek. Just as chil-dren are of a nature identical to their parents, so interest, being of a similar nature to money, is the offspring of money, an idea which is completely against nature, therefore to be resisted at all costs. Of all means of acquir-ing wealth, it is the one most in contradiction with nature. Arising out of this analysis, we find the famous formula of the Middle Ages: 'money does not beget money'. This argument was frequently used to back up condemnations of interest-bearing loans.

Aristotle, who laid down the basis of scientific knowledge in so many domains, has only value judgements to offer when it comes to economics, particularly in his analysis of interest rates. He set little value by trade, holding paid labour to be degrading, and gave pride of place to agriculture. His economic doctrine is marked by a social prejudice in favour of the great lord, for whom the only honourable occupations are those of warrior and landowner. Other occupations, such as trade and industry, should be reserved for slaves and metics. His condemnation of usury is first and foremost based on contempt for the money-lender.

CREDIT AND SOCIETY IN REPUBLICAN ROME

As in all ancient societies, Roman law was initially based on custom. However, from the foundation of the Republic onwards we see common law giving way to statutory law. The most important example is the *XII Tables*, which the Romans saw as the basis of their laws up until Justinian. Tradition has it that the 22 propositions of an economic and social nature contained in the *Tables* were decreed in 450 BC. Somewhat like Solon's reforms, they are an attempt to resolve the social crisis which, in the fifth century BC, opposed the aristocracy, masters of the city and the plebeians. The ordinary people – victimized by wars and plundering, and burdened with debts which left them subject to servitude – were demanding a share in the lands taken from enemies. But the Senate, being Patrician, wanted to keep the monopoly of its own members over these lands. As a concession, however, it adopted a series of economic measures which, among other things, set ceilings for interest rates. The interpretation of the maximum rate authorised by the *XII Tables*, the *foenus unciarum*, is open to discussion. Some set it at 1 per cent per month that is 12 per cent per annum, others suggest $8\frac{1}{3}$ per cent that is one-twelfth of the capital. The latter interpretation tends to be the more widely accepted of the two. In 88 BC the limit was raised to 12 per cent, and became the famous *centesima usura*, which governed all transactions for a few centuries (Bernard *DTC*; Gaudemet 1982; Homer 1963). The *mutuum* obliged the borrower to pay back exactly what he had borrowed, both in quantity and in quality. Linked with a stipulation of interests, a *usura*, it became the *foenus*.

The *XII Tables* were complemented by the Licinian laws, introduced by the plebeian tribune Licinius Solon in 376 BC, to respond to the people's demand for a reduction in debts. These laws grant a remission of interest to insolvent debtors, and a moratorium of three years in which to pay back the capital sum outstanding. An insolvent debtor was, however, still liable to seizure of his person by the creditor who could imprison him, sell him, or even put him to death. The death penalty for insolvent debtors was finally abolished by the *Poetelia Papiria* law in 326 BC. The law protecting the borrower, which was introduced by the conservatives at the time, seems to be more of a compensation granted to the people in order to avoid other economic and social difficulties; a process which still enjoys great success!

Fed by conquest, the Roman economy in the second century BC, was expanding rapidly. The Punic and Eastern wars procured vast tracts of land for the State, especially for the leaders of the armies, who were members of the Senate class. In 219 BC, a law was introduced forbidding maritime trading for the Senate class. They increased their wealth, however, by buying land cheaply from landowners ruined by the wars. Booty and tributes filled the public coffers and, by ricochet effect, increased the influence of the Senators, military leaders, and their opposite numbers in allied cities (Rostovtsef 1988).

The influx of money, slaves, livestock and foodstuffs of all kinds had a salutary effect on the economy. The majority of the nouveaux riches owed their fortune to speculation and were hoping for an idle life of comfort. The way they were most likely to achieve their goal was by investing in land. Thus, in the second century BC, we find a rapid and regular increase in the ownership of landed property. The owners lived in the towns and cities, and the land was cultivated by tenant farmers. Labour was cheap and plentiful. Trade increased, particularly imports. Rome consumed, but produced little, and had to pay for foreign purchases with gold taken from the spoils of war.

The social stability which had been the cornerstone of the Republic during the third century BC, was shattered by economic transformations, the diversity of activity and the concentration of large fortunes among the *nobilitas*. With military might on the decline, the traditional roman aristocracy, based on an army of free peasants, was degenerating progressively into an oligarchy of opulent families. The equestrian order, once the military élite, through farming taxes and levies, favouritism and arms sales, had become a group of rich businessmen. Distant trade brought about the appearance of exchange bankers who opened their offices near the *forum* and saw to payments in the provinces. Useful, though not very scrupulous, they often amassed rapid fortunes and thus scandalized society. In opposition to this small group of economically powerful people, without any intermediary well-established middle class, was the Roman proletariat, consisting largely of freed slaves, out-of-work veterans, foreigners, and down-and-outs living frugally with neither work nor property. The largely agricultural provinces suffered the exorbitant demands of Rome, abusive governors, and the risk of seeing part of their property confiscated (Gaudemet 1982).

After nearly a century of troubles and political disorder, ending with the establishment of the Empire, social reforms were introduced in answer to the demands of the masses. Aside from measures to help people in trouble, debts were reduced and a moratorium was introduced for small rents. In other words, credit relief was used to dress the wound, but deeper general problems were ignored.

USURY, AN ENDEMIC EVIL IN THE EMPIRE

Even at the height of their Imperial splendour the Romans invested little in industry. Unlike the Greeks, they produced little and transported little.

Roman society can be generally categorized as having its population dispersed, little buying power except in a few major centres, and the upper classes ignoring trade through prejudice and even forbidden by law to indulge in it. Although the élite lived off the produce of their rural properties and bought almost nothing, with the exception of a few luxury items which they imported from distant lands, they were nonetheless very extravagant in their spending. From the time of Cicero onwards, lavish public games and great generosity towards the plebeians were an essential part of any political career. Often suffering from a lack of ready cash and devoid of an entrepreneurial spirit, the dominant families concentrated on three types of business: farming of taxes owed by Roman subjects living in the provinces, property investment based essentially on an attempt to gain social prestige and usurious loans.

It has even been said that usury was the great Roman industry, the pillar of the Empire. Montesquieu put it superbly: 'Awful usury, continually beaten down and continually rising up again, was established in Rome'. Small-time lending was looked down on socially. However, it was perfectly acceptable and in no way shameful to indulge in large-scale usury. More than that, it was a noble means of increasing one's wealth. Knights and senators lent to the all powerful, to Eastern kings, to cities, to corporations, to wealthy private individuals and particularly to nobles embarking on a political career. In this case, the loan created multiple obligations to the point where a provincial governship was acquired with the possibility of making a fortune. Thus, extortion of funds often became a personal necessity in the provinces. Money problems in the upper strata of Roman society created constant and considerable tensions. Bankruptcy, in particular, led to disaster when the creditors left the debtor to his fate: he could then be excluded from the Senate and his domains seized. Each wealthy head of a family had a safe, a *kalendarium*, in which he kept a calendar of payments due, proofs of debt and also the sums of money destined to be lent. The *kalendarium* could be left in his will to his inheritors, as therefore could his rights over the debtors (Lot 1961; Veyne 1987).

In the course of the first two centuries of the Christian era the economic situation continued to develop: overseas trade became the major source of the Empire's wealth. This increased the importance of movable fortunes and fostered the growth of a provincial bourgeoisie whose fortunes reached a high point in the second century when transactions across *mare nostrum* were guaranteed by the *pax Romana*. This prosperity was short-lived, however, owing to the weakness of its economic basis. Imperial finances continued to be fed by booty from conquests. When these came to an end, the principal source of wealth dried up. The crisis broke out in the third century. Trade declined and the ruin of the active bourgeoisie was felt in the lack of taxes. Simultaneously, the needs of the occupying armies and the cost of a growing bureaucracy put a serious strain on the Treasury. A demographic crisis further compounded the situation. And to crown it all, the religious crisis called into question the very structures of adherence to the great imperial model.

The fruits of conquest were dissipated. Small farmers were hit heavily for taxes and for land rights. In the end they were forced to join the ranks of the ruthlessly exploited. The true freeholder farmer lost all protection against a series of bad harvests, compulsory military service, or against endless pillaging, now that wars were endemic. Chaos and misery reigned throughout the Empire. In the fourth century Rome could no longer feed its citizens, maintain its administration, or pay its troops.

In Athens, the borrower was often a trader anxious to make a profit from the money he borrowed. In Rome, the borrower was often a farmer in a terrible plight, threatened with ruin by the war, bad weather and soon the arrears from previous loans. The relationship between the patricians and the plebs was somehow balanced out curiously, between increasingly sumptuous feasts offered to the people on the one hand, and generalized usury on the other. The historians called it evergetism. It was one of the most constant and most efficient forces in Roman society. *Panem et circences* lived on in the popular imagination. Financing was managed by means of *usura*.

The free feast was paid for with the gains from usury. In other words, it was the plebs themselves who paid for their feast! This eminently vicious circle was responsible for a large number of popular revolts. But usury, like a fatal flaw in society, continued to wreak havoc. The most highly respected members of the priviliged class indulged in the greatest excesses. Cato the Elder pressurized his debtors mercilessly and Seneca, whilst condemning usury in his books, indulged in it unscrupulously in order to increase his already immense fortune. Saint Jerome, a Church Father, is one of the experts on the Empire in the fourth century, having widely travelled and occupied important positions in both the East and the West. He records with horror that current interest rates were as high as 50 per cent. Thus, usury appears to have been an endemic evil which worsened daily, as the cities and the Empire became engrossed in their problems. For this reason, the fledgling Church, which derived vitality from its total reinterpretation of society, saw usury in the forefront of its enemies. In order to combat it, the Church undertook a serious examination of its own philosophical sources, as revealed in sacred scriptures (Taveneaux 1977).

In a similar spirit, reformers believed that by fixing interest rates they could remedy the crisis of the Empire. The most important of these was Justinian, who totally revised the legislation on money-lending. He did not go so far as to abolish it, as the Church demanded, but he reduced it, setting rates at 6 per cent for ordinary private loans between individuals, while banks and other traders could stipulate rates of up to 8 per cent. A rate of 12 per cent was allowed for maritime loans or for foodstuffs. Justinian decided that a loan should cease to produce interest when the amount of the interest became equal to the capital.

When a plaintiff's case was upheld by the court, execution of the sentence – whether seizure of goods, in kind, or in exceptional cases, physical constraint – was no longer left to the initiative of the plaintiff, but was the direct responsibility of the judge. Justinian's text is historically the first large legal corpus devoted to credit, in so far as it defines the activity as a whole, from the maximum legal rate to means of recovery, and distinguishes types of loans and types of borrowers. It dates from 533 AD. Wholly praiseworthy for its attempt to introduce a moral dimension, the Justinian Code was obviously only a partial answer to the serious problems besetting society, which brought about the notorious downfall of the Roman Empire. Here again, credit was mistaken for the cause rather than a compounding factor of the problems of the time. The measures stipulated in the Justinian Code were only applied in the Byzantine part of the Empire. In the West, society had become so shrivelled up under the effect of invasions and their corollary, the progressive feudalization of the provinces, that credit disappeared from everyday life. A society without credit has no horizons.

REFERENCES

BERNARD, A. 'Usure', in *Dictionnaire de théologie catholique* (DTC).

Encyclopédie de La Pléïade, Histoire Universelle, Paris: T.I. Gallimard, 1956.

FINLEY, M.I. *The Ancient Economy,* 2nd edn Berkeley: University of California Press, 1985.

FINLEY, M.I. *Economy and Society in Ancient Greece,* New York: Penguin Books, 1985.

FRANCOTTE, A. *'Aristote et le prêt à intérêt'*, *Journée d'étude Philosophie perennis et analyse économique* Université Paris I Panthéon-Sorbonne.

GAUDEMET, J. *Institutions de l'Antiquité*, Paris: Sirey, 1982.

GLOTZ, G. *Histoire grecque*, 5th édn Paris: PUF, 1986.

HATZFELD, J. *Histoire de la Grèce ancienne*, Paris: Petite Bibliothèque Payot, 1969.

HOMER, S. *A History of interest rates*, Rutgers, 1963.

Lois de l'Ancien Orient, Editions du Cerf, supplement to *Cahier Evangile* n° 56, 1986.

LOT, F. *The End of the ancient world and the Beginning of the Middle Ages*, New York: Harper, 1961.

ROSTOVTSEF, M.I. *Histoire économique et sociale de l'Empire romain*, Robert Laffont, coll. Paris: 'Bouquins', 1988.

SCHUMPETER, J.A. *History of Economic Analysis*, London: George Allen & Unwin, 1963.

TAVENEAUX, R. *Jansénisme et prêt à intérêt*, Paris: Librairie philosophique J. Vrin, 1977.

VEYNE, P. 'The Roman Empire' in Aries, P. *A History of Private Life*, Cambridge, MA: Harvard University Press, 1987.

2 Almsgiving versus Usury

BIBLICAL BANS

The Hebrews were the first people to condemn interest-bearing loans. The Old Testament forbids it in three different places:

> Exodus XXII: If you should lend money to one of my people, to the afflicted among you, you must not become like a usurer to him. You must not lay interest upon him.

> Deuteronomy XXIII: You must not make your brother pay interest, interest on money, interest on food, interest on any thing on which one may claim interest.

> Lastly, *Leviticus XXV*: If your brother grows poor and he is weak beside you, you must sustain him. As an alien resident and a settler he must continue to live beside you. You shall not lend him your money for interest and you shall not give him food for profit.

These three passages, written between the ninth and the sixth centuries BC, are the bases for more than 2000 years of European legal bans on usury. They also lie at the root of more than 2000 years of legal breaches and loopholes. They have almost always been interpreted and analyzed in the context of a religious doctrine. It is interesting to consider their historical context before examining their philosophical and moral development or consequences.

The nation of Israel first appeared on the historical horizon in regions where civilization was already more than 1000 years old. In historical times, the Israelite tribes were born out of a gradual transformation of the old Hebrew tribes as they settled in the land of Canaan, at the beginning of the first millennium BC. The ancestors of these tribes were nomadic, tent-dwelling shepherds. In such an egalitarian society which advocated the same very simple staple food, the same coarse garment and the same movable dwelling for all, pastures and springs belonged to the community. The social structure was based on the extended family that is the clan. Power and influence resided not with the wealthy but with the elders.

When they first settled in Canaan the Hebrews tried to perpetuate this system. But from the beginning of the historical period we find only a few faded vestiges of the older system. The Israelite masses assimilated the principle of division of land. Quite quickly only landowners could claim full membership of the tribe and soon the first signs of social differentiation began to appear, based on the value of property (Lods, 1948).

In this respect the more advanced civilization of Canaan imposed its values on its conquerors: the clearest indication of this is that the settlers quickly adopted the lifestyle of the original population. The Israelites learned the science of agriculture and began to live in cities. They even modified their language to a certain degree, and did not remain indifferent to the worship of local divinities. Each district had its own legends and holy places. These were adopted by the new arrivals, who embraced the ancient feasts related to such things as the seasons. Israelite society, based on the clan, was slowly but surely changing into a society based on territorial structures, and the historical awareness of its ethnic unity was beginning to blur. However, a small but influential group remained faithful to the teachings of the Mosaic tradition. These were the priests of Leviticus. Outlying shepherd areas also remained faithful to the traditions of their desert ancestors.

After the wars with the Philistines, which fostered the development of an homogenous and powerful kingdom, agriculture was intensified and began to show high yields. Similarly, trades and commerce increased noticeably. Now that greater security reigned in the country, the more talented farmers could make a fortune by skilfully manipulating land and cereals. Moreover, an aristocratic class, grown rich on exterior plunder, or favoured by the sovereign, was coming into existence. Solomon's court adopted a lifestyle which was more and more removed from the primitive simplicity of the desert. This tended to accelerate the division of Israelite society into increasingly differentiated categories. In order to satisfy their suddenly extravagant needs, local dignitaries used all the force at their disposal. Pressure was put on law breakers, the poor were stripped of their goods, and the least misfortune was seized as an opportunity to lend to small farmers and demand ruinous pledges from them. Finally, they would appropriate the land of the insolvent debtor and sell him and his family into slavery. Thus, small holdings disappeared progressively, and a new minority of powerful landowners came into being alongside an increasingly impoverished peasant class. It is easy to understand the bitterness provoked by such a complete overthrow of the egalitarian system of nomadic times.

However, the prosperity was short-lived. Under threat from Assyria, war became permanent. Economic decline accentuated class differentiation and social problems. Each succeeding catastrophe hit the small farmers with greater force. Foreign invasions, earthquakes, grasshoppers, alternating drought and flooding, all mercilessly depleted the accumulated fruits of years of work. The poorest and least fortunate farmers lost their patch of ground sooner or later, while possession became concentrated among a relatively small group of large landowners. It should nonetheless be remarked that transfer of property could only take place when an insolvent debtor was constrained to cede his rights of ownership to his creditors, or when a thief was forced to sell his land in order to pay a fine. Even in this latter case, the legal system echoed the ancient clan laws in so far as his relatives had a pre-emptive right to the property. Such relatives were morally bound to acquire the land for the family. However, in the absence of someone who could do this, the land often passed into the hands of a stranger.

Whereas the monopolization of property in Babylon and Egypt had taken place in the vague and distant past, Israel went through the experience at an advanced stage in its evolution.

PROPHETIC INSPIRATION

Economically exhausted by wars and exceptional taxes, the country was suffering from a dearth of capital. Whereas Assyria, with all the wealth of a great empire, had an average interest rate of about 25 per cent, credit in the now impoverished Palestine was at a much higher rate. Poor farmers were often ruined merely by the cost of the debt. Israelite law, like that of other ancient nations of the Middle East, allowed the creditor to demand payment in the form of work for a period of up to six years. Consequently, many Hebrews became the slaves of their creditors. At the end of their period of service they had no option but to join the growing masses of landless day labourers. The majority worked without any guarantee of tenure, hence the seasonal, indeed permanent, unemployment. This strained social situation inevitably provoked a religious backlash, since religion and politics were closely interwoven in ancient Israel. Consequently, money-lending, as a symbol of a deranged society, aroused the passion of the prophets (Baron 1986).

Their often radical condemnations came from the pastoral regions to the south and east. Economic development had been slow in these provinces and thus there was a living memory of property being owned collectively by the clan. These areas were relentlessly opposed to private ownership. Harking back to the period of the patriarchs and the first settlers, which they believed to represent an ideal society, the Rechabites demanded common ownership of property and the supremacy of herd-based society over industry, agriculture and commerce.

In general, the prophets did not share these extremist nomadic ideas. Much like the legislators, they were willing to praise the merits of an idealized past, but this did not mean they wanted to return to a nomadic life. With the vague sentiment that it might perhaps have been better to have kept the simple lifestyle of the Fathers, and that all of Israel's ills came from infiltration by foreign culture, particularly Canaan, they left it to the tribunal of history to judge the rights and wrongs of their people. The prophets of Israel rose up against Canaan and its ways. Interest-bearing loans came from Canaan. Let them perish! Then the Mosaic tradition could be restored.

Laws at this period were still considered to be of divine origin. Thus, under the influence of the prophets, a restrictive interpretation of usury, as the cause of all social ills, was adopted. Of all the codes making up the body of Jewish law, the first *Decalogue* is, without doubt, the most profoundly imbued with the prophetic spirit. This explains why the Deuteronomical school and, later Judaism and Christianity, gave it such importance (Lods 1971).

The collection of *Civil Laws* incorporated in the *Book of the Covenant,* and which seems to have been written about nine centuries BC, prescribes that Hebrews enslaved for non-payment of debts should be set free after six years, much as the Code of Hammurabi prescribes three years. It should nevertheless be stressed that kings often assumed powers which were traditionally forbidden them. There is a striking difference between law in theory and in daily practice. The majority of laws were decreed by the priestly class who had the legal right to do so, but who had no material means of implementing them. Hence the particular flavour of doctrine and idealism which we find in biblical laws, most notably in Deuteronomy, written in the seventh century BC.

Josiah was the sixteenth king of Juda and helped provide the conditions under which Deuteronomy was written. He was also the only king who felt legally bound by its stipulations. He saw to it that a large part of prophetic teaching was incorporated into the laws. There is a direct organic link between the reforms introduced by Josiah and the whole of the laws and exhortations making up the book of Deuteronomy as we know it today. The Code of Josiah is one of the greatest reforms in Hebrew history. It was passed as the law of the land in 622 BC, 30 years before Solon's reforms and more than a century before the *XII Tables* of Roman Law, and had a considerable influence on Christian theological thought. The fact that the ban on usury was retained as central to Christian thought, whereas it was only one article of the Code, and applied only to money-lending within the Hebrew fraternity, is doubly indicative. Firstly,

Josiah, caught between his great rivals, the Babylonians and the Egyptians, was trying to reestablish the social cohesion of his people by pulling them into line with the prophets. Secondly, this declaration of identity was later to be both reduced and generalized by Christian theologians to a simple ban on usury, without taking into account the historical conditions under which the laws were drawn up and their symbolic importance in affirming social cohesion.

We get a better view of the importance of these biblical bans by looking at Christianity's slow moulding of mentalities. We only have to bear in mind that the essential prayer of the Christian, dictated by Jesus himself, the *Pater Noster*, states specifically '*dimitte nobis debita nostra sicut et nos dimittimus debitoribus nostris*, forgive us our debts as we forgive the debts of our debtors'. This text, initially in Aramaic, then Greek, then Latin and finally in the vernacular the world over, comes to us from Matthew (VI), whose gospel, we should not forget, is the most concrete of the four, probably because the author was a former tax collector. Hence the seventeenth century French expression for a money lender 'fesse-Mathieu' (fait-ce-Matthieu, do this Matthew). This fact constituted a stumbling block in relation to the parable of the unfaithful servant, a text which is important in the context of condemning credit, since we find in it the practice of physical constraint of the debtor until the debt is paid. The parable is sure proof of the widespread existence of money lending, in spite of the repeated anathemas of the Scriptures (Matthew XVIII)! Luke (XI), a doctor, is more figurative in his rendering of the *Pater Noster*. He speaks of forgiving sins and only keeps the image of the debtor in the second part 'as we forgive those who are indebted to us'. For centuries, morning and evening, this assimilation of debt with sin formed the grounds on which, first the theological ban, then the civil ban on interest was based.

RELIGIOUS SANCTIONS AND THE CHURCH FATHERS

When Justinian published his compilations regulating credit in the sixth century, the Church Fathers had been fighting against interest-bearing loans for two centuries, and had already condemned usury, that is any surplus gain, either in currency or in kind. Christian morality is often seen as having emerged from the Roman world as some kind of a phenomenon which had been imported from the fringes of the Empire. In fact, the Stoics and the Epicureans had long prepared the soil from within, and the dominant mentality was already imbued with disdain for commercial activities, money and the practice of credit. Thus the fledgling Church found a favourable reception for its ideas in the temporal world. In the third century, in the name of charity and love of one's neighbour, the Church Fathers adopted Old Testament rules forbidding interest-based loans. The practice of usury, which was simply regulated by the civil laws of the time, became punishable by eternal damnation.

Saint Clement of Alexandria, a Greek Church Father who died in 220, was one of the first to denounce credit on the basis of Old Testament writ. More particularly, two Cappadocian Fathers, Saint Basil (329–79) and Saint Gregory of Nysse (331–400) led a campaign against wealth and attacked usury by toughening the spirit of Holy Scripture. In a spirit of revolutionary fervour for the new faith, the early Church took an extreme moral stance, delving into its own sources, much as Josiah had done with the Mosaic tradition.

Saint Basil, bishop of Caesarea and initiator of the coenobite life, states that if in need it is better to beg than to borrow. 'On the whole, it is better to beg for alms, if one has been stripped of all and can no longer bear the burden of work.' This practice of institutionalized begging for alms was one of the foundations of Christianity for centuries, poverty idealized in the extreme by the practices of the Eastern monks, and later brought to its Western culmination by Saint Francis of Assisi. Usury occupies the opposite repulsive pole to almsgiving in the collective unconscious of Christians: sublimation of the self on the one hand and the utter banality of everyday life on the other. Not until the great Reformers of the fifteenth and sixteenth centuries would almsgiving be denigrated as a sign of parasitism and lending seen as proof of an enterprising spirit.

The sermons of Saint Basil constitute the first great study of Holy Scripture (Cremona, 1991). Taking his position from the precepts of Deuteronomy and the famous phrase from the gospel of Saint Luke:

'Do good and give alms, asking nothing in return', the bishop of Caesarea unleashed his fury against usury. His condemnation is terrible for it concerns day to day life. To the borrower he says:

> You came in search of support and found an enemy. You sought medicine and found only poison. Having received money, you are happy and at ease for a while. But the money disappears and time marches on, increasing the interest. Night no longer brings rest, the day provides no light, the sun looses its radiance and you begin to hate life.

To the usurer whom he considers as less than a dog he says:

> You never stop barking, always demanding more. If your debtor swears, you do not believe him. You find out what he has at home, take up position in front of his house, and knock at his door. You disgrace him

before his wife and before his friends too. In the market place you way-lay him and make his life unbearable. Usury is the beginning of lies, it fosters ingratitude and perjury. Its fruits are full of vipers. It is said that at birth vipers eat their way out of their mothers' bellies. Interest is born by devouring the house of the debtor. Against that, he who has pity on the poor gives to God, and God will compensate him.

In all the Christian tradition there is no more demanding prosecutor of interest-bearing loans than Saint Basil. He had considerable intellectual influence. He is, in fact, at the foundation of more than 1000 years of a total ban on interest by the Christian Churches, and his distant echo can be heard right up to the *Cantos* of Ezra Pound.

Saint Gregory of Nysse, his younger brother, is less concrete but more theoretical. He advanced the argument of the sterility of money which Saint Thomas was later to borrow from Aristotle. He also stresses the social dangers of usury: more poor, ruined homes, lust and debauchery, despairing debtors faced with nothing but misery (Bernard *DTC*).

The Fathers of the Latin Church also attacked usury from the fourth century. Saint Ambrose of Milan (340–97) devotes his *Book of Toby* to it. In the name of religion, he condemns loans on interest because they seriously compromise eternal salvation and are against the natural law. Stressing the ban on lending between 'brothers', as defined in Deuteronomy, he allows for the practice of usury between 'non-brothers' that is between strangers.

Moreover, it is interesting to remark that this biblical distinction between 'brothers' and 'non-brothers' is also strictly applied in the two other religions deriving from the Bible, Judaism and Islam. Resulting more or less naturally from this distinction we find the appearance of money lenders on the fringes of each of these worlds which, though enemies, were not ignorant of each other. In the Middle Ages the Catalans, the Lombards and the Cahorsans each specialized in lending money to their 'non-brother' Muslims and were condemned several times by the Pope, not as money lenders, but for being politically two-faced (Nelson 1949). As for Jews, their reputation as money lenders in the Christian and Muslim world need only be recalled. Along with these premises of a doctrinal nature, certain Church Fathers maintained a philosophical stance borrowed from Aristotelian thought. What they condemned initially, however, was not so much the practice of interest-bearing loans, but its abuse, which was one of the bitterest social scourges of the Roman world. The usury they condemned was abusive rates imposed on the poor; they equated abusive interest rates with a kind of enslavement of the debtor. For them, free lending to the unfortunate was a sort of divine commandment.

The names of the Greek Church Fathers are often associated with the cities where they preached and where misery was rampant. For them, a debtor was a potential pauper. But the money lender was not their only target. They also fought fiscal oppression: the arbitrary nature of the equivalences established between charges in kind and taxes paid in coin, capricious levies by landlords and the excessive frequency of compulsory services. In this respect, they represented the moral conscience of society.

It was always easy to spot the poor, particularly when they are concentrated in cities. Maimed and needy, vagrants and immigrants from badly afflicted areas, they gathered round the doors of basilicas and slept under the porches of the inner courtyards. They were the anonymous human dregs of the economy. And it was this very anonymity which caused them to be chosen as the remedy for the sins of the Christian community. Almsgiving to the poor became an essential part of the ongoing amends of penitents and the standard atonement for venial sins.

The fourth-century Church was still on the fringe of the great world, which continued to develop and modify its principal structures under powerful pressure from authority and hierarchy. The Christian spirit, although Christianity was now the official religion of the powerful, was still in a minority position.

Progressively, the Christian community was welded together by the very powerful notion of religious solidarity. By giving alms and the opportunity of work to the less fortunate members of their community, the Christians, but also the Jews, were able to protect their vulnerable fellow believers from ungodly employers and money lenders. The practice of almsgiving to the poor became the principal sign of solidarity between believers. The replacement of the Roman model of games and usury, with a model based on the implicit solidarity between the rich and the hapless poor, is still one of the clearest examples of the change from the pagan to the Christian world (Brown 1987–1991).

From the beginning of the fourth century the councils, particularly the Council of Nicea in 325, forbade the practice of usury among clerics, because it was incompatible with Christian solidarity and detachment from riches. However, although the ban on clerics was generalized in the fifth century, it was not extended to the lay community until the time of Charlemagne.

THE FIRST CIVIL BAN: THE *ADMONITIO GENERALIS* OF CHARLEMAGNE

Economic development at the beginning of the Carolingian era was based on war and plunder, not on production and trade. Charles Martel,

Pépin le Bref and Charlemagne amassed such wealth wherever they could and rewarded their followers with gifts. Not only did they not consider increasing their wealth by saving and lending, but they were even totally opposed to such an idea (Duby 1978).

The economic organization of Carolingian society allowed for only one form of credit: bridging loans. The Carolingian empire, apart from its Northern shores, was a land-based empire, producing and consuming essentially in the context of great domains. This situation was the result of an internal development which began in the Roman Empire after Constantine, and was accelerated by external factors. Ravaged by Germanic invasions, deprived of part of its Mediterranean regions by devastating reconquests of Justinian, the barbarian West was knocked off its feet by the Arab invasion: pirates at sea, brigands on the coasts, Sarrasin incursions as far as Provence and Aquitaine, war and economic competition between Islam and Byzantium. But poverty was nothing new in the West. The exodus of Germanic populations had left vast areas uninhabited between the Elbe and the Rhine. Moreover, the barbarian peoples of the invaded lands had proved unable to compensate for the losses caused by massacres and famines, particularly in the South of France. With production, exportation and means of payment all on the decrease, the West became a rural civilization again. The village became the central focus for the peasant class which was beginning to settle and take root by the ninth century.

Wealth was mostly landed property. The domain, supplying for local consumption, was at the centre of the economy. Trade and monetary exchanges were rare, slow and unwieldy. Gold coins became a rarity, city life was paralysed and the majority of professional traders disappeared. The centre of gravity moved from South to North and became more Germanic. However, money was never totally absent from transactions, even among the peasant class. Most important of all, it never ceased to play the role of exchange standard. Nor was society at this time completely ignorant either of buying and selling, but it did not live from it. Exchange had a lesser role in the economy than services. With service there was a general subservience of the rural population in Europe as a whole, a relationship of simple economic subjection, which made all the humble subject to the great, the poor subject to the rich (Bloch 1989).

In such a society there was no place for credit as a force of economic development. But usury remained a normal practice in such a primitive rural society, deprived as it was of monetary reserves and nonetheless criss-crossed by exchange networks of a commercial or other nature. Every man, whatever his level in the social hierarchy, found himself obliged to borrow from time to time in order to meet his obligations.

For the peasant it would be a bridging loan, usually in the form of seeds for the spring sowing. For the nobleman, it would be to maintain his role in society, equip a knight, or other symbolic expenditures. (Duby 1978).

This general power of symbols is essential in order to understand the toughness of Charlemagne's attitude to interest-bearing loans. The Carolingians came to power through a *coup d'état* and had themselves crowned in order to forget their background. The Pope's personal envoy, Saint Boniface, by pouring the holy oil on the head of Pépin le Bref, transformed the Carolingians into God's chosen monarchs at the same time as he made them the people's favourites. The ceremony of crowning the king dates from Biblical times, and bestowed and invested the Carolingians with the divine right of kings.

When Pope Leo III raised Charlemagne to the status of Holy Roman Emperor, he enabled him to usurp simultaneously the crown of the Merovingians and the august powers which the 'Roman Emperors' of Byzantium had not ceased to wield until the middle of the eighth century. By virtue of the coronation, his authority derived from God and he became God's representative; his responsibility came from God. Like Saul or David or Josiah, he became the leader the Almighty had chosen to lead the new chosen people, the people of Christ, to salvation.

The laws passed by Charlemagne bear witness to his constant desire to apply a programme identical to that of the biblical kings. In one of his most famous capitulars, the *Admonitio generalis*, made public at Aachen in 789, he outlined the general principles he had set for himself. He first reminds us of the example of king Josiah who, according to The Book of Kings, worked ceaselessly to establish throughout Israel the worship of the true God. Charlemagne considered that his principal mission was to lead the people of God to salvation. In his own mind there was no distinction between his spiritual and temporal roles. Consequently, he set out to make sure that economic activities did not interfere with the divine order. Still taking his example from Scripture, he sought in particular to introduce a moral dimension into commercial practices and the handling of money, into all transactions where people might forget the spirit of Christian charity (Halphen 1977).

The moral principles underlying the Carolingian prescriptions tolerate trade only in order to compensate for occasional deficits in domestic production. Buying and selling could only be justified as a means of restocking one's own house and to have some to give to others, in other words an economy based on self-sufficiency and gifts. Trade was seen as an exceptional, almost bizarre practice, and those who indulged in it should not draw any profit from it, other than the just cost of their own labour (Duby 1978).

Charlemagne's attention was particularly focused on two areas where there was greater risk of sin: slave trading and interest-bearing loans, the two being often linked. Usury was forbidden to the lay population for the first time by secular legislation in the *Admonitio generalis*. It refers back to and implements the wish of the Council of Clichy, expressed in 626, giving it the full symbolic weight of the new imperial power.

Dating from the insistence of Saint Basil onwards, Christian morality requires that we help our neighbour freely. Based on a passage from the Book of Exodus, the 806 capitular proclaims that 'a loan consists in giving something; the loan is fair when what is asked back is what was given, and no more.' According to the capitular, usury is 'asking for more than one has given, for example, if you have given ten sous and you ask for more in return, or if you have given a hogshead of wheat and then you ask for two back.' Usury was punishable by the supreme sanction: excommunication. The principal had been laid down clearly and would not be forgotten.

Lothario, who was the author of a *coup d'état* against his own father, continued the work of Charlemagne. In 825, he reinforced the ban on the practice of usury in the capitular of Olonne. He expressly granted power to the bishops, not only to seek out and punish usurers, but also to demand the support of counts in order to impose their decisions, by force if necessary. Moreover, he laid down penal sanctions for the misdemeanour of usury by decreeing reprimands, fines and imprisonment as punishment for usurers. In an 832 capitular, Lothario ordered the *missi dominici* to seek out usurers and to deliver them up to their bishops for public punishment (Bernard *DTC*).

Thus, in the Frankish world, more than elsewhere, usury was vigorously fought against throughout the ninth century, while a general reform of Church and State was being carried out simultaneously. Moreover, on the initiative of Charlemagne and his successors, Council pronouncements multiplied, confirming the ban for both lay and clerics. By the end of the Carolingian era, the Church had in its hands the tools necessary to continue its struggle against usury, a struggle it would continue by its own methods until the thirteenth century.

CREDIT AND CIVILIZATION IN VISIGOTH CATALONIA

Unlike Carolingian law, Gothic law imposed no ban whatsoever on money lending; it was regulated, as had the Greeks and Romans. The example of

Catalonia, one of the centres of European civilization at the time, is a good illustration of the difference between the Gothic and the Franco-Germanic world. The oldest deed of pledge in Catalonia dates from 973 and is in the archives of Saint Cugat. This type of contract was still rare in the latter decades of the tenth century, though whole series of them are to be found in the first half of the eleventh century. At the same time, wills give a greater and greater place to the problems raised by recovery of credit and the settling of debts left by testators. Of 150 wills, 72 make reference to credit operations (Bonnassié 1975).

This period is characterized by the massive influx of gold and silver from the Islamic world and by the intensification of commercial exchanges. Between 980 and 1050, the flow of Muslim dinars had such an influence on the Catalan economy that the very name for money throughout the Mediterranean world derives from the Latin word which the Arabs had borrowed: *danaro* in Italian, *dinero* in Castillian, *diners* in Catalan. The country produced more than was necessary for the survival of the population and the surplus fostered exchange. The economy flourished to such a degree that coins, which were in abundance, were not sufficiently plentiful to regulate exchanges, hence a great development of credit.

Everybody lent in this economy. Lenders were so common among the clerics that they were to be found, in cities, among the very lowest ranks. There is the example of Guillem, a clergy's member. Creditor to some of the most highly placed persons he seems, above all, to have been the official money lender to the local peasants. It would seem that he organized a veritable credit organization, having recourse to the services of a priest, Gauzfred (whose job it was to update the list of loans), to satisfy its needs, and to another person, Onofred described as a ministerial (who was responsible for the objects taken in pledge). Was Guillem working for himself only or was he an agent for the Barcelona chapter? The two theories are not mutually exclusive: on the one hand his profits enabled him to acquire numerous properties, although he seems to have been directly subject to canons and to the bishop Deudat whom he salutes as his lord. Whatever the case, he represents the first clearly documented example in Europe of an organized pawnbroker. The simple fact that Gothic law allowed interest means that today we have access to his archives. The forbidden, though nonetheless practised, usury of countries subject to Frankish law remains cloaked in anonymity (Bonnassié 1975).

Only very occasionally did monasteries play the role of sponsors. Moreover, credit was not in any way specialized: today's borrower could very well be tomorrow's lender, while some accumulated debts and credits simultaneously! Amounts borrowed were sometimes modest, as in the case of bridging loans, but sums were also massive when the aristocracy borrowed.

The majority of loans were signed for a period of less than one year, against the remission of a pledge of valuables or property. Generally speaking, the value of the pledge was distinctly greater than the amount of the loan. Legally speaking, the creditor became the owner of the pledge, but in the case of land or a dwelling, the borrower continued to reap the fruits and to enjoy all the benefits of ownership. The borrower was not free to dispose of property entered into pledge, nor to pledge it a second time. Recovery of the loan, in case of non-payment, was precisely described in the Code of Réceswinth. The creditor had to allow a minimum deadline of ten days after the repayment date and then had to deliver a public summons to the debtor. If the debtor still did not pay, the creditor could then formally lodge a complaint against him. A judge then convened a commission of three members who decided on the outcome of the affair. If there was no breach of the legislation relative to money lending, the creditor was then free to dispose of the pledge.

Although documents from the period are very explicit on the subject of loans, they remain vague on one point: interest rates. The law set a ceiling of 12.5 per cent, whereas 25 per cent was often admitted to and considered reasonable. Rates of between 50 per cent and 70 per cent were not rare. Although these rates may appear exorbitant, they should be placed in the context of the times with the demand for credit far in excess of the supply.

When credit is legal and regulated by law it becomes a growth factor and enhances the well being of an expanding society. Compared to the sombre outlook for the Carolingian empire, Catalonia was one of the principal poles of European development. The complete body of archives at our disposal enables us to study the first historically recorded examples of credit and to establish the link between the level of civilization and the availability of credit. We shall encounter this link on many more occasions.

REFERENCES

The decalogue, two versions: (a) Exodus XX 2–17 (b) Deuteronomy V 6–21.
Code of the Covenant, Exodus XX, 22 XXIII, 33.
Deuteronomy, Deuteronomy XII à XXVI.
BARON, S.W. *Histoire d'Israël,* Paris: P.U.F., coll. 'Quadrige', 1986.
BERNARD, A. *'Usure',* in *Dictionnaire de théologie catholique* (*DTC*).
BLOCH, M. *Feudal Society,* 2nd edn London and New York: Routledge, 1989 (© 1961).

BONNASSIE, P. *La Catalogne du milieu du Xe à la fin du XIe siècle. Croissance et mutations d'une société*, Publications de l'Université de Toulouse-Le Mirail, Série A, T.23, 1975.

BOUTRUCHE, R. *Seigneurie et féodalité*, Paris: Aubier/Montaigne, 1968.

BROWN, P. *A History of Private Life*, Cambridge MA: Harvard University Press, 1987–91.

CREMONA, D. '*Carità e interesse*' in *San Antonino da Firenze*, Aleph, 1991.

DUBY, G. *The Early Growth of the European Economy: Warriors & Peasants From the 7th to the 12th century*, 2nd edn, Ithaca, NY: Cornell University Press, 1978 (©1974).

DUBY, G. *Rural Economy and Country Life in the Medieval West*, Columbia: University of South Carolina Press, 1976 (©1968).

DUBY, G. *Histoire de la France*, Paris: T.I, Larousse, Coll. 'Références', 1986.

HALPHEN, L. *Charlemagne and The Carolingen Empire*, Amsterdam and New York: North Holland Pub. Co., 1977.

LODS, A. *Israël, from its beginning to the middle of the 18th century*, London: Routledge, 1948.

LODS, A. *The Prophets and the rise of Judaism*, 2nd edn, Wesport, Conn.: Greenwood Press, 1971.

MOLLAT, M. *The Poor in the Middle Ages*, New Haven: Yale University Press, 1986.

NELSON, B. *The idea of usury, from tribal brotherhood to universal otherhood*, Princeton University Press, 1949.

TAVENEAUX, R. *Jansénisme et prêt à intérêt*, Paris: J. Vrin, 1977.

3 The Two-sided Attitude of the Church

Founded as it was on Scripture and the Church Fathers, particularly Saint Basil, the principle of an absolute ban on usury remained intact until the twelfth century. The prevalent theological reasoning was based on fraternity and natural morality, although the thinking was philosophically vague, the rational justification quite summary, and definition of types hardly touched upon.

The two main theoretical texts from the twelfth century, the *Decree* of Gratien and the *Sentences* of Pierre Lombard, both monks from Northern Italy, arose from a train of scholastic thought which favoured the maintenance of a traditional economy centred round the domain. They sum up Christian doctrine in one organic whole, comprising Holy Scripture, the writings of the Church Fathers, conciliar canons and Papal decrees. Their conclusions on the subject of credit can best can be expressed thus: lending is recommended in the Bible (particularly in Ecclesiastes) but to demand in return, either in coin or in kind, more than had been lent, is an act of usury; it is also usurious to lend a sum of money in return for a quantity of merchandise, knowing that by the time of maturity the value of the merchandise will have outstripped that of the sum lent. All interest-bearing loans are theft, and therefore to be condemned in cleric or lay. Pierre Lombard ranked usury among the sins against the seventh commandment, usually concerned with sacrilege and rapine (Bernard *DTC*). It was also the primitive scholastic tradition which placed *avaritia,* that is greed, of which usury was the supreme expression, at the head of the list of the seven deadly sins, in the place previously occupied by *superbia,* that is pride (Le Goff 1988, *Your money or your life*). Historically speaking, this is of extraordinary symbolic importance: the replacement of pride, the feudal sin par excellence, with greed, reputed to be a more bourgeois sin, gave perfect expression to current social developments, particularly in the Italian cities, and showed that primitive scholasticism, which is much disparaged as a mere compilation of older traditions, was also capable of subtle observation.

MEDIEVAL CHANGES

With the twelfth century the world began to change. Interest-bearing loans, under different forms, became an important element in economic life, and an essential growth factor, particularly in Italy.

Economic developments were undermining the foundations of the old military, clerical and rural society. Lending, which enriched the bourgeoisie at the expense of the aristocracy, was violently attacked by the defenders of the old system. But it was also at the centre of the intellectual writings of the new mendicant and urban orders who were seeking a compromise. The Papacy, although it had everything to gain from the new redistribution of power within the Church, hesitated: it condemned lending, then tolerated it, then listed exceptions to the rule and generally adopted a pragmatic attitude.

In the Early Middle Ages, in a context of endemic warfare, the two principal bases of the economy were slavery and pillage. At the Lateran Council in 1059, the Church succeeded in imposing 'God's peace', granting divine protection to a certain number of persons and goods. This protection was progressively extended to cover the whole of economic life. This was the end of the first feudal age, based solely on brute force. Economic structures ceased to be founded on pillage. Aggression was then turned against the world outside the Christian arena. This was the beginning of the Age of the Crusades. The more Christian activity was focused in Mediterranean countries, the more the lords left their earlier isolation. The corollary of this was their growing taste for luxury, travel, finery and ostentation. To satisfy their growing needs, they had to increase the revenue from their estates. The peasantry was encouraged to produce more and more in return for the lord's protection (Duby 1976).

At the beginning of the twelfth century, society was still essentially rural and development was marked by peasant conquests, but money had an increasingly important role to play in exchange. The commercial horizon broadened. The towns, with artisans and the bourgeoisie beginning to prosper, awoke from their millenary slumber. Progress was being fostered everywhere, as merchants were protected. Canals were opened up, ports built and security increased at fairs and on the highways. Thus, towns began to have a central role in the structures that were developing out of feudalism. Money became the most powerful instrument of power. It was by using money that a prince acquired faithful auxiliaries, that he succeeded in exploiting the financial difficulty of the 'barons', that he enlisted cavalry in his service and recruited mercenaries. A prince allowed the bourgeoisie to amass wealth, then he squeezed it out of them, either by means of taxes or by forced borrowing. The growing financial fluidity, which allowed the princes to consolidate their positions, was based on bourgeois credit. But the lords were not the only ones indebted to the merchants: money had begun to flow outward from the towns, in increasing quantities over larger and larger areas of the countryside, to progressively feed the rural economy. Money went from town to villages, enabled people to buy their way out of compulsory duties, to pay transfer taxes and to make harvest purchases. While the volume of business continued to increase regularly, money as an instrument and the practice of negotiation, progressively infiltrated rural lifestyles (Duby 1976).

The growing ostentation, which characterized aristocratic life at the time, put increasing pressure for funds on the lordly dwellings, be they lords of the Church or temporal lords. But land was practically their only fortune. Of necessity, therefore, they liquidated a part of that fortune. Their attitude to money began to be characterized by debts. They had always had recourse to small short-term loans. By the end of the twelfth century, the situation was becoming chronic. The first affected were the richest and most powerful of the lords, who were also the most spendthrift: princes first of all, then large religious establishments, then local lords. By 1140, the monastery of Cluny was so deeply in debt that it would never manage to extricate itself. Five years later the Cistercian abbeys began to take out loans also. For religious institutions in the area around Metz, 1170 was the critical year.

Lower, more widespread, social strata would later follow this example. Sources show that in the regions around Macon the lower aristocracy began to run heavily into debt in the early thirteenth century. It appears that a large part of the noble classes throughout Europe were going through financial difficulties at this time. Although they owned vast fortunes, there was little return, except in terms of agricultural produce. However, it was becoming more and more expensive to celebrate festive occasions, follow dress fashions, make war or stock a stable. They had no choice but to go to creditors. Increased sales of land and land rights correspond closely with increasing numbers of loans. This phenomenon can be considered as one of the most characteristic of this new phase of European economic development, opening up at the end of the twelfth century (Duby 1976).

The increasing use of currency, was not limited to the nobles, clerics and monks. Villagers too, felt the pressure to buy more. They needed more and more money for any one or more of a variety of different purposes: to buy livestock and increase their farming activities; to concentrate more on breeding; to acquire property which was constantly increasing in price; to acquire the legal status of a freeman and the franchises the lords offered; or finally to acquire the objects, tools and garments produced by town-dwelling artisans. Throughout these centuries of prosperity, the increase of rural debts is one of the surest signs of economic expansion, and better standard of living (Duby 1976).

In spite of the bans, Christian traders in towns, like their Jewish counterparts, gave interest-bearing loans to country people. In this way, they kept in circulation the money they earned which was not needed to replenish their stocks. The same holds for the religious institutions which were constantly receiving alms in the form of money or precious metals. They were often deeply in debt, and when the stipulations of donors prevented them from paying their creditors with money or valuables received, they were prompt to lend it out themselves.

Naturally, in all countries where interest-bearing loans were forbidden by civil law, as was the case in France and Italy, people had resort to legal ingenuity in order to avoid being condemned as usurers. Nothing simpler! Since money could not be used to make more money, the pledge for the loan could be used to earn money! Thus, from the tenth century onwards the system developed of giving false donations to be returned to the pawner-lender at the end of the period of guarantee. The system was improved in the twelfth century: the borrower sold an annuity to the lender, the annuity corresponding exactly to the repayments to be paid by instalments, consisting of the capital sum and of interest. If the borrower failed to pay, the lender kept the pledge.

The sale of annuities quickly became the principal system of credit in France. Everybody, abbeys, lords, bourgeoisie and peasants found it to their satisfaction. It has been shown that in certain regions there was a high correlation between a strong economic revival (salt pans, vineyards, Romanesque churches and so on) and the increased sales of annuities, which account for as much as a quarter of the records kept in civil and ecclesiastical registers. During these same centuries, Italian jurists were even more daring. They used a contract of purchase with sale agreement. The credit was obtained by simulating the purchase by the creditor of an item that will be sold later to the debtor at an increased price.

The religious authorities were not taken in for a moment. Conciliar and Papal bans continued to rain down for a long time, indicating their ineffectiveness by their very repetition. In 1139, the second Latran Council confirmed the excommunication of usurers and in 1179 the third forbade them private burial. In 1148, Pope Eugene III condemned mortgages as indirect usury, a condemnation which was confirmed by Pope Urban III. In this increasingly flagrant conflict between the needs of the economy and

Church tradition, the next three centuries would see profound changes. Interest-bearing loans became a major focal point for philosophical reflection, from which modern society would be born.

OPPOSITION OF THE FEUDAL WORLD TO CHANGES IN SOCIETY

The economic development which shifted the centre of activity from country to town was accompanied by a centralizing political development which was also visible in the Church. The progress of the monetary economy was leading to an overthrow of traditional power.

Naturally, feudal and ecclesiastical hierarchies resisted these changes with force. The old agrarian economies reacted against the intrusion of a new power, money, the instrument of progress and modernization, with all its implicit social changes. One of the most effective brakes to development lies in the tenacious resistance of certain mental attitudes and the cultural models which support them. Most resistant of all was the system of chivalry. This system offered as the only attitude worthy of the perfect man *vis-à-vis* wealth: not to produce, to live as a lord, owning land and wielding power over men, the only proper sources of income, then to spend lavishly on feasts as a sort of substitute for war (Duby 1978).

At the very moment when financial difficulties increased at the highest levels of the lay aristocracy, when the lords' debts to the bourgeoisie were beginning to accumulate, when the art of governing through money was inclining princes to choose their best servants not from the nobility but from mercenaries and men who knew how to count, this ethic of warrior idleness and waste was taking an even greater hold on feudal Europe. It formed the armature of the class consciousness of a group which was beginning to feel threatened in its superiority. While the progress of the money economy accelerated, this gentlemanly morality condemned with more insistence than ever the spirit of profit and the desire to increase one's resources.

The economy was totally subject to ethics and would continue so for a long time to come. Progress was still measured by the accumulation of power over men and land, not by the accumulation of capital. But whatever the feudals thought, about 1180, all over Europe, the age of commerce was about to begin; the spirit of profit was pushing back the spirit of generosity (Duby 1978).

The Church, whose wealth lay most of all in property, was also drawn into the crisis of feudalism and the rural economy. Consequently, opposition to the new order also came from that part of the clergy which was closely linked to the feudal and rural world. Interest-bearing loans became one of the symbols around which this opposition would crystallize. The most virulent attacks, those which made the greatest mark on the collective consciousness, were the work of preachers like Saint Bernard, a Cistercian monk, the youngest son of a family of Burgundy nobles, who was fiercely opposed to scholasticism.

In the model sermon *Ad status 59*, Jacques de Vitry, one of the most brilliant preachers of the first half of the thirteenth century, imbued with the feudal and rural spirit, gives a clear picture of how he sees the new bourgeoisie class, as symbolised by the usurer: 'God ordained three types of men, the peasants and other labourers to ensure the survival of the others, knights to defend them, clerics to govern them; but the Devil ordained a third type: usurers. They have no share in the work of men and they will not be punished with men, but with demons. For, to the quantity of money they receive through usury corresponds the quantity of wood sent to Hell to burn them. The thirst for greed makes them drink tainted water and makes them acquire filthy money through lies and usury. It was of this thirst that Jeremiah (III, 25) said: "Forbid this thirst in your mouth". And as if in violation of this overall ban, the usurers feed on dead bodies and carrion, eating the food acquired by usury, this food which cannot be sanctified by the sign of the cross or any other blessing, thus we read in Proverbs (IV, 17): "For they eat the bread of wickedness and drink the wine of iniquity"' (Le Goff 1988, *Your money or your life*).

At the beginning of the thirteenth century the same Jacques de Vitry denounced the merchant cities as 'nests of heresy' and accused them of being one of the reasons for the spread of Catharism, because this doctrine did not demand that people go to confession nor, consequently, that they give back what they had gained unduly.

FROM OPPOSITION TO COMPROMISE: THE SCHOLASTIC DOCTRINE ON USURY

Progressively the Church advanced from feudalism to the new influence of nascent capitalism. It was assisted in this progression by the growing numbers of the rich merchant classes joining religious orders. The golden legend that grew up around Saint Francis of Assisi gives a symbolic illustration of this change: the son of a rich merchant from a prosperous town in central Italy, he had frequented all the fairs of Europe, yet he espoused the vow of poverty with a passion, whereas his order was to promote *monts-de-piété* (state-owned pawnshops), the first major social innovation with regard to credit. The fact that Italy adopted him almost immediately as its patron saint illustrates his emblematic quality in a society hesitating between the old and the new and which was finding a synthesis in the form of a morally tempered market economy. Later, the new orders of the thirteenth century, the mendicant orders, would become the most ardent defenders of the merchants. Familiar with the urban world and faithful servants of a Papacy desperately trying to extricate itself from feudalism, they were to furnish the ideological and religious justification of the market economy.

Thus, torn between the invective of crusading preachers and the necessity of adapting to contemporary economic changes, the Church slowly but surely elaborated a complete systematic doctrine with precise definitions, exceptions and punishments. Counterbalancing this development – as Jacques le Goff highlighted so well – the invention of Purgatory, private confession and penance, were the necessary milestones to calculate and evaluate the after-life in such a way as to save from hell the merchants, money lenders and other adepts of a capitalism which was still in its infancy. This joint emergence of capitalism and Purgatory with its principal application in interest-bearing loans, forms the foundation of the modern world. Half way between Saint Bernard and Pierre Lombard, between primitive scholasticism and the crusading spirit, the Church, in a gesture that was not lacking in audacity, donned its new theological robe. It is not without significance that the conjunction of clerics from Northern Italy and the merchant cities of Champagne and Flanders (the schools of Laon and Tournai) was at the root of this essential *aggiornamento*. From the Italians came the example of credit and the defence of the bill of exchange; from Flanders came the adoption of Purgatory and the abolition of public confession (Le Goff 1984). Modern Europe was born out of this ideological reconciliation; the great economic adventure, linking the bank of Florence to the industries of Bruges, is no more than its secular reflection.

Through the scholastics of the golden age, particularly Saint Thomas Aquinas (1225–74) who, as his name indicates, came from the kingdom of Naples, Aristotelian philosophy, which was rediscovered in the thirteenth century, became one of the essential elements of theological reasoning. When joined with evangelical teaching it led to a rationalization of moral life. Virtue was everything that respected the harmony prescribed by reason; sin was everything that upset that order. The ideal lay, neither in the accumulation of wealth nor in extreme privation, but in respecting the balance willed by God. Commerce and industry could make a positive contribution to that balance, on several conditions: that they be socially useful, that the resulting profit remain moderate and, above all, that the profit be the reward for personal work or risk. Although this was admitted, and we shall see why it was such a big step to make, interest-bearing loans, consumer loans or loans to industry, still remained illegitimate and irrational.

Saint Thomas' argument was based on the principle developed by Aristotle, whereby money was sterile, since it was fungible: money does not beget money. Usury (in the etymological sense of using away) was the price paid for the use of money; but from the point of view of the possessor, money was consumed when it was used. Consequently, its use could not be separated from its substance, as it could, say, with a house. Therefore, to charge for the use of money was charging for something that did not exist. To these arguments, Saint Thomas added those of Revelation. Basing his reasoning on Old Testament texts, particularly Deuteronomy, and on the tradition established by Saint Basil, he asserted that usury, in essence the opposite of charity and Christian duty to one's neighbour, was a mortal sin (Taveneaux 1977; Noonan 1957).

Saint Thomas' motives were essentially spiritual: usury is a sin because it is the indication of a too great attachment to the world, a challenge to eternal values, contempt for Christ's poverty and a negation of the gratuitous act of almsgiving as expiation. In this context the scholastics identified lending money with almsgiving. A conception which was eminently coherent, given the chosen aims of the mendicant orders found at the beginning of the thirteenth century. Essentially preachers, whose principle aim was to combat heresy, they worked to communicate the evangelical message in order to have it pervade and permeate both minds and institutions.

According to the scholastics, the term usury should be applied in all cases where profit accrued from a loan, also when the principal intention was to derive profit from a loan. The usurious nature of a contract did not depend on its rate of interest, whether excessive, fair or minimal. All profit, however small, was usurious, if it derived from a loan. No consideration was given to the use to which the borrowed money was put. For the scholastics, a loan, termed *mutuum*, could only be applied to fungible items, that is items that could be measured, weighed or counted. The *mutuum* was, in essence, a free contract. Once it ceased to be, it became, *ipso facto*, an usurious contract that is a mortal sin.

The doctrine thus formulated is clear. However, its range of application was greater in the intellectual sphere than in the practical. Its transfer to the realm of business raised far more difficulties than did its theological definition. The need for and the inflow of wealth increased the occasions for lending and usury. An intelligent grasp of the interests of both the

Church and of lay society led to the elaboration of numerous mitigating circumstances. One might even wonder whether Saint Thomas and his followers had not, perhaps very cleverly, toughened their theoretical condemnation of interest-bearing loans in order, later, to be able to propose, in all theological sincerity, practical remedies for its development. In order to get around the ban on usury, they suggested two legitimate means: the use of a legal contract which would not be classified as a disguised loan (which obviated the need for the legal ingenuity of earlier jurists) and the demand for compensation or damages for deeds not included in the loan.

Besides *mutuum*, Roman law distinguished another free contract, the *commodatum*, which concerned non-fungibles, such as a horse or a house, the use of which was separable from the thing itself. When the 'commodat' was onerous it became a *locatio* that is a perfectly legal lease contract. A *cambium* or contract of exchange was also legal. It consisted of an advance loan repayable in another place and more often than not in another currency. The *societas*, in which each associate bore his own share of the responsibility and received a share of the profits, also slipped through the net of usury. Finally, the doctrine ratified the *poena,* that is the practice of stipulating the payment of a certain sum in the case of non-repayment of the capital sum at time of maturity.

Transferring these concepts to interest-bearing loans, the scholastic doctrine allowed the lender the right to receive compensation in four cases which are now classic: in the case of *damnum emergens* that is when he suffered damages such as late repayment, the case of *lucrum cessans*, when by lending he deprived himself of an advantageous investment, *stipendium laboris* that is payment for work or service accompanying the loan and, finally, *ratio incertitudinis*, when the issue of the operation was uncertain (Le Bras *DTC*; de Roover 1971).

These four scholastic cases constituted an extraordinary breach. The theoretical condemnation of the scholastics has often been seen as a sort of curse placed on a monetary economy; but their analysis is in fact the best guarantee for the development of credit, at once both a moralization and a base, since it is easy to class the principal actuarial characteristics of interest rates under one of the four possibilities allowed for by these theologians. In what some still consider, even today, as an example of obtuse theology, there lies a lesson in economic pragmatism. (One is easily reminded of the theological justifications of some banks which have been influenced by Islamic fundamentalism and which, to this very day, do not charge interest but demand that their clients pay a *stipendium laboris* and a *ratio incertitudinis*.)

MEDIEVAL PRACTICES

During this period, merchants often granted short term credit by having recourse to *cambium* or a contract of exchange. Long term credit took the form of annuities which could be compared to *locatio*, whether perpetual annuities or life annuities. Perpetual annuities, which appeared in France about the end of the twelfth century and were widely used around 1240–50, were the most common practice. As we have seen, by constituting an annuity the owner of a property did not relinquish possession; he merely sold the right to a yearly and theoretically perpetual income from the property. The annuity of course reduced both the income from and the capital value of a property thus entailed. On the other hand, the investment was a particularly solid one since, in the event of default, for just one annuity, the recipient of the allowance had a right to all the goods of the debtor, or to a property specified in the contract. Thus the lender ran no risk in the long term, except if the annuity was specified in a cash amount, given that money depreciates. For this reason, amounts were often stipulated in quantities of grain, particularly in rural areas.

The annuity market remained very lively until the fourteenth century. When the economy was good, its advantages far outstripped its disadvantages: rents dwindled and the value of the land continued to increase. Thus people did not hesitate to sell an annuity in order to improve their livestock or to acquire new equipment. Consequently, in the thirteenth century, annuities helped to equip under-stocked small farms. After much hesitation, the theologians finally gave their seal of approval to both rural and State annuities.

Independently of the rural economy, interest-bearing loans were practised throughout society at large, by princes, merchants, simple folk and the Church itself. It was a hypocritical society, trying to disguise the forbidden practice, condemning it publicly but having recourse to it privately, turning away from those who practised it, yet tolerating them (Braudel 1981–4)! Jews and Christians both used the same means: simulated sales, false bills of exchange, false figures in notarial deeds. Although people practised loans on interest they were nonetheless not free from pangs of conscience. At the last minute, remorse led many to make amends for usurious practices, the most famous case being that of the Scrovegni Chapel in Padua, decorated so sumptuously by Giotto. The son of the most famous usurer in Italy commissioned it in an attempt to buy his way out of the *Inferno* to which Dante had condemned his father. Another example is the famous *Tryptich* by Jan Provoost in the Groeningen Museum in Bruges. The theme of the painting is greed and death. In it we see Death haggling over the value of his ticket with the money lender, and then the same money lender expiating his usury by praying to Saint Nicholas, while offering the painting to the Dominicans of Bruges.

In the *Divine Comedy*, usury is one of the pillars of the *Inferno*. Since Aristotle it had been considered as an act against nature; it was therefore relegated to the seventh circle of the *Inferno*, alongside the other sins against nature, sodomy, suicide, blasphemy and acts of violence.

The Church took up the idea and popularized it by helping to spread rumours about usurers being carried away to hell. She was preaching to the converted. Artisans in towns and peasants in the country often rose up in passion against money lenders who took advantage of their neighbours' misfortune by mortgaging their goods. This was a natural result of the two-sided situation: ordinary people had long cursed the quibbling attitude of the schoolmen jurists, and corporations even forbade their members to plead before ecclesiastic courts! They finally finished by establishing rules for conducting business which bore a strange resemblance to Canon Law. The lay community was not particularly virtuous, nor was the Church all-powerful, but its teachings made their way into the minds of men and stayed there as an attitude long after the ban had been lifted. Among peasants and artisans, borrowing and lending were everyday acts imposed on them by the economic situation. It was therefore in relation to their petty transactions, and not to high finance, that their traditional attitude to the money lender crystallized (Tawney 1984).

The Church transcended this popular attitude, giving it a religious dimension, and consolidated it into a system which preached economic morality from the pulpit, developed it in the confessional and applied it in the last resort through the courts. The sanctions applicable in cases of usury were extremely severe, and uncovering usurers was one of the major preoccupations of the ecclesiastical police. Since the usurer was committing both a crime and a sin, the punishment was both spiritual and temporal.

A usurer who died in a state of sin was excommunicated and deprived of the rights of a Catholic burial. The *restitutio* for usury or its equivalent was required both by natural law and by divine law. The usurer was therefore struck by civil incapacity and corporal or ignominious punishment, excluding him partially or totally from society (Le Bras *DTC*).

These sanctions came to bear with all their weight on pawnbrokers, often Jews or Lombards who advanced small sums to ordinary people. The interest rates indicated by trials suggest fabulous profits. It sometimes suited the borrower to go to the judge and denounce the usurer, rather than pay the interest. Naturally, the judge could only condemn the usurer. The bond between them was then declared illegal and the borrower freed of his debt. Such examples are deceptive. In fact, the real profit made by pawn-brokers was quite small. The miserable fellow who pawned his threadbare coat for three sous and accepted to pay a high interest rate, knew quite well that he would never come to reclaim his coat and that he had in fact sold it for as much as the ragman would have paid.

The high point of Church attacks on usury was reached at the time of the Councils of Lyon (1274) and Vienne (1312). Here the money lender was condemned as a veritable outlaw. Under pain of excommunication or interdict, no individual or company was to let a house to a usurer. They were refused confession, absolution and Christian burial until such time as they returned the goods in their possession, and their wills were not accepted as valid. Any person who persisted in claiming that usury was not a sin was punished as a heretic. The Inquisition ruled. Under pain of excommunication, all secular legislation allowing usury had to be abolished (Tawney 1984).

We may well seek the meeting point between Saint Thomas' liberal attitude and the Inquisitorial severity practised in reality. Although inclined to make exceptions in the case of big business, banking and public financing, the schoolmen denied the same privileged treatment to small-time consumer credit. This discriminatory attitude is the first striking example in a series of refusals, on the part of moral or political guardians, to understand consumer credit. This refusal to understand is often found today in the form of a bad image which has lived on since the Middle Ages. As if it was only big-time credit, that is bank credit that has the privilege of benefiting from 'damages' for late payment or uncertain risk.

Indeed, the charge of usury was practically never brought against the vast transactions of kings, feudal lords, bishops or abbots not to mention the Papacy. The top of the money market escaped the anathema. But from the end of the thirteenth century, a few princes and some towns had become aware of the lack of coherence in the system and granted Jews, Lombards and Cahorsins the right to set up lending tables, even between 'brothers', in return for a fair charge.

From the twelfth to the sixteenth century, the principles of the doctrine remained unchanged. Their application in civil legislation, however, was somewhat relaxed in order to adapt to economic changes. Credit reigned everywhere, in towns as in the heart of the countryside. There are monographs describing it being practised more and more openly and authenticated by notaries. The accounts book of the Sienna branch of the Ugolini bank has even been found. This is the bank that covered the Champagne fairs between 1255 and 1262. The book records a large number of loans to a very broad clientele, ranging from lords to abbeys, but also including the bourgeoisie, traders and small artisans (Cassandro 1987). Of course the interest rate is never mentioned, but it is estimated to have been in excess of 20 per cent. It is generally calculated to the least, the amount of the real loan being less than the sum indicated in the contracts, which is the equivalent of the total of the repayments (often with tapering annuities). But the phenomenon was not restricted to big business in Flanders and Italy. It is also found in remote parts of the country in a more rudimentary form. We only have to look at the case of the Guillaume family with its nine members. Between 1310 and 1378, that is at the very time when the Councils were taking a harder line, the family took out an impressive series of loans with due security and interest, all this in Haute-Saintonge, around the little hotel de Pons.

Confronted with such a social trend, the Church had no choice but to turn a blind eye and to leave the question as a matter of conscience, which the faithful could resolve for themselves. It was to introduce some elasticity into their thinking that they invented Purgatory, and to give the faithful some leeway between Heaven and Hell. The city of Sienna is a good example. Modern banking began there with interest-bearing loans being practised on an increasing scale from the twelfth century onwards. It was also in Sienna, and during the very same period, that the greatest number of flagellant fraternities developed. Long processions of clients, led by the bankers themselves, came to flagellate themselves before the palace of the bankers. 'One of the possible keys to Siennese mysticism is the bad conscience of the city, due to the success of its bank' – thus writes Franco Cardini, historian of the city (Cardini 1987). In 1319, during one such procession of penitents, the banker Bernardo Tolomei decided to withdraw from the world and to found, in atonement for his sins, the hermitage of Monte Olivetto Maggiore, the mother house of the Olivetan order.

The mentality of the times is easily illustrated, without going to such extremes. It was very frequent for merchants, bankers or usurers to leave money in their wills to pious institutions, thus making amends for what they had earned during their lives, in order to atone for their sins and have a seat in heaven. The story of Francesco di Marco Datini (circa 1332–1410), a famous merchant in Prato, is a good example: on the advice of his notary, the good Ser Lapo Mazzei, he left his complete and not inconsiderable fortune to the hospitals of Florence, in order to avoid the seventh circle of hell, to which his banking activities would have condemned him (Origo 1992).

Although the Church threatened and punished both borrowers and lenders, it was well known that interest-bearing loans were indispensable in a world where the most destitute had no other means of facing up to the unforeseen, whether illness, unemployment or bad harvests. Very early on she began to show favour for loans at easier rates than those available from professional money lenders. The ecclesiastics created institutions where the poor could acquire capital at reasonable rates. Parishes, religious fraternities, corporations, hospitals and monasteries lent wheat, livestock and even money. And in 1462 the Franciscans led a movement which resulted in the institution of *monts-de-piété* (State-owned pawnshops).

THE FIRST *MONTS-DE-PIÉTÉS* IN ITALY

The first *mont-de-piété* opened in Perousa in 1462 and the second at Gubbio in 1463, right in the middle of Saint Francis country. Supported by the Franciscans, they quickly spread throughout Italy. As public pawnshops at low rates, their vocation was to help poor people and to protect Christians from the sin of usury.

What really allowed them to develop was a new advance in theological thought. Saint Bernardin of Sienna (1380–1444) established the basic principles and Saint Antonin of Florence (1380–1459) popularized the doctrine. Saint Antonin was Prior of Saint Mark's and directed Fra Angelico's work there, going on to become Archbishop of the city at a time when it was becoming the banking centre of Europe, as well as a vast and teeming agglomeration which was frequently shaken by social movements. While observing the principles of Saint Thomas, wrote the two saints, it is advisable to complement them with the idea that monetary capital may bear legitimate fruits if it is 'fertilised by human industry', that is work, however humble (Cremona 1991). This was an essential addition to current philosophical and economic thought, and in perfect accordance with the historic role that Florence was to have under the Pazzi, the Bardi, the Strozzi and of course the de Medicis, once it had Sienna under its banner.

In the very same year that Saint Antonin elaborated his theory, Felice Brancacci, the Florentine banker and silk merchant, commissioned Masaccio to decorate the Chapel of Santa Maria del Carmine. This gesture he considered as his *restitutio* before the Almighty. Masaccio paid particular attention to the subject of Saint Peter giving alms. His frescos, which use Florentine models of his time to illustrate Church history, are unanimously considered to be the forerunners of a new world. Emerging from the conjunction of the splendour of Saint Mark's and the poverty of the Carmelites, Saint Antonin and Masaccio, charity and interest, Florence opened the road to modern economics.

Although rich with this intellectual climate, Florence did not open its *mont-de-piété* until ten years after Perousa, and one year after Sienna, (which operated both as a pawnshop and as a rural bank, hence its name Monte dei Paschi de Siena, that is the Hill of Pasturage). The opening in Florence nonetheless affirmed the importance of the new institution, and set an example for all of Europe. The birth of the Florence *mont-de-piété* was preceded by a difficult period of gestation, due to the rigidity of old practices and privileges and ingrained ways of thinking.

The first attempts to establish its statutes date from 1473 and gave rise to a heated controversy on whether its loans were usurious or not. The two opposed factions in this debate were the Dominicans, guardians of the Inquisition, and the Franciscans, defenders of the *monts-de-piétés*. In fact, the opening of the Florence *mont-de-piété* was delayed for want of the 6000 ducats necessary to set it going. Moreover, numerous illustrious citizens, among them Piero and Lorenzo de Medici, were against its opening because they were afraid that its existence might put it into competition with the Jewish community, with which they were deeply involved. In 1495, a new oligarchy came to power and gave the *mont-de-piété* its stamp of approval. Under pressure from the 'left', the Republic finally institutionalized it in the same year. All the religious orders organized an enormous fund raising procession. Thanks to the vehement actions of Bernardino de Feltre and Savonarola, nearly half of the required sum was collected. In 1498, the Republic confiscated 6000 lira from Pisan rebels and allocated them to the fund (Magini 1992).

The Florence *mont-de-piété* was well organized and financially stable, and from 1542 it was authorized to serve interest to depositors on the grounds of *lucrum cessans*. It later became the principal bank of the Tuscan State. It nevertheless continued to lend money to the poor in order to justify its existence, until 1947 when it was absorbed by the Florence Savings Bank.

Initially, the start-up capital for *monts-de-piétés* came from non-refundable deposits, which were considered to gain spiritual merit for the depositors, and free loans from Jews, in return for being allowed to continue their business. Getting a loan, however, was no easy matter. Administrative procedures were awkward and unwieldy, so much so that the population quickly came to consider them compromising and degrading.

The first *monts-de-piétés* created in the fifteenth century were extremely shaky. Many of them closed down for any number of reasons: lack of cash, too many bureaucrats living off them, embezzlement by employees, fraud on the part of customers, sacking of cities, the rapacious nature of certain princes, lending to insolvent cities and so on (Poliakov 1967).

However, in spite of all these difficulties, they were protected by the Church and the Popes, and so they spread progressively throughout all Catholic Europe. Florence affords the best example. But although the institution was conceived of as a victory of ordinary people over the business and banking oligarchy, *monts-de-piétés* in France, Spain and Austria quickly became one of the official tools of the Counter-Reformation in its struggle against Protestant theological excesses, one of the main preoccupations of which was greater flexibility in matters of interest-bearing loans.

REFERENCES

BRAUDEL, F. *Civilization and capitalism,* New York: Harper & Row, 1981–4.

CARDINI, F. 'L'argento e i sogni: cultura, immaginario, orizzonti mentali'*, in Banchieri e mercanti di Siena,* Monte dei Paschi di Siena, 1987.

CASSANDRO, M. 'La banca senese nei secoli XIII e XIV,' in *Banchieri e mercanti* di Siena, Monte dei Paschi di Siena, 1987.

CHAUNU, P. *Le temps des réformes,* Brusells: Complexe, 1984.

CREMONA, D. *'Carità e interesse' in San Antonino da Firenze,* Aleph, 1991.

DANTE, ALIGHIERI *The Divine Comedy, Hell,* London: Penguin Classics, 1949.

DEMPSEY, B.W. *Interest and Usury*, London: Dennis Dobson Ltd, 1948.

DUBY, G. *The early growth of the European Economy: Warriors and Peasants from the 7th to the 12th Century*, Ithaca, New York: Cornell University Press, 1978.

DUBY, G. *Rural Economy and Country Life in the Medieval West*, Columbia: University of South Carolina Press, 1976 (©1968).

DUBY, G. *Histoire de la France*, Paris: Larousse, coll. 'Références', 1986.

JULIEN-LABRUYERE, F. *Paysans charentais*, preface by J. LE GOFF, La Rochelle Rupella-where, 1982.

LE BRAS, G. 'La doctrine ecclésiastique de l'usure à l'époque classique (*XIIe-XVe siècle*)'*, Dictionnaire de Théologie Catholique.*

LE GOFF, J. *Marchands et banquiers du Moyen Age*, Paris: 'Que sais-je?', P.U.F., 1956.

LE GOFF, J. *The Birth of Purgatory*, Chicago: University of Chicago Press, 1984.

LE GOFF, J. *Intellectuals in the Middle Ages*, Oxford and Cambridge, MA: Blackwell, 1993.

LE GOFF, J. *Your Money or your life*, New York and Cambridge, MA: Zone books (Distributed by MIT Press) 1988.

LE GOFF, J. (ed.), *Histoire de la France religieuse*, Vol. I, Paris: Le Seuil, 1988.

MAGINI, M. *La cassa di risparmio di Firenze*, Florence: Olschki, 1992.

NOONAN, J.T. *The scholastic analysis of usury*, Cambridge, MA: Harvard University Press, 1957.

ORIGO, I. *The merchant of Prato, The daily life in an Italian city*, Harmondsworth: Penguin Books, 1992.

PERNOUD, R. *Histoire de la bourgeoisie en France*, Paris: Le Seuil, coll. 'Points', 1981.

POLIAKOV, L. *Les banquiers juifs et le Saint-Siège*, Paris: Calmann-Lévy, 1967.

ROOVER, R. de *La pensée économique des scolastiques*, Paris: J. Vrin, 1971.

ROOVER, R. de *Business, banking and economic thought in late medieval and early modern Europe*, Chicago: University Chicago Press, 1974.

SCHUMPETER, J.A. *History of Economic Analysis*, London: George Allen & Unwin Ltd, 1963.

TAVENEAUX, R. *Jansénisme et prêt à intérêt*, Paris: J. Vrin, 1977.

TAWNEY, R. H. *Religion and the Rise of Capitalism*, New York: Penguin Books, 1984 (© 1926).

4 The Cleavage of the Reformation

To the scholastic mind, economic activity was justifiable only insofar as it had a moral purpose. The Church taught the faithful to distrust purely economic motives. It warned of the evil of commerce which, though necessary, was dangerous for the soul. Most particularly it warned of the dangers of finance which, at best, defiled the soul and often rendered it vile and loathsome. Of course there were distinct differences between the attitude of the primitive Church, the Church of the martyrs and of sublimation, and that of the institutionalized Church of the late Middle Ages. The institution it had become could not remain blind to the forces which were shaking society. With time, Church doctrine became less rigorous and more adaptable in its application. Nevertheless, the basic doctrine remained intact: interest-bearing loans were forbidden and were sometimes punishable by civil law.

Thus, in the age of discovery, the most active members of the population were imbued with religious fervour and torn between the opportunities offered by the opening up of a new world and the fear of eternal damnation. This feeling of profound impotence before the forces of the new world is recounted by the chroniclers of the time and heightened by the series of misfortunes which had befallen Europe since the beginning of the fourteenth century for example food shortages, the plague, the Hundred Year War, the War of the Roses, the Schism, the Turkish invasion and so on. The West was suffering from a feeling of guilt, no doubt fostered by the sermons of the preachers who, throughout the fifteenth century, like Old Testament prophets, tirelessly stressed the sinfulness of the people, the punishment awaiting them and the urgency of doing penance. Numerous pictures bear witness to the terror in which the people lived on the eve of the Reformation, a terror which was heightened by the fear of death, the threat of Hell or protracted suffering in an, as yet unknown and vaguely defined, therefore all the more terrifying, Purgatory (Delumeau 1988; Duby 1986).

The Church's teaching was quite simple: salvation was to be obtained, by being a member of the Church, by believing the teaching of the priest and nothing else. The next duty of a Christian was to confess his sins to a priest, to repent and thus obtain soul-saving absolution. Finally, the Christian was to perform good deeds which were essential in order to escape eternal damnation in hell, which was the inevitable destiny of all who died in a state of mortal sin. There was an ever-widening gulf between the aspirations of the bourgeoisie – who were keen to see their actions mirror their faith – and the sometimes ridiculous, sometimes inappropriate solutions offered by a Church which had become anachronistic.

Out of this gulf appeared the Reformation. More than anything else, it relieved people of the spiritual anguish caused by economic success. The only precondition for eternal bliss, and to be able to live without constantly fearing the judgement of God, was faith. Thus the early reformers reinvented a more human, a more living God, who understood their weaknesses and their earthly labours which bore the characteristic mark of economic activity.

Moreover, by advocating a more personal relationship between man and the Scriptures, the Reformation did away with several centuries of Church development, and radically changed both its nature and its functions. The reformed Church was no longer supposed to play the role of an intermediary policeman of souls. The Catholic, in order to confess and wash away his sins, to face death and win God's favour, had to turn to the Church for comfort and consolation and to mediate for him with God. The Church was the repository of grace and held the power of absolution. The Protestant, on the other hand, found himself alone with his own conscience, and alone before God (Lüthy 1959; Delumeau 1988).

Two main schools arose out of this more intimate encounter with one's own conscience: Lutheranism and Calvinism. By affirming that God is not a judge, but a father, Martin Luther (1483–1546) offered a radical cure for the Christian anguish, which found expression in the extraordinary abundance of *Last Judgement* paintings in the fourteenth and fifteenth centuries. All men were guilty, but already saved by faith. It was enough to have faith in the saviour: faith alone could save. Thus, for a sincere believer, there was no hell, nor even Purgatory, since it had never existed (Duby 1986). For such a believer, to give a formalized, exterior shape to his inner faith was a degradation of that same faith. Similarly, the maintenance of Christian morality should not be left in the hands of the clerics who had shown themselves incapable, but should be transferred into the hands of the State. Luther believed it was possible to maintain the social teachings of the Middle Ages while rejecting the sanctions which had accompanied them. Based on the belief that the Bible was a guide for the private and collective practice of the faith, he demanded the abolition of Canon Law (Tawney 1984).

Although Luther was indulgent of human weakness and placed his trust in God, he nonetheless continued to look toward the past. Being a monk of peasant origins, he saw no place in society for the middle classes. International trade, banking and credit, capitalist industry, the whole complex of economic forces which, in the aftermath of the Lutheran revolution, were to be the greatest forces in the dissolution of the medieval world, all these he saw as belonging to the world of darkness, on which every Christian should turn his back (Tawney 1984).

When he discussed economic problems in detail, in his two *Sermons on Usury*, in 1519 and 1520, he drew his teaching from the strictest and narrowest interpretation of ecclesiastical jurisprudence, without any regard for the reserves which even the canonists had tried to introduce, in order to make the law more adaptable to the necessities of everyday life. Not only did he insist on the fact that loans should be free, but he stigmatized the *damnum emergens* that is payment of interest in compensation for losses suffered. He also condemned the practice of investing in constituted annuities (*Zinskauf*). All of which were allowed by Canon Law in his own time.

At the time of the *Sermons on Usury*, Luther was using the discontent, which was to erupt in the peasant war, to further his own cause. In his teaching he adopted a demagogic position, which his disciples reject, but which consisted in joining theological ranks with the most hard-line scholastics, and then proposing a general moratorium on all debts. One of his followers, Jacob Strauss, took up the idea and in 1524 he started a veritable revolution because of the Eisenach annuities, which were the principal source of income for that monastery. There followed a long public debate between German theologians and University professors of the time. The debate on the Eisenach moratorium is traditionally given as the first philosophical break away from Deuteronomical ideal (Nelson 1949).

In fact, when peasant discontent turned to outright revolt, Luther, who had proposed the idea of a general moratorium, went back on his position, because he saw the risk of social disorder involved. This realization, and the influence of Melanchthon, who was to succeed him at the head of the reformed Church, brought Luther round to the idea that interest-bearing loans were a civil question, to be decided by each prince, and that theological condemnation only came into play in cases of gross abuse. The parallel he drew between usury and circumcision is still famous. According to Luther, sixteenth-century Christians were no more bound to respect the civil laws which governed the ancient Hebrew tribes than they were to celebrate the ceremony of the excision of the foreskin of young boys.

Melanchthon took up the same argument, applying it to the jubilee which granted remission of debts every 50 years.

Other reformers, such as Zwingli (1484–1531) in Switzerland and Bucer (1491–1551) in Strasbourg, also contested the idea that we could conclude from Scriptures that all interest-bearing loans are usurious. The tone was set: usury was not to be confused with interest. It was an abuse of interest and should be defined in civil law.

Between the 1525 revolution and the economic crisis of 1539, Luther contributed nothing new to the debate on usury. In 1539, he declared war on usurers and encouraged preachers to do the same. He was, however, careful to distinguish between lenders who offered reasonable rates of between 5 per cent and 6 per cent, and real usurers who demanded rates of up to 60 per cent. On the ever-controversial question of annuities (*Zinskauf*), he found a maximum rate of 8 per cent to be reasonable, on condition that the annuities be repurchasable, based on land which brought in a stable income (*Unterpfand*) (Nelson 1949).

Melanchthon and Bucer were even more lenient than Luther in their attitudes to annuities and interest-bearing loans. After this, civil laws came more into line with the ideas of 'moderate' reformers, although an intense polemic continued with traditional Catholics, and extremist Anabaptist Protestants who found themselves united in their absolute condemnation of interest-bearing loans. In 1541, Melanchthon publicly supported the Catholic, Charles V, thus helping him to get the diet of Regensburg to adopt an order legalizing interest-bearing loans, with a limit of 5 per cent. In 1545, Henry VIII of England followed this example, as did Christian III of Denmark in 1553, also with the support of Melanchthon.

Under Luther's influence, and because of the similarity between *die Schuld* – debt, and *die Schuld* – fault, the text of the Protestant *Pater Noster* was changed, dropping Matthew's image: the prayer no longer asked for forgiveness of debts but for forgiveness of offences. The new version, which even went further than Luke's version, was not adopted by the Catholic Church in vernacular versions of the prayer until the nineteenth century, whereas Matthew's image is still the official Latin version.

CALVIN'S CONTRIBUTION

Calvin (1509–64) had the approach of an enlightened, cosmopolitan city dweller; a man of the world. He accepted the essential institutions of a commercial civilization which was already well-developed in the flourishing Italian and Flemish cities. His work consisted in giving a new faith to the classes who, through their social skills, were destined to dominate the future. This supposes a relatively advanced economic organization, and Calvin built his moral system on such an organization.

In fact, Calvinism is a faith which sets out, not only to purify the individual, but also to reconstruct the Church and State. In order to do this, society had to be renewed by permeating every sector of private and public life with religious influence. The movement was essentially urban, carried from country to country by traders and emigrating workers. After Strasbourg, Calvinism set up its headquarters in Geneva. Later, its most fervent followers would be recruited from large business centres such as Antwerp, Leyden, Edinburgh, London and Amsterdam. Its leaders addressed their teachings to the commercial and industrial classes who constituted the most modern and most progressive elements of the century.

They started by openly recognizing the necessity of capital, lending, banks, big business and finance, and all the other practical aspects of the world of business. Thus they broke with the tradition which considered all preoccupation with economic matters 'beyond what is necessary for subsistence' to be reprehensible, and which had stigmatized the middleman as a parasite, and the money lender as a thief. They held that profits from finance or commerce were just as respectable as the worker's wage or the landowner's rent.

Calvinism was the first systematic body of religious doctrine which recognized and approved of economic virtues. Its enemy was not the accumulation of wealth, but the misuse thereof. Thus, the sacrifice of the monk, who accepts the rigors and privations of monastic life, for the salvation of his brothers, was no longer seen as worthy but as simple social parasitism. The true Christian should abolish begging and promote the virtues of work and economizing. The world was sanctified by effort. Consequently, the laziness of the beggar was both a sin against God and a crime against society. Against that, the activity of a prosperous trader was a Christian virtue, and a blessing for the community.

Calvinism is deeply imbued with the work ethic and the sanctification of work, and these ideas also ran over into Lutheran Protestantism. It is a question of discipline, not dogma, and it applies, not to the members of a religious order who have renounced the temporal life, but to temporal society itself. Work was no longer seen as a penance, the deplorable consequence of the Fall; it became, like prayer, an exercise in piety. It was not a punishment, but was given to man for his own salvation, and for the glory of God. In the Catholic Church, holiness, meditation and charity were more highly valued than utilitarian work. The needs of the body were far less important than the salvation of the soul. For Calvin, work was prayer. The holiness of work deprived begging of all justification and therefore, almsgiving. In Catholic piety, begging was a state of grace, and almsgiving was the supreme good deed. In Calvinism, begging was debasing and almsgiving a sin, because it encouraged laziness and maintained a social weed instead of uprooting it (Lüthy 1959).

The famous distinction between the deserving and the undeserving poor illustrates a basic Calvinistic view of society. The former were exclusively those who had suffered a setback in life. Moreover, it is significant to note that half a century later, in Catholic countries, the notion of the 'disgraceful pauper' appeared to describe someone to whom we should still give alms, but with contempt. This nuance between the undeserving whom we reject and refuse, and the disgraceful, whom we scorn, could well be found today by comparing the images and practices of consumer credit in traditionally Calvinist and traditionally Catholic areas. The undeserving attitude gives rise to a positive file, recording all the debts of the population. The disgraceful attitude results in a curative exclusion in a negative file, that is, which only records the past mistakes of the potential client.

For Calvin, the only good deed was worldly success. Giving work, therefore, became the supreme good deed. Thus, the capitalist could consider himself chosen by God. However, the capitalist praised by Calvin is not one of the idle rich, a landowner or a man of independent means. The Calvinist capitalist is active and makes his capital work by employing workers, he is a trader who opens up new markets and increases his capital through his own labour. Calvin's attitude to usury must be seen in the light of this change of social perspective and its personal reflection (Lüthy 1959).

In Geneva, two centuries before Calvin, the bishop had allowed a certain freedom in the practice of money lending. In January 1538, the town council set a maximum interest rate at 5 per cent. This rate, which was ratified by a 1547 decree, was raised to $6\frac{2}{3}$ per cent in 1557 and to 8 per cent soon after. In this context, Calvin's writings, which continued from 1554 until his death, highlight and introduce a system into the positions taken by previous Lutheran reformers. His ideas are summed up mainly in *Letter to Claude de Sachin*, the *Commentaries on the Four Last Books of Moses*, *Commentary on the Book of Psalms* and *Commentaries on the Book of the Prophet Ezedriel*.

Jean Calvin, whose real name was Cauvin, born in Noyon of a bourgeois background, was a humanist, a philologist, a jurist, a logician, a Master of Arts who had a complete mastery of scholastic philosophy,

Greek, Latin and Hebrew. As a philologist he was critical of the translation of the Hebrew word *nesech* into Latin with the word *usura*, because the meaning of the Hebrew word was 'bite' that is 'putting the bite on the poor'. Thus, he concluded that the Scriptures did not condemn interest-bearing loans, only excessive interest. This criticism had already been brought to bear in the same terms by Bucer in Strasbourg (Hauser 1931).

The Scriptures placed a moral ban on 'the bite'. However, the general ban on Jews, forbidding them to lend money 'between brothers', was a political measure corresponding to a time of need for a holy union of the Jewish people. The ban, which could be dated historically and was introduced for political reasons, was not the result of a divine commandment. What one civil law introduced could be rescinded by another civil law. Moreover, the notion of fraternity, as reduced to the chosen people, was debatable. All men are brothers before God. If God banned loans on interest 'between brothers', it would be against the 'common good', something which, obviously, God could not allow (Nelson 1949).

Calvin rejected the much-quoted passages from the Old Testament and the Church Fathers as being inadequate, because they were conceived for conditions which no longer prevailed. A keen observer of economic life in his time, he knew that credit was both normal and inevitable in social life. For Calvin, payment of interest on capital was as reasonable as paying rent for land. He left it to the private conscience of the individual to make sure that the interest did not exceed the amount set by natural justice. A financier was not a pariah but a productive member of society, and interest-bearing loans, if the rate was reasonable, were no more usurious than any other economic transaction in human affairs.

Like other reformers, Calvin pleaded for civil laws recognising interest-bearing loans and setting the limits beyond which they became illegal. So far, there was no innovation. It had all been said before. Calvin's essential contribution, which delivered the *coup de grâce* to scholastic theory on usury, was the work of a logician demolishing Aristotle's famous argument: 'Money does not beget money'. In practice it was possible to get around this argument, but it was nonetheless at the heart of official Catholic theories.

Firstly, Calvin proved the productivity of money. He accepted that if money was kept locked in a box it was sterile, but did a trader leave his money sleeping in a box? No, he bought goods which he sold again at a profit, or he bought a field and when the harvest came it would be impossible to say that money did not generate more money (Hauser 1931). Moreover, he added, a loan of money could be legal and a loan in kind usurious, if the quantity required in return was excessive. For Calvin, it was not the nature of a contract which made it usurious, but its rate. Thus, he legitimized a practice which divine Scripture does not condemn, and which is necessary for a healthy social and economic life, but he subjected the practice to the laws of divine equity (Hauser 1931).

By generalizing the legitimacy of interest-bearing loans, not only with theological argument but also with sociological, legal and philological analysis, Calvin contributed to eliminating an important obstacle to economic progress.

THE ABOLITION MOVEMENT

This doctrine flourished in England under the reign of Elizabeth I. It was, in fact, in England that the decisive battle concerning usury was fought between new economic forces and ecclesiastical morality.

In Tudor England, most families owned some land and simple tools. The trader, the peasant and the artisan were the chief occupations. In this world of small, independent and often prosperous landowners, serfs and wage earners were a minority. With the exception of some branches of the textile industry, the principal grievance behind social agitation, reform programmes, new legislation and new administrative organization was not the exploitation of the proletariat, but the general need of all to have recourse to the money lender. In matters of economic morality, the English theologians of the sixteenth century adopted almost completely the doctrine that had been elaborated by the Papacy and interpreted by the scholastics in the Middle Ages. The effect of their sermons was that the usurer became so unpopular that anyone who was unpopular could be called a usurer. Similarly, any unfair market was called usurious. Although the Reformation constituted a veritable cultural revolution, it initially left the hierarchical structures of the ecclesiastical organization more or less intact, and consequently so was their effect on the transmission of values (Tawney 1984).

However, the century of Elizabeth saw the rapid development of capitalism in the textile industries and in the mines, a great increase in foreign trade and, as a consequence of the increase in scale, the birth of joint-stock companies. It also saw the beginning of deposit banks in the person of the first notaries. The financial needs of the English government meant that when Antwerp began to decline, London became the centre of the foreign exchange market, equipped with most modern techniques: futures market, arbitration and so on.

Usury is a term which can mean both the simple practice of an interest-based loan (interest, in the etymological sense of the word) and abuse of the system, that is extortion and the whole associated social scourge.

A controversy arose about the term in relation to the idea of a 'clean conscience', in the context of trade and commerce. This controversy gave expression to the contradiction of an expanding commercial civilization on the one hand, and on the other, a Church whose moral teaching still took its inspiration from the Church Fathers and the scholastics.

For a large manufacturer, or for a trader doing business between London and Antwerp, an usurious rate, that is an excessive rate, was not a sign of bad moral standards, but of bad business standards. Their experience led them naturally to defy the traditional bans with all in their power. They were irritated by the efforts of preachers and popular movements to apply the doctrines of charity and good conscience to the impersonal mechanisms of big business. They were more interested in getting the theory to fit their economic practices.

With finance becoming more technical, markets opening up to all of Europe and the organization of industry becoming more capitalist, the old theological vision of society no longer had any specific solutions to offer. It had been formulated to prevent abuse and to protect the peasant from exploitation. The problems that arose, when individuals came together for economic activity on a large scale, revealed the obsolete nature of the old system. Its lack of practical efficacy paved the way for its theoretical abandonment. The social teaching of the Church ceased to count, because the Church itself had ceased to think.

For those who were to remain Catholic, the major result of the Reformation was the realization that Church doctrine was not adapted to the way the world was developing. For the Protestants, not to put too fine a point on the differences between Luther, Calvin and Zwingli, the major awareness coming from the Reformation was the need for a new philosophical basis for the modern society which was coming into being. As a semi-technical symbol of new societal structures, interest-bearing loans were at the centre of the debate. Just as Saint Antonin gave expression to Florence's modernism, fidelity to the Reformation, therefore to good economic conscience, split Europe in two. Protestantism, with its new social doctrine, was to become the spearhead of modernism, while Catholicism, entangled with theological constraints, would lag behind. The dominance of Northern over Southern Europe dates from this period, the division itself centring around no more than a few old maxims about interest-based loans.

Of course this revolution did not take place in one day, nor without fierce opposition, even persecution and wars. The importance and often the violence of the debate, which was the fundamental criterion of modernity in Germanic and Anglo-Saxon countries, is perfectly illustrated by the ups and downs of British legislation. In 1545, Henry VIII authorized interest-bearing loans and set the ceiling at 10 per cent. In 1552, Edward VI, under pressure from the traditionalists, repealed the law and made those who continued to practice such loans liable for imprisonment. Two trials in Germany also illustrate the difficulties encountered in this country to implement the new laws. In 1565, the bishop of Rudolfstadt in Thuringia, refused to serve communion to two nobles on the pretext that they practised money lending at a rate of 6 per cent. The nobles took the bishop to court, and after much deliberation and consultation with German Universities, the court ruled in favour of the nobles. A similar event took place in Regensburg in 1587: two brother preachers accused the local bankers of robbery for lending money at 5 per cent. The bankers also had recourse to law and, like the nobles, won their case (Nelson 1949).

In fact, from the beginning of the sixteenth century, ecclestical authorities who tried to enforce traditional morality had to cope with a current of counter-opinion which denied them the least jurisdiction in economic matters. The idea that the Church possessed independent value criteria, on which social institutions depended, was progressively called into question. Soon the Church no longer had any say in matters of commercial morality, since a healthy morality always coincides with commercial wisdom.

Under Elizabeth I, the Puritan movement, which drew its strength from the citadels it had made for itself among the commercial classes, succeeded in rendering the moral jurisdiction of the clergy odious to an ever-increasing portion of the population (Chaunu 1986). A striking indication of this development was the definitive abolition, in 1571, of the ban on loans at interest, according to the 1554 conditions, that is with a ceiling of 10 per cent. This came to pass, in spite of Dr Thomas Wilson's famous Parliamentary discourse on usury. Wilson was to be, among other things, Master in the Court of Requests, Ambassador to the Netherlands and Secretary of the Council. Later, ordinary ecclesiastical tribunals were deprived of all penal jurisdiction. And from 1640, neither ecclesiastical tribunals nor the High Commission, nor the Star Chamber continued to function. With the Restoration, the usurer disappeared from episcopal condemnations.

The Crown had become the supreme head of the Church, now royal. And who could be more royalist than the king himself? The Church bowed to his will, and all of society benefited.

In this century of reform the meaning of the word usury evolved. This was a major event for the image of credit. Usury came to mean the practice of excessive interest rates. It was up to each individual, therefore, with the assistance of civil tribunals, to evaluate rates.

Wherever the Reformation triumphed, the entrepreneur, the financier and the trader felt at peace performing operations which, under the influence of the theologians, they had previously learned to consider with powerful guilt feelings. With the sixteenth century the practice of *restitutio* disappeared from Protestant areas, though it would continue to flourish for a long time in Catholic countries. This was the system whereby the death-bed penitent, in order to salve his conscience, felt obliged to make restitution in his will by giving back interest acquired on money loaned.

It is easy to understand that the legitimation and positive recognition of interest-bearing loans was of enormous importance for the organization of credit, which was so important for the development of modern economies. It should also be stated that this legitimation of interest in no way favoured the work of the money lender. It was precisely because of the freer market in Protestant countries that money lending fared less well than elsewhere. The usurer was one of the standard images of medieval economies. However, as we come closer to modern times, we find that the image is more deeply rooted in countries with a ban on usury than those practising the new liberalism.

The effect of the religious Reformation was immense. This need hardly be said for Protestant countries: the British economists and philosophers, who were to lead the movement for European emancipation, were its direct inheritors. But outside of Protestant countries and circles, its influence was felt more and more as time went on. In the European Jewish world, the realignment of Deuteronomy, so dear to Luther and Calvin, was made official in 1655 by the British Rabbi Menassah Ben Israël. This meant that interest-bearing loans were authorized, even between brothers, that is within the Jewish community itself (Nelson 1949). The evolution of mentalities in Catholic countries was slower and more chaotic, but was insidiously marked by the example of Northern Europe.

REFERENCES

BESNARD, P. *Protestantisme et capitalisme*, Paris: Armand Colin, coll. 'U', 1970.
CHAUNU, P. *Le temps des Réformes*, Brusells: Complexe, 1984.
CHAUNU P. (ouvrage collectif sous la direction de), *L'aventure de la réforme, le monde de Jean Calvin*, Paris: Hermé, 1986.
DELUMEAU, J. *La civilisation de la Renaissance*, Paris: Arthaud, 1984.
DELUMEAU, J. *Naissance et affirmation de la Réforme*, Paris: P.U.F, coll. 'Nouvelle Clio', 1988.
DUBY, G. *Histoire de la France*, Paris: T.II, Larousse, coll. 'Références', 1986.

FEBVRE, L. *Au coeur religieux du XVIe siècle,* Paris: Le livre de poche, coll. 'Biblio, essais', 1983.

HAUSER, H. *Les débuts du capitalisme,* Paris: Alcan, 1931.

LÜTHY, H. *La banque protestante en France,* T.I.1959, T.II. SEVPEN, Paris: 1961.

NELSON, B. *The idea of usury, from tribal brotherhood to universal otherhood,* Princeton: Princeton University Press, 1949.

TAVENAUX, R. *Jansénisme et prêt à intérêt,* Paris: J. Vrin, 1977.

TAWNEY, R.H. *Religion and the Rise of Capitalism,* New York: Penguin Books, 1984, (© 1926).

WEBER, M. *L'éthique protestante et l'esprit du capitalisme,* Paris: Plon, 1967.

WEBER, M. *Histoire Economique,* Paris: Gallimard, 1991.

WILSON, T. *A discourse upon usury,* with a historical introduction by R.H. TAWNEY, New York: Harcourt Brace & Co, 1925.

5 The Hypocritical Masks of the *Ancien Régime*

In a sort of anachronistic backlash to the Reformation, seventeenth- and eighteenth-century theologians in Catholic countries made the crime of usury one of their chief studies. Simultaneously, Church condemnations started again and became even more severe. This movement was, in essence, driven by the desire to establish a Counter-Reformation. Moreover, it was assisted by persisting conservative structures in the two main Catholic countries. Their economies had remained weak because of slow agricultural progress and were unable to satisfy the needs of a growing population. These same economies were also weakened by the ravages of war.

THE IDEOLOGY OF THE COUNTER-REFORMATION

Having perfectly understood the temporal importance of the subject, the Counter-Reformation was rigid in its opposition to interest-bearing loans. People were afraid to show any tolerance, however slight, for the liberal precepts of Calvin. The Council of Trent (1545–64) was particularly severe in its condemnations. It ranked usury among the different categories of theft expressly forbidden by the seventh commandment and reiterated the old definitions, that is usury is 'all that a man receives above and beyond the capital he has lent, be it money or any other item which can be evaluated in terms of money'. Papal bulls and catechisms in the sixteenth century restated the same condemnations.

It was the very class mentality of the first Jansenists, coming as they did from established legal families, that provoked them to further toughen the Tridentine teaching. Their hostility to usury also extended to all other forms of credit. Some Jansenists saw their strict maintenance of classical bans as an essential defence of Catholic tradition and the magisterium of the Church. The first bishops who sympathized with Jansenism saw themselves as reacting to the laxity of Calvinism. Coming mostly from the country squire and lawyer class, they gave expression to a caste mentality which looked down on trading and money. Jansenism was a kind of French Protestantism, but without the 'capitalist spirit'. Its influence on the people remained quite limited, except perhaps in the Catholic part of the Netherlands where the bishop of Utrecht led the fight against the pervasive Reformation. In France, anti-usury sentiment found its audience and acceptance under the leadership of Bossuet, 'the father of French bishops'. Although not a Jansenist himself, he shared their moral theological standpoint and showed keen support for Tridentine teaching. At his request, in 1700, the assembly of the clergy formulated official condemnations of interest-bearing loans (Taveneaux 1977; Lüthy 1959). Not content with theoretical condemnation, some particularly zealous bishops waged a merciless campaign against the practice. Through them and their incessant homilies, anti-usury feeling spread throughout the masses of the faithful. The catechism also took up the struggle, which quickly proved to be of a rearguard nature. In the seventeenth century, catechisms, which relied for their authority on theological faculties, were unanimous in their condemnation of interest, usually equating it with theft.

This position of the Catholic hierarchy is easily explainable in historical terms: they were trying to maintain order in a society which had been torn apart by questioning and schisms. They were trying to take the initiative and to answer the challenge of the Reformation with their own Counter-Reformation. To a certain degree, they succeeded. The Church consolidated the social order, but to do so it had recourse to what was increasingly considered as doctrinal demagogy, thus slowing up the development of intellectual adaptability which is necessary for a modern society.

Europe at the time of the Counter-Reformation was still a society of aristocratic lace and stuccoed chancels, doggedly refusing to fit in with the economic models developing in the North. There was a progressive slowing-up of social development, felt most particularly in the Iberian and Italian peninsulas. It was as if, by having missed the bus which would have delivered them from the guilt created by infringements of the ban on interest, the Catholic countries had been drawn into a relative regression in their basic institutions, that is their philosophy, their teaching and their economic vigour – to the advantage of the emancipated Northern religions.

THE SPIRIT OF THE *ANCIEN RÉGIME*

In these countries, the aristocracy did not hesitate to become entrepreneurs, to invest money in trade and shipbuilding, thereby supporting the economic activity of the bourgeoisie. Britain quickly became the model for these active societies, where prejudice against business and industry no longer existed. The urban bourgeoisie did not invest exclusively in public finances and office peddling, nor was it below the country gentry to take an interest in drapery manufacture and agronomic improvement of the land. In Britain, the social standing of those managing the economy improved as their role in society became more important. Similarly, in the United Provinces, the merchant occupied a position of prime importance in the town, the province and in the Estates General.

As a contrast, Spain was practically devoid of a business bourgeoisie. There was no group comparable to the merchants of London, Amsterdam or even Rouen, to challenge the monopoly of commercial profits and financial speculation held by foreigners and Marranos. By giving themselves up to an obscure obsession with '*limpieza de sangre*' (purity of blood lines), the whole country opted for social immobility.

In Italy, the power of bankers and merchants reached its high point in the middle of the sixteenth century. It was based on old, medieval foundations which had been slowly established over several centuries through a flexible adaptation to social, philosophical and political circumstances. This system which, in its time, had been new, hardy, original and of incomparable modernity, latter became rigid and unable to benefit from the financial needs of States and from the broadening horizons of trade. The Italians lacked sufficient State support to implement a policy and organize a navy capable of defending the interests of the merchants. Most of all, they lacked the consistency of business thought, which had stood by them so well a few centuries earlier. The bankers, who had been so skilful in using their influence to develop economic attitudes, no longer sought anything except ways to take advantage of the system by infiltrating it. Thus, what is generally considered to be the glory of the de Medicis, their rise to power in Florence crowned by the creation of the grand Duchy, royal alliances with France or the white smoke of the Papacy, were nothing more than signs of a loss of vigour and economic creativity. It cannot be said too often that Lorenzo the Magnificent was without any doubt a great aesthete, but that he led his bank to bankruptcy. By not continuing to modernize its social and economic thought, Italy became entrenched in the kind of mannerisms which we find in all decadence.

In France, maritime and colonial trade showed prosperity for a while. To accommodate this trade the monarchy was to create joint-stock companies for example, the East and West Indian companies. However, like the first private factories, they were only moderately successful. The French bourgeoisie preferred to invest in land and offices. Commercial or industrial capitalism, with a system of loans, shares and bonds, was to remain the domain of socially restricted milieus. In domestic traffic it developed only in the wholesale market and in the form of local companies in a few large markets. Foreign trade remained a monopoly, in the hands of a caste of big dealers and ship owners in the Atlantic ports, who formed the link between the artisan class and the nobles. However, this emerging *grande bourgeoisie* really only played a small role in a society where the forms of a true capitalism remained sporadic, principally because of the precarious nature of the credit system. Commerce continued to take the form of small private or family businesses, in which interest-bearing loans normally had no place.

Why did France, the richest and most populated kingdom in Europe, with its coasts well endowed with ports and harbours, not build up a commercial empire like the English or the Dutch? Why did a powerful group of merchants, capable of influencing the laws on interest, not appear on the French scene as they did in Great Britain? The answer can doubtless be found by examining state structures and social laws more closely.

The prosperity of the first half of the sixteenth century promoted the merchant class as a whole. They nevertheless remained a discontented group because, in the consensus view of society, the nobles were the only estate worthy of consideration. Trade, a contemptible occupation, was at best a step on the way to achieving noble status, insofar as it enabled some to buy titles and offices (Gascon 1977). The nobility itself rejected all economic enterprises, through a fear of loss of status. This attitude was quickly picked up by the neo-nobles. Following in the same steps as the de Medicis, they hastened to abandon business as soon as they acquired the letters of nobility. The State, having an administrative conception of France, played along with this phenomenon, by multiplying the means of access to nobility. From 1520 onwards, the expanding number of monarchical institutions, along with the financial needs of the Crown, were the cause of a veritable inflation in the number of officers (Gascon 1977). The hereditary status of such officers was established in the seventeenth century, in return for an annual tax equal to one sixtieth of the value of the office. Thus the king acquired considerable resources and won the near-absolute fidelity of the office bourgeoisie and of its natural development, '*la noblesse de robe*', titled legal officers. By concentrating their ambition, and a large part of their resources, almost exclusively on these offices, the French bourgeoisie, and therefore the whole country, forgot the race for commercial, maritime and productive supremacy, which was lining the pockets of Northern Europe.

Throughout the seventeenth century this gap would only increase. The mediocre nature of the French economic scene was directly related to the restrictive training available for traders and manufacturers, their lack of knowledge of business methods, and their reticence to use the instruments of credit and payment – all of which were perfectly familiar to foreign traders. Some educational reforms were introduced in an attempt to modernize. No place was accorded, however, to the knowledge required in business. The reforms centred around Jesuitical humanism, and totally ignored the despicable realities of the economic world.

At the beginning of the seventeenth century, agricultural methods were still traditional and yields were mediocre. Metallurgy industries of the time seem obsolete in comparison with innovations in Great Britain. The navy lacked ships; banking and stock market organization was non-existent; and trading companies were rare and short-lived, being composed of too few associates with insufficient capital. In order to help France to play a role in international trade and colonial development, Richelieu hatched a vast plan to form large companies and encourage merchants to join them by offering great privileges. In an attempt to involve the nobility in this maritime adventure, the great edict of 1629 allowed gentlemen to indulge in maritime trade without fear of loss of status, and promised nobility to the greatest ship owners. This attempt, on the part of the government, ran into numerous obstacles. Social prejudice and religious scruples combined to turn many of the bourgeoisie away from business, and the edict of 1629 did not succeed in diminishing the disdain of gentlemen for manufacturing and mercantile professions (Gascon 1977; Deyon 1978).

The ban on interest, which many theologians and moralists of the Counter-Reformation kept harking back to, impeded the development of companies and hampered the circulation of promissory notes and bills of exchange from one place to another within the kingdom. This only goes to show that every technique depends on the state of society; on the state of mind. Once a bourgeois family had secured its fortune, it invested in land, seigneuries and offices, and its capital was sterilized in status-related expenses or in usury lending. History is paradoxical in that the ban on usury was applied rigorously to commercial operations which were thus rendered more difficult, but on a local or family level a solution was always found when it was a question of expanding landed estates. For this bourgeoisie of legal offices knew very well how to get around the bans when, in a case of, for example, a loan accompanied by an option of repurchase of land, they could hope to acquire the land in question if the borrower, usually a peasant, could not make the payment. There are numerous examples of this kind of practice throughout provincial France from the sixteenth to the beginning of the twentieth century, which saw the introduction of agricultural credit funds. Seeding loans, bridging loans, farm implements or livestock loans and the obligation to repay the loan, all indicate the presence, locally, of small-scale, credit sources. For all the French petit bourgeoisie, often described as smallholders, this credit was the basis of their success.

Although attempting to broaden the options offered by Richelieu, Colbert's policy of protecting the national market, strengthening manufacturing industries and the navy, and investing in commercial and colonial conquest, was no more successful than his predecessor's. Not only were the French distrustful of state intervention in economic affairs (Goubert 1977), but the faculty of theology's reiterated condemnation of interest and banking continued to weigh heavily on economic life. Moreover, the profits from state loans and traffic of financial and judicial offices still remained more substantial and sure than the exercise of commercial activity. The tax system was oppressive. In France, given the various taxes on the circulation of merchandise, and also the taille (direct tax payed only by plebeians), the farmers and merchants were the most heavily hit by taxes. Against that, the nobles were spared and, moreover, acquired the majority of the money collected by the state, and redistributed in the form of pensions, offices and favours.

The French economy was lacking in dynamism, adaptability and availability of money, because the class which should have created a modern economic system had become a caste of hereditary title-holders, and wielders of judicial and administrative power. In a country subjected to the heavy yoke of the magistrature and an awkward and onerous administration, the ideal to which all society aspired was still that of seigneurial positions and landed property, which gave access to independent incomes.

The tragedy of Colbert was that he was trying to replace a non-existent capitalist spirit with bureaucratic intervention, and with a system of privileges, monopolies, concessions, state supplied capital and official regulations (Lüthy, 1959). For the economy of the kingdom to progress it would have also required appropriate credit and payment facilities, that is a banking system. This was absent. Banking never really formed part of *Ancien Régime* society. It was foreign in its origins, and continued to be so in its development, its major orientations and its organizers. This situation continued until the middle of the nineteenth century.

Moreover, the confusion of banker and usurer was still quite current, and made not only by the people ignorant of business. It was a collective feeling derived from the civil and canonical bans, and fed by the repercussions of a bad economic situation on a great general indebtedness.

DEBT: REMEDY, POISON, OR PROPITIETARY VICTIM?

In the sixteenth century, Europe went through a period of vigorous growth. The expenses of war, although increasing, did not consume all the wealth.

The possible bankruptcy of States did not necessarily have an affect on prosperity. On the contrary, the seventeenth century appears as a period of depression aggravated by wars, revolts, devastation, food shortages and even sporadic reappearances of the plague. There was a climatic chill, monetary debasements and arrested agricultural production. Politically, States engaged in long rivalries. France and Spain, the two main Catholic powers, therefore rivals, both became countries of soldiers and men of independent means, both of them sorely affected by the European crisis.

Beyond the brutal oscillations of the short-term economic situation, due to bad weather or caused by the excesses of campaigning troops, the end of the sixteenth and the seventeenth century were characterized in France by a progressive deterioration of the different aspects of economic life. The periodic return to hostilities helped slowly but surely to reduce the productive elements of the rural world: men, capital and technical ability. The period was marked by an increase in taxes levied by the monarchy in order to support its foreign policies. Taxes and wars became the two essential elements in degrading the conditions of the humble. The indebtedness of the majority of the peasantry and the religious wars, at the end of the reign of Louis XIV, are fundamental to the social history of France. Although hardly noticeable under the reign of Francois I, the impoverishment of the rural masses became glaring from 1600 onwards (Jacquart 1978).

The great demographic growth of the sixteenth century led to over-population of the country areas and progressive land division. The difficulty of the situation was further aggravated by the hardships of the time. In almost all the French provinces, political and religion crisis reduced by more than half the extension of land owned or rented by farmers who had to deal with the devastation of the country, the increase of taxes and the rise of rents.

Harvests were often poor whereas costs were constantly rising: rents, taxes of all kind and particularly the royal tax which, in real terms, more than doubled in half a century. The humblest peasants who needed money to face up to these circumstances were often forced to borrow. A comfortably-off labourer, a merchant from the nearest burgh, or an owner of smallholdings from the town, would advance money to the poorest part of the population. A bond was signed. The maturation date came round, and the payment could not be met. A new debt was contracted, or a rent on goods was opened with the creditor, thus mortgaging the meagre income from the inheritance. The slightest hitch along the way, a bad harvest or passing roughneck soldiers, and arrears accumulated. Sometimes a patch of land had to be sold in order to get out of debt (Jacquart 1974).

Indebtedness also affected some of the ruined old nobility, now deprived of all public or official function and transformed into a courtisane clientele, or relegated to the obscure and often miserably crude existence of country squires. The progressive indebtedness of individuals was mirrored by that of rural communities. Their incomes, like those of individuals, also suffered from the setbacks of the times.

The trend of rural indebtedness, which began in the 1540s, accelerated in troubled times and slowed up with a return to peace, only to begin again around 1630–40 (Jacquart 1978). This was the period of great peasant revolt throughout France, particularly in the poorest area, that is Southwest Aquitaine. Increasing ground rent combined with successive royal taxes to compromise the fragile viability of the agricultural economy, which was already finding it difficult to feed an over-abundant population. Once again wars disrupted agricultural production. Tax demands, rents and a series of unfavourable climatic conditions impoverished the peasant class. From 1642 to 1652, famines and epidemics raged. Moreover, the mediocre banking and technical capacity of the kingdom left it destitute, with increasing scarcity of precious metals in European circles. The shortage of precious metals led to a decrease in prices in certain areas, such as the south of France, which began after 1600 and became general after 1650, the trend continuing until the early eighteenth century. This accentuated the real value of debts which, in the seventeenth century, were of long duration, sometimes exceeding 50 years (Le Roy Ladurie 1974). Thus the burden of debts increased and caused further deterioration in the rural standard of living. Subsequently the consequences of foreign policy at the end of the reign of Louis XIV delivered the *coup de grâce* to the population, already crushed by the events of a terrible century. The depression of the seventeenth century was further compounded by the dearth of precious metals, caused by the interruption of their flow from Latin America, and the cost of imports from the Far East.

In the context of a long-term crisis, credit facilitated deferred payment, which prolonged the life of the farm. But then it became the instrument of impoverishment which crystallized the grievances of a population crushed by the misfortunes of the times and the bad management of a society suffering from over-rigid structures. In this sense, the massive indebtedness of the French rural world, during the *Grand Siécle*, would seem to be the scapegoat of a society which had become unhinged. Both a poison and a remedy, the indebtedness is, above all, the glaring sign of the hypocrisy of a society which maintained its bans on that which could have helped it to develop, that is big business and the spirit of enterprise.

Instead of changing this, it became increasingly trapped, in a more or less secret manner, in the forbidden practice of usury, which was justified only by the desire to increase one's landed property. In short, a lesson in how to fail to modernize an economy, while retaining one's guilt feelings!

THE SPANISH CARICATURE

Spain adds its own horrific touch to this already grim picture. Representing the spearhead of the Counter-Reformation, and profoundly imbued with the feudal spirit, when the flow of riches from the Americas began to dry up in the seventeenth century, Spain entered a period of decadence from which it would take several centuries to recover. Here again we find idleness, wars, rents and debts constituting the fabric of a society which had pushed things so far that it became a caricature of itself.

For centuries, the reconquest of territory from the Arabs led to distribution of booty in the form of lands, flocks, gold and functions, and afforded rapid access to honour and riches. Soldiers, state officials and servants of the victorious faith became models of society. The conquest of the Americas prolonged and amplified the old mental attitudes. Thus the Castilians became accustomed to seeking fortune and honour by means other than those which could foster abundant production and active exchange. And, as in ancient Rome, when there was no more booty from conquest, but only the expenses incurred in defence of the Empire, the economy came tumbling down. With that, debts ceased to be a way to increase wealth and became a sign of misery.

At the beginning of the sixteenth century, peasants were selling annuities in order to buy land or to improve it, but by the end of the century the situation had changed. From that moment on, they no longer borrowed to develop their farms or to buy land, but to meet their obligations. The loans were usually bridging loans at sowing time, or quite simply in order to have food to eat. The nobles also got massively into debt as inflation eroded the real value of their fixed incomes. The principal lenders were Church people, collectives (monasteries, confraternities and hospitals), as well as the *letrados*, the legal bourgeoisie and law officers. Progressively, these annuities, constituted on peasants, nobility or state, became the sole investment of the country, a means, in some sense, of fleeing work. The bourgeoisie and the well-to-do farmers abandoned their jobs, their lands, their flocks or business, to live from annuities (Benassar 1967; Vilar 1956, 1962, 1974).

In his *Memorial*, dating from 1600, Gonzalez de Cellorigo makes the point that 'a man who works has to support himself, the lord of the domain, the rent lord, the one who claims the tithe, the overlord's collector, all those who have a claim … and … between those who work and those who do nothing, the proportion is one to thirty!' It should be added that the proportion is totally insufficient in a country with low-yield agriculture, barely competitive industry and which knows nothing about modern commercial developments. With the end of the sixteenth century, collective bankruptcy set in: annuities were no longer guaranteed, except by abandoned houses, or where the rent was low, or again by lands which had been mortgaged under an infinity of costs.

Naturally, as is the case throughout history, the voices of the self-righteous could be heard violently calling credit into question as the destroyer of the social fabric whereas, in fact, it was nothing more than the symptom of an overall shock to society. Corresponding to an open and conquering Castille in the first half of the sixteenth century was the theological research of the famous school of Salamanca which, from the works of the Italian scholastics and those of Saint Antonin of Florence, had further broadened the four exceptions to the ban on interest-bearing loans. A century later, the country confined itself in its own glory, the purity of its blood lines and its inability to waive a principle, to producing its own wealth.

Successive expulsions of Jewish and Muslim who lend and work only heightened the ideological isolation. The more Castille enclosed itself in its own fantasy world, the more it hindered the mechanisms of modernization. In this regressive process, the ban on interest-bearing loans represents a sort of black hole into which no decline can fail to fall. Whereas small-time usury for the hypocritical purposes of family property flourished all over, the only real justification for credit as a tool for economic development remained in the realms of the sulphurous!

In contrast, first in Antwerp, then in Amsterdam and London, numerous new tools were being invented: sale on commission, joint-stock companies, maritime insurance, modern specialized banking. In each case, the technique of interest was at the basis of the concept. In Spain, as in all Catholic Europe, the interest-bearing loan constituted the major pole of repulsion in the development of mentalities. The feeling which we often find, even today, of Northern Europe being more advanced in its day to day life, comes from this break between a world which had its cultural revolution, and a world which preferred the myths of the past.

REFERENCES

BENNASSAR, B. *Valladolid au siècle d'Or*, Paris: Mouton, 1967.
BRAUDEL, F. *La Méditerranée et le monde méditerranéen*, Paris: Armand Colin, 1966.
BRAUDEL, F. *Civilisation and Capitalism*, New York: Harper & Row 1981–4.
BRAUDEL, F. LABROUSSE, E. *Histoire économique et sociale de la France*, Paris: T.II, PUF, 1970.
CHAUNU, P. and R. GASCON, 'Histoire économique et sociale de la France,' F. BRAUDEL and E. LABROUSSE (eds), *Histoire Economique et sociale de la France* T.I, Vol. I, Paris: PUF, 1977.
CLAVERO, B. *Usura, del uso ecónomico de la religión en la historia*, Madrid Tecnos, 1984.
Collective, *Catéchisme de l'Eglise catholique*, Paris: MamePlon, 1992.
DEYON, P. 'Théorie et pratique du mercantilisme' in P. Leon, (ed.), *Histoire économique et sociale du monde*, T.II, Paris: Armand Colin, 1978.
DUBY, G. *Histoire de la France, 1348 à 1852*, Paris: Larousse, coll. 'Références' 1986.
FEBVRE, L. *Philippe II et la Franche-Comté*, Paris: Flammarion, coll. 'Science de l'Histoire', 1970.
GASCON, R. 'La France du mouvement: les commerces et les villes' in F. Braudel and E. Labrousse (eds) *Histoire économique et sociale de la France*, T.I, vol. I, Paris: Puf, 1977.
GELPI, R.M. 'Mécanismes de la création monétaire et régulations économiques', Doctoral thesis, Université de Paris Dauphine, 1982.
GOUBERT, P. *Cent mille provinciaux au XVIIe siècle*, Paris: Flammarion, coll. 'Science', 1968.
GOUBERT, P. 'Le tragique XVIIe siècle' in F. Braudel and E. Labrousse (eds) *Histoire économique et sociale de la France*, T.II, Paris: Puf (1977).
GOUBERT, P. *Louis XIV and 20 million Frenchmen*, London: Allen Lane, 1970.
GRICE-HUTCHINSON, M. *Early Economic Thought in Spain*, London and Boston Ma: Allen & Unwin, 1978.
JACQUART, J. *La crise rurale en Ile-de-France, 1550–1670*, Paris: Armand Colin, 1974.
JACQUART, J. 'Des sociétés en crise' in P. Leon (ed) *Histoire economique et sociale du monde*, T.II, 1978, Paris: Armand Colin.
JULIEN-LABRUYÈRE, F. *Paysans charentais,* preface by J. LE GOFF, Rupella, 1982.
LE GOFF, J. *Histoire de la France Religieuse*, T.II, Paris: Le Seuil, 1988.
LEON, P. (ed.), *Histoire économique et sociale du monde*, T.II Paris: Armand Colin, 1978.
LE ROY LADURIE, E. *The Peasants of Languedoc*, Urbana: University of Illinois Press, 1974.
LÜTHY, H. *La banque protestante en France*, T.I, Paris: SEVPEN, 1959.
PASCAL, B. *Les Provinciales*, Paris: Gallimard, coll. "Folio", 1987.
TAVENAUX, R. *Jansénisme et prêt à intérêt*, Paris: J. Vrin, 1977.

VILAR, P. *'Histoire de l'Espagne'* Paris: 'PUF, *Que sais-je?'*, 1971.
VILAR, P. *Or et monnaie dans l'Histoire*, Paris: Flammarion, coll. 'Science', 1974.
VILAR, P. *La Catalogne dans l'Espagne moderne*, T.I, Paris: SEVPEN, 1962.
VILAR, P. *'Le temps du Quichotte'*, *Europe*, January 1956.
WEBER, E. *Une histoire de l'Europe*, Paris: Fayard, 1986.

6 The Contrast of the Enlightenment

The great eighteenth-century movement of emancipation redirected theories on usury. European economic expansion, particularly in the North, the increased volume of commerce, the first great spread of colonial companies, the appearance of finance in the focus of attention as shown by the Law affair, all led to a considerable development of credit. Seen as a sign of progress by some, and as the road to perdition by others, interest-bearing loans remained at the centre of a debate which continued in ecclesiastical circles, and became one of the favourite subjects of controversy for many economists and philosophers.

In countries where the ban had remained in force, there was a flowering of lay articles attacking the scholastic doctrine either openly or indirectly: in the name of orthodoxy, legitimate interest was often opposed to usury. The term 'legitimate interest' was used to denote compensation for damages suffered by an individual who, because of a loan, had to forgo other possibilities of investing his money at a profit. Others tried to introduce a new extrinsic term: *lex civilis* or *auctoritas principis* that is an authorization granted, either by civil or common law, to stipulate and receive a moderate interest (De Roover 1953).

In 1745, Pope Benedict III, who was famous for his doctrinal rigour, published the *Vix pervenit* encyclical. It reaffirmed the traditional attitude of the Church in a most striking manner: the practice of usury was to be found only in money lending. Usury was the demand for anything over and above the principal. Under no circumstances could a claim be advanced that the gain was moderate and not exorbitant, that it was claimed from a wealthy person and not from someone poverty-stricken, or that the borrower intended to make the sum bear fruits. Compensation could only be justified for reasons non-intrinsic to the loan, and by virtue of contracts essentially different from the said loan.

The sudden conservative swing is obvious, it even goes back on the principals elaborated a few centuries earlier by the modernist scholastics of Florence and Salamanca! How can we explain this? It amounts to an ideological hardening of the Church's position, based on the idea of a return to basic principles, although perfectly aware of the economic explosion taking place in Protestant countries and of the philosophical movement all over Europe which was taking the Enlightenment as a symbol of progress. A return to basics could have fitted into a swing towards modernization, as Calvin had succeeded in doing. However, draped in pomp and tradition, it was not to prove credible and would fail when confronted with the reality of economic facts, thereby dragging the Church into a process of alienation in terms of social representation, a position from which it is still, today, trying desperately to recover. In any case, the encyclical provoked a controversy. It was no longer just a moral or religious debate, but a veritable philosophical battle which was being fed by the coexistence in different European countries of opposing laws and practices.

In the United Provinces, from 1658 onwards, the fixing of interest rates was left to the discretion of the contracting parties, therefore to the free play of economic laws. Merchants in Amsterdam had no scruples about lending money 'for certain profit', in other words, for interest, pure and simple. In spite of this, throughout the seventeenth and eighteenth centuries, the interest rate on the Amsterdam monetary market remained lower than anywhere else. It went as low as 3 per cent and English mercantilists were constantly complaining about the money market which favoured their Dutch competitors.

But the Dutch were not spared passionate debate, any more than anyone else. Until the middle of the sixteenth century, when money was needed, instead of asking for a forbidden loan, it was possible to obtain the same amount of money selling a real rent with a repurchase option. Real rents were perpetual annuities payed with the product of the exploitation of land. They were mainly bought with the widows' and orphans' funds, managed by the Dutch Senate. In 1567, the purchase option was extended to the acquirer as well as the seller. The economic situation of the public concerned, whether borrower or lender, justified this measure. However, it was later extended to all solicitors of funds and was no longer reserved for the poor. Thus, taking the example of the orphans and widows, many financial backers responded to the demand. This practice was not without its defenders. Saumaise, a French refugee jurist in Holland, claimed that money could be rented out and that it could earn interest, that this interest rate should be left to the discretion of the contracting parties. Moreover, the Estates of Holland pronounced themselves in favour of these interest-bearing economic practices which were widely accepted, and added that they concerned civil power only (Du Passage *DTC*).

Such a view was not held unanimously. It was severely criticized at the beginning of the eighteenth century by the French Jansenists, who had fled to the diocese of Utrecht. There were some exceptions, such as Nicolas Broedersen, who abandoned the traditional standpoint and formulated a synthesis between the opinions of Calvin and the most progressive Catholic teaching.

If Holland represents a veritable laboratory of modernity, Italy by contrast represents the pole of essential doubt, where the most cloistered tradition was confronted with the most open practices. Since the Middle Ages, interest-bearing loans were widely practised by merchants there, but they masked their credit operations with greater or lesser degrees of success. With the beginning of the modern era, no further attempt at dissimulation was made. Thus the banks paid interest, aptly termed *discrezione*, on time deposits. The Church forbade usury, but it said nothing about gifts! In theory, however, all interest remained forbidden until the end of the *Ancien Regime*. In his *Universal and reasoned dictionary of mercantile jurisprudence*, published in 1787, Azuni, one of the finest specialists on commercial law, still upheld the principle of the free nature of a loan, referring to the *Vix pervenit* encyclical to denounce the, as he claims, subversive theories of Scipione Maffei and the Neapolitan abbot, Antonio Genovesi, who rallied round the liberal theories of Broedersen, the Dutch Jansenist. Azuni states that usury is any lucre accruing directly from a loan, and the only remuneration he admits is interest on arrears which could be sought before a court (De Roover 1953).

Here we have an example of the subtle distinctions between interest and usury made by Catholic economists from the seventeenth century onwards. Such distinctions served to open the breach which would finally abolish the old scholastic teaching.

In England, where the legal maximum rate of 10 per cent had been reduced to 8 per cent in 1624, 6 per cent in 1651 and 5 per cent in 1714, economists abandoned scholastic teaching and were unanimously in favour of interest-bearing loans. However, a controversy raged over a market problem. The question was whether to maintain or abandon legally imposed restrictions on interest rates. The debate was fuelled by the example of the Dutch market and the official counter-position of the Papacy. From the idea of a ban pure and simple, the debate moved on to the question of legally fixed rates. Some claimed that the prosperity of Holland was due to the low interest rates, and advocated the reduction of British rates. Others, who would finally win the day, claimed that a low interest rate is the consequence of a prosperous economy and not the cause. The principal defender of this position was the philosopher and jurisconsult,

Jeremy Bentham (1748–1832), famous throughout Europe for his spirit of social renewal.

BENTHAM'S TREATISE

Jeremy Bentham was the leading figure in the utilitarian school, which was devoted to the idea of the greatest good for the greatest number of people. In his treatise, published in 1787 under the title *Defense of Usury*, (Bentham 1962) he developed a series of arguments to show the evils of the system of fixed ceilings, which were in force in England at the time.

> No man of ripe years and of sound mind, acting freely, and with his eyes open, ought to be hindered, with a view to his advantage, from making such bargain, in the way of obtaining money, as he thinks fit: nor (what is a necessary consequence) anybody hindered from supplying him, upon any terms he thinks proper to accede to. (Vol. 3, p. 3)

Bentham then looks at the reasons that one can imagine to restrict the freedom that he advocates, and lists five of the arguments developed by his opponents: prevention of usury; prevention of prodigality; protection of indigence against extortion; repression of the temerity of projectors; and finally, protection of simplicity against imposition. They correspond quite well to those used today by consumer protection associations. Rather than try to regulate everything by means of a clear conscience dictating from above, Bentham preferred a concrete analysis of reality. Point by point, he takes up the five arguments, and proposes, in opposition to them, a veritable emancipation of the market.

According to Bentham, the necessity to prevent usury is based on an assumption which had been accepted without question throughout the centuries, that is 'that usury is a bad thing, and as such ought to be prevented: usurers are a bad sort of men, a very bad sort of men, and as such, ought to be punished and suppressed.' Acceptance of this supposes that the nature of usury has been identified correctly. But this is not the case. Bentham gives two essential definitions: one legal, which can be summed up as a taking of a greater interest than the law allows of; another of a moral order, the taking of a greater interest than it is usual for men to give and take.

The modern character of these definitions is striking. When the European Commission in Brussels discusses consumer credit, the theoretical bases put forward by Bentham still form the ground plan for

Directives. Bentham points out that custom is the only base on which either the moralist or the legislator can build their respective precepts and laws. However,

> what basis can be more weak or unwarrantable, as a ground for coercive measures, than custom resulting from free choice? ... Nor has blind custom, thus made the sole and arbitrary guide, anything of steadiness or uniformity in its decision: it has varied, from age to age, in the same country – it varies, from country to country, in the same age, and the legal rate has varied along with it; ... Much has not been done, I think, by legislators as yet, in the way of fixing the price of other commodities; and, in what little has been done, the probity of the intention has, I believe, in general, been rather more unquestionable than the rectitude of the principle, or the felicity of the result. Putting money out at interest, is exchanging present money for future: but why a policy, which as applied to exchanges in general would be generally deemed absurd and mischievous, should be deemed necessary in the instance of this particular kind of exchange, mankind are as yet to learn. For him who takes as much as he can get for the use of any other sort of thing, a house for instance, there is no particular appellation, nor any mark of disrepute. ... Why a man who takes as much as he can get, be it six, or seven, or eight, or ten per cent, for the use of a sum of money, should be called usurer, should be loaded with an opprobrious name, any more than if he had bought a house with it, and made a proportionable profit by the house, is more than I can see. (Vol. 3, p. 4)

Bentham then goes on to question the efficacy of such restrictive laws with regard to the prevention of prodigality. He states that it is neither natural nor habitual for spendthrifts to pay a higher than normal rate for money. Nobody with the required guaranties at their disposal will borrow money at a rate higher than that commonly practised. Therefore a law restricting rates would be of no use to a true prodigal because, as long as he has securities to sell or mortgage, if he cannot find a lender, he will sell instead of borrowing. Finally, those who have no guarantees to offer and who cannot find a lender at the rates fixed by the law, will only be able to find credit at much higher rates than if there were no restrictions. The number of possible lenders is restricted, because in this case the operation would be illegal, consequently the lender would demand more and would also benefit from the lack of competition.

In other words, laws governing usury only offer an apparent protection for those who might be considered as weak; moreover, they tend to foster illegal practices, which are completely outside the market and in flagrant contradiction with the stated purpose of such laws. Continuing his analysis, Bentham states that there are three other classes of people who can be said to be protected by laws against usury:

> the indigent, the rashly enterprising, and the simple; those whose pecuniary necessities may dispose them to give an interest above the ordinary rate, rather than not have it; and those who, from rashness, may be disposed to venture upon giving such a rate, of from carelessness, combined with ignorance, may be disposed to acquiesce in it. (Vol. 3, p. 7)

With regard to the indigent,

> in the case of his wanting it to save himself from a loss, ... though, in proportion to the amount of the loss, the rate of interest were even so great as that the clear saving should not amount to more than 1 per cent or any fraction per cent, yet so long as it amounted to anything, he would be just so much the better for borrowing, even on such comparatively disadvantageous terms. If, instead of gain, we put any other kind of benefit or advantage – if, instead of loss, we put any other kind of mischief or inconvenience of equal value, the result will be the same.
>
> A man is in one of these situations, suppose, in which it would be for his advantage to borrow. But his circumstances are such, that it would not be worth anybody's while to lend him, at the highest rate which it is proposed the law should allow – in short, he cannot get it at that rate. If he thought he could get it at that rate, most surely he would not give a higher: he may be trusted for that, for by the supposition he has nothing defective in his understanding. But the fact is, he cannot get it at that lower rate. At a higher rate, however, he could get it: and at that rate, though higher, it would be worth his while to get it: so he judges, who has nothing to hinder him from judging right – who has every motive and every means for forming a right judgment – who has every motive and every means for informing himself of the circumstances upon which rectitude of judgment, in the case in question, depends. The legislator, who knows nothing, nor can know anything, of any one of all these circumstances – who knows nothing at all about the matter, comes and says to him – 'it signifies nothing; you shall not have the money: for it would be doing you a mischief to let you borrow it upon such terms'. And this out of prudence and loving-kindness! There may be worse cruelty, but can there be greater folly? (Vol. 3, p. 8)

As for the need to protect the simple:

> but in what degree soever a man's weakness may expose him to imposi-
> tion, he stands much more exposed to it in the way of buying goods,
> than in the way of borrowing money … it is the borrower always, who,
> according to the indefinite or short term for which money is lent, is on
> the safe side: any imprudence he may have committed with regard to
> the rate of interest may be corrected at any time; if I find I have given
> too high an interest to one man, I have no more to do than to borrow of
> another at a lower rate, and pay off the first. (Vol. 3, p. 8)

In his treatise Bentham also develops arguments in favour of lenders,
underlining some of the reasons responsible for their bad image.

> The business of a money-lender, though only among Christians and in
> Christian times a proscribed profession, has nowhere, nor at any time,
> been a popular one. Those who have the resolution to sacrifice the pre-
> sent to future, are natural objects of envy to those who have sacrificed
> the future to the present. The children who have eaten their cake, are
> the natural enemies of the children who have theirs. While the money
> is hoped for, and for a short time after it has been received, he who
> lends it is a friend and benefactor; by the time the money is spent, and
> the evil hour of reckoning is come, the benefactor is found to have
> changed his nature, and to have put on the tyrant and the oppressor. It
> is an oppression for a man to reclaim his own money; it is none to keep
> it from him. Among the inconsiderate, that is, among the great mass of
> mankind, selfish affections conspire with the social in treasuring up all
> favour for the man of dissipation, and in refusing justice to the man of
> thrift who has supplied him. In some shape or other, that favour attends
> the chosen object of it through every stage of his career. But in no
> stage of his career can the man of thrift come in for any share of it.
> (Vol. 3, p. 17)

Echoes of Bentham's extraordinary text are still to be heard today in
the smallest debate on overindebtedness. It would be in the interest of
all three actors in the discussion – professionals, regulatory authorities
and consumer representatives – to study his text in order to relativize
their points of view. Rather than being naïve, Bentham has the lucidity to
recognize that when regulations are too restrictive or inadequate, human
nature strives and finds the means to get around, always at the expense of
the poor.

1 The Code of Hammurabi, engraved on a stele. The Code, dating from c. 1760 BC, constitutes the earliest example of credit regulation. The upper section shows Hammurabi receiving the Code from Shamash, the sun god.

2 *Saint Basil*, or *The Absolute Ban*: by Herrera.

3 *Saint Thomas,* or *The Moderate Ban* – taking economic practices
into account: by Manuel-Deutsch.

4 'The Usurer's Shop' by Jacques
Le Grant in *Livre des bonnes
moeurs.*

5 Jan Provost's famous triptych *Der Geizige und der Tod*.

6 Luther, by Lucas Cranach.

7 Calvin.

8 Jeremy Bentham.

9 Jacques Turgot, from a lithograph by Delaruelle after the portrait by Douais.

10 An 18th century engraving, 'Credit is dead, bad debts killed it'.

11 Balzac's famous hero, Gobseck, by Jacque from *Les dangers de l'inconduite*.

12 'The British Pawnbroker', from an illustration for *Sketches by Boz* by Charles Dickens.

13 The French *mont-de-piété*: the pledging of goods, from a painting by Heilbuth.

14 The distinctly more lively 'redeeming room' of the *mont-de-piété*.

15 'A Year of Credit', with a down-payment of 10 per cent for the famous Singer sewing machine.

16 A 1955 Cetelem brochure.

His *Defense of Usury* (Bentham 1962) bore fruit, although somewhat tardily. Fixed ceilings, beyond which interest rates were considered to be usurious, were abolished in Britain in 1854. They have never been reintroduced.

TURGOT'S *MÉMOIRE*

The French kings of the early fourteenth century allowed merchants frequenting the fairs of Champagne to charge interest between 15 per cent and 20 per cent. This was the only part of the kingdom – a sort of free zone between Flanders and Northern Italy – where a commission could be charged. But this tolerance fell into disuse with the decline of the fairs. Interest on loans remained forbidden until the French Revolution. It was impossible to claim interest before the courts and a debtor who had paid interest unnecessarily could even take action against the creditor.

Until the middle of the seventeenth century most Catholic doctors of law objected to arguments based on the service given to the borrower as a justification of the 'hiring of money'. They condemned the widespread practice of 'commercial loans' as well as all the different loans, which were very common in rural areas. The rate of interest, considered as unacceptable by the theologians and the civil legislators, was nevertheless the daily lot of almost all merchants who, from fair to fair, insured their supplier credit, and of the peasants who, thanks to the bridging loans, from harvest to harvest, overcame the uncertainties of the weather. Obviously, as if to bear out Bentham's theories, the terms of these forbidden loans often verged on usury.

Pasquier Quesnel, the mercantilist, was the first to diverge from the old scholastic opinions and to draw closer to Calvin's view, but his liberal opinions remained obscure for a long time. It was not until 1682 that the priest, Jean Le Correur, in his *Treatise on the practice of bills between merchants* put forward his renovated theology of credit. The practice consisted of receiving 'for a given time, money on interest in the form of promissory notes between persons agreed on a pure principle of commerce'(Tavenaux 1977). According to Le Correur, money, thus used for useful purposes which became capital, is not sterile. Lending money to a business was the equivalent of a contract between persons joined by a commercial bond. In this sense, a commission was legal. He distinguished between a charitable loan, that is the pure transfer of usage of the thing lent, implying consumption, and a business loan based on use. Only the first was usurious if it was not completely free. It was in response to

Le Correur's book that Bossuet wrote his *Treatise on Usury*, a traditional attack on interest (Taveneaux 1977).

In the wake of the new British liberalism, Anne Robert Jacques Turgot (1727–81), a disciple of Quesnay and intendant of Limoges, took the Angoulême affair as an example of the perversions stemming from the old bans; Turgot's report was irrefutable. The city of Angoulême was not a great centre of business because as soon as a man made a fortune there, he set out to acquire a noble title. The little commercial activity there was, was therefore in the hands of people almost without money, who had to run their business on loans and who, because it was illegal, could only borrow at very high interest, as much because of the scarcity of money as because of their lack of sureties. Bankruptcies were commonplace and, just before Turgot presented his *Mémoir* to the Council of State in 1770, a scandal about fraudulent bankruptcies erupted. Several merchants had agreed to sign promissory notes for each other without there being any real counterpart for them. The bills, which were successively endorsed by all parties to the scheme, were then used to make payments or to borrow money. One of the conspirators, who had thus acquired considerable sums, absconded. The lenders were prepared to pursue the endorsers, however, the latter had the idea of intimidating the lenders by threatening to report them for usury. The family of one of the lenders tried to appease the informers, and to get out of a charge of usury, by offering to return the interest already paid. This led to an avalanche of demands for restitution of commission from all the lenders in the region. The greed and determination of the informers on the one hand, the terror of the lenders on the other, and the ease with which the legal officers of Angoulême lent themselves to these accusations of usury, led to a serious economic crisis which spread to the whole province.

Hence the emphatic tone of Turgot's famous *Mémoir*:

The laws recognised by the courts and governing interest on money are wrong; our laws correspond to rigorous prejudices with regard to usury which were introduced during centuries of ignorance by theologians whose understanding of Scripture was no greater than their understanding of natural law. The strict observation of these laws would mean the destruction of all trade, consequently they are not strictly observed. They forbid all stipulations of interest without alienation of the capital. They declare illegal all interest stipulated beyond the rate fixed by the edicts of the Prince. It is a well-known fact that there is not a market place in the world where the majority of transactions are not conducted through money borrowed without alienation of the capital, and where interest is not fixed by convention, depending on the greater or lesser abundance of money on the market place, and the greater or lesser solvency of the borrower. The rigidity of the laws has given way to the force of circumstances: jurisprudence has had to moderate its theoretical principles in practice. We have come to openly tolerating loans, whether on bills, discount or any other form of money transaction between traders. It will always be so, as long as the law forbids what is, in the nature of things, necessary. However, this situation, whereby the laws are not observed, but subsist without being revoked, and are even still partially observed, leads to very unpleasant consequences. On the one hand, the known disregard for the law reduces the respect in which all citizens should hold all things legal; on the other, the existence of this law maintains an unfortunate prejudice, condemns something which is in itself legal, something without which society cannot survive, and which, consequently, a large group of citizens are obliged to practice. This group of citizens is degraded by doing so, and this beginning of debasement in the eyes of the public weakens the group's sense of honour, the cornerstone of honesty. The author of *l'Esprit des Lois* remarked that 'when the laws forbid something necessary, they only succeed in making dishonest people of those who practise it.' Moreover, since the law itself does not stipulate the cases in which it is to be observed and those in which its infringement can be tolerated, the fate of those breaking it is left to a shifting jurisprudence which changes like public opinion. What one group of citizens practices openly and, practically with the seal of public approval, will be punished in others as a crime. Thus, in order to ruin a citizen who relies confidently on a well-known public tolerance, all that is required is a misinformed judge, or one blinded by misplaced zeal. (Vol. 3, p. 163, Turgot 1919)

Turgot observed that the law turned a blind eye, even to loans at exorbitant rates which were hardly more than compensation for the risk taken, and which did not really enrich the lenders. The borrowers did not complain, for without these loans they could not conduct their business and earn their living. Since the authorities turned a blind eye to loans of up to 75 per cent interest, we may well ask at what rate did they intervene? Turgot wonders whether the public prosecutor was not waiting for the borrower, who considered himself wronged, to complain or to inform on the lender.

He would be no more than the instrument of the bad faith of those knaves who would wish to go back on freely contracted commitments, and the law would only protect those who are unworthy of its protection, and their lot would be better than that of honest men, who, faithful to their agreements, would blush at the idea of using the law to get out of them. (Vol. 3, p. 165)

Turgot then pleads for legislation authorizing loans on interest, arguing that God could not have forbidden 'a thing absolutely necessary to the prosperity of societies'. He goes further. He advocates not only the legalization of loans, but also the liberalization of interest rates. He thus takes the side of the English economists who, at the same period, were leading an offensive against ceiling rates. According to Turgot, the interest rate should be a market price which depends on the supply/demand ratio, and also on the risk to the capital in the hands of the borrower.

Here Turgot's arguments are not far from those that Bentham will develop later. Turgot states that different rates are perfectly justified.

Why deprive the man who is lacking sureties of the right to borrow that which he absolutely needs? Why should he be deprived of the means to undertake enterprises in which he hopes to grow rich? No civil or religious law obliges anyone to give him free assistance. Therefore, why should civil or religious law make it forbidden to assist him at a price which he accepts to pay for his own advantage? (Vol. 3, p. 169)

He also attacks the argument concerning the sterility of money, raised by Aristotle and the scholastics:

They forget that money is the necessary tool in all enterprises in agriculture, manufacturing and trade; that with it the farmer, the manufacturer and the merchant procure immense profits and cannot procure them without it; that, consequently, its so-called sterility in trade is nothing more than a palpable error, based on a petty misunderstanding.

He continues his defence of the legitimacy of interest.

Equity requires that in a contract which is not free, the sureties given by both sides should be of equal value, and that neither give more than they receive, and receive no more than they have given. Whereas, all that the lender demands in the loan, beyond the principal, is something he receives beyond that which he gave, since by receiving only the principal, he receives the exact equivalent of what he has given. (Vol. 3, p. 173) Yet it is remarkable, having started from the principle of equality of sureties in an agreement, to establish a system whereby all the advantage is for one of the parties, and non-existent for the other. Nothing could be more flagrant; for, when, after some years, the sum of money I had lent without interest is rendered to me, it is obvious that I have not gained anything, and that, having been deprived of its use and having run the risk of losing it, I have no more nor less than exactly what I would have if I had kept it locked away all that time! It is equally clear that the borrower has taken advantage of this money, since he had no other motive for borrowing it than that advantage. I have therefore given something for nothing, I have been generous; but if in my generosity I have given something real, then I could also have sold it without injustice. (Vol. 3, p. 180)

Turgot goes on to refute the Scriptural arguments against interest-bearing loans. He claims that jurists banned these loans, having been misled by scholastic theologians who thought they found confirmation for their prejudices in the Gospel passage: 'lend without hope of interest' (St Luke, VI) Reasonable people would have seen no more in this passage than a charitable precept. Transforming it into a rigorous precept of justice is both an abuse of reason and of the text. Moreover, this passage occurs in the same chapter as a series of maxims known as Evangelical Counsels, which are offered as a means of arriving at a perfection to which all men are not called. This becomes more clear when the passage is quoted in its entirety: 'Love your enemies, do good, lend without hoping for something in return, and your reward will be great and you will be sons of the Most High, because He Himself is kind to the unthankful and the wicked'. (Vol. 3, p. 182)

The true origin of the opinion which condemns interest-bearing loans is to be found, according to Turgot, in historic circumstances:

how could it have happened that, in spite of the simple nature of the principles governing the legitimacy of loans on interest, in spite of the futility of the sophisms which have built up to confuse something simple, public opinion condemning interest-bearing loans as usury could have become so general? (Vol. 3, p. 183)

It is not hard to find the origin of the theologians' prejudice. They only invented reasons for condemning interest-bearing loans because of the harm already done by usurers. The pleasure of being helped in time of need is forgotten with the need; but soon the need returns, the debt remains, and is felt as a constant burden until it is acquitted. Besides, the lender only lends what he has in excess of his needs whereas the borrower usually borrows what is necessary for the satisfaction of his needs. And

> although the rigour of the law is on the side of the lender–creditor, who is only claiming what is rightfully his, human sentiment and pity always side with the debtor. We feel that by paying what he owes he will again be reduced to misery, but that the creditor can quite well live without that which is rightfully due to him. (Vol. 3, p. 183)

> The greater the likelihood of the lender losing his money, the more the interest rate should increase. He must gain on the interest from the small number of reliable borrowers, the interest and capital that he will lose through the bankruptcy of the unreliable ones. (Vol. 3, p. 184)

> In all the ancient republics, the abolition of debts was always the wish of the people, and the cry of the ambitious who sought their favour. Sometimes the rich were forced to concede, in order to calm the ire of the people and to avoid more terrible revolutions, but that was just another risk for the lenders and, consequently, interest rates only continued to rise. (Vol. 3, p. 185)

Turgot then goes on to develop the advantages of a law liberalizing trade in money:

> the effect of this freedom would be competition, and the effect of this competition would be lower interest rates: not only because the stigma and the risks attached to borrowing at interest are a surcharge which the borrower always pays ... but also because a very great quantity of money which is left sitting in coffers would enter into circulation as soon as the prejudice, no longer reinforced by the laws, had little by little given way to reason. The economy would become all the more active in accumulating capital, once currency exchange became an open market. (Vol. 3, p. 193)

Turgot's long, ardent and perfectly documented plea, based on 'palpable' reality, with the Angoulême case as evidence, became the essential text on which French jurisconsults were to deliberate. It fits perfectly into the context of a deep desire for emancipation, which characterizes the age of Enlightenment. In this respect it is dated; but its subtle analysis, subjecting fixed mental attitudes to the light of reason, makes it still, today, one of the most enriching texts available to credit professionals. Its immediate influence was great, both for the world of ideas and for Turgot's career!

In 1789, the Constituent Assembly proclaimed freedom of property, freedom of work, freedom of trade and freedom of credit. Interest-bearing loans were legalized in 1804. Article 1905 of the *Code Civil* states that 'it is permitted to stipulate interest on a simple loan, be it of money, food-stuffs or any other movable properties'. Faced with this Napoleonic legislation which was soon to spread throughout Mediterranean Europe, the Church, without the slightest retraction, confined itself thereafter to condemning excessive interest rates. With neither pomp nor ceremony, it laid to rest a doctrine which had been raised to the status of dogma and which, throughout the centuries, had been nourished with Papal and Conciliar approval.

REFERENCES

BENTHAM, J. *'Defense of Usury: Showing the impolicy of the present legal restraints on the terms of pecuniary bargains'* in *The Works of Jeremy Bentham*, Vol. Three; New York: Russell & Russell Inc., 1962.

LEVRON, J. *Le crédit à la Banque d'Anjou*, Angers Crédit de l'Ouest, 1950.

PASSAGE, H. Du *'Usure'*, Dictionnaire de théologie catholique (*DTC*).

RIST, C. *History of Monetary and Credit Theory from John Law to the Present Day*, New York: Macmillan, 1940.

ROOVER, R. De *L'évolution de la lettre de change*, Paris: Armand Colin, 1953.

TAVENEAUX, R. *Jansénisme et prêt à intérêt*, Paris: J. Vrin, 1977.

TURGOT, *Mémoire sur les prêts d'argent, Oeuvres de Turgot*, Paris: T.III, Gustave Schelle, 1919.

7 Toward an Economic Concept

From the nineteenth century onwards, credit – the cornerstone of growth – was no longer a subject of heated theological debate. It became a subject of study and of controversy for the principal schools of economy, each one trying to a greater or lesser extent to answer the question: what is the effect of a change in purchasing power on the real national revenue? Of course, consumer credit, as such, would not claim the serious attention of economists until the twentieth century, and almost exclusively in the United States. However, throughout the nineteenth century, economic thought was sensitive to the negative image resulting from the classical model. This image, which still persisted at the beginning of the twentieth century, is well illustrated or rather, caricatured, by the German Professor Taussig. In 1911, he wrote that a loan to a spendthrift 'causes labor to be directed to producing truffles and champagne, not factory and machinary'! (p. 81). Nevertheless, the majority of economic theorists and practitioners already believed in the usefulness of interest-bearing loans. Claude-Frédéric Bastiat hammered the message home in the following phrase: 'giving credit is giving time, it is giving up time to another, it is giving up something precious for him; consequently, he must pay for the exchange of something present for something yet to come'.

THE DANGERS OF CONSUMPTION

It was principally through the master work of Adam Smith, *An Inquiry into the Nature and Causes of the Wealth of Nations*, published in March 1776, that certain eighteenth-century ideas about human nature reached the economists of the following century. Adam Smith divided the wealth of a country into three parts: the part which is consumed and which, consequently, creates neither income nor profit; fixed capital which secures an income or a profit without circulating; circulating capital which produces an income only when it changes hands.

According to Adam Smith, capital growth, obtained through saving, is the principal source of real wealth and income. In the majority of cases, a wealthy man will annually consume a not inconsiderable share of his revenue which he will distribute to a series of idle guests and servants.

There is nothing to show in return for this consumption. However, the share of his revenue which he saves is immediately used as capital and consumed also, but by different people, farmers, artisans and so on, who reproduce at a profit the annual value of their consumption. If the prodigality of some is not compensated for by the frugality of others, the country will be impoverished. Every prodigal individual appears to be a public enemy, and every frugal individual a public benefactor. But great nations are never ruined by private, though they sometimes are by public prodigality, and misconduct. Fortunately, the frugality and the good behaviour of most individuals are upon most occasions sufficient to compensate, not only the private prodigality and misconduct but the public extravagance of government.

The consumption of durable goods is preferable to immediate consumption that is feasting and so on, since durables sustain productive workers and, more than other forms of expenditure, contribute to growth of public opulence. 'The man who borrows in order to spend will soon be ruined, and he who lends to him will generally have occasion to repent of his folly. To borrow or to lend for such purpose, therefore, is in all cases, where gross usury is out of the question, contrary to the interest of both parties.' These ideas were mainly inspired by the behaviour of the nobility, whose members mortgaged their property to pay grocers, traders, showmen and other entertainers.

They were already contained in *Poor Richard's Almanac*, which Benjamin Franklin began to publish in 1732 to illustrate with this character many contemporary moral and social attitudes. Thus we read:

A fat kitchen makes a lean will .... (Vol. II, p. 32) If you would know the value of money, go and try to borrow some; for he that goes a borrowing goes a sorrowing; and indeed so does he that lends to such people, when he goes to get it again .... (p. 34) Fond pride of dress is sure a very curse; Ere fancy you consult, consult your purse .... (p. 36) Pride is as loud a beggar as Want, and a great deal more saucy. When you have bought one fine thing you must buy ten more .... (p. 36) It is easier to suppress the first desire than to satisfy all that follow it. And it is as truly folly for the poor to ape the rich as for the frog to swell in order to equal the ox .... (p. 34) Pride that dines on vanity sups on contempt. Pride breakfasted with Plenty, dined with Poverty, and supped with Infamy. And after all, of what use is this pride of appearance, for which so much is risked,n so much is suffered? It cannot promote health, nor ease pain; it makes no increase of merit in the person; it creates envy; it hastens misfortune .... (p. 35) But what madness must it be to run in debt for these superfluities! We are offered by the terms of this sale six months' credit; and that, perhaps, has induced some of us to attend it, because we cannot spare the ready money, and hope now to be fine without it. But ah! think what you do when you run in debt; you give to another power over your liberty. If you cannot pay at the time, you will be ashamed to see your creditor; you will be in fear when you speak to him; you will make poor, pitiful, sneaking excuses, and by degrees come to lose your veracity, and sink into base, downright lying; for, The second vice is lying, the first is running in debt.... (p. 35) Lying rides upon Debt's back.

It is easy to recognize the tone of the old bans, worked into this Protestant bourgeois ethic which imposed its model of society on a part of Europe. What is new about the texts of Adam Smith and Benjamin Franklin, one economic, the other personal philosophy, is the importance given to consumption.

In this ongoing debate, the Christian tradition attacked interest rates, therefore credit. It condemned credit in all its forms, often confusing without reason equipment credit, commercial credit (including maritime) and bridging loans. With Adam Smith and Benjamin Franklin begins a new era wherein credit was widely accepted, but for professional or investment purposes, the only forms of credit reputed to create wealth ... and morality. For them, consumption connotes futile, extravagant, even irresponsible spending, a sort of social lasciviousness caricatured by the old aristocracy of the Catholic countries, with Versailles leading the pack, its love of splendour being its only prestige. The new model of society was based on the black-clothed bourgeois bending over his account books to whom the very idea of consumption was something painful.

Since tradition had it that credit was suspect, if not directly involved in creating wealth, the association of the two words, consumer and credit, conjured up the very opposite of the rising bourgeois model: bad man, carefree, prodigal, the famous cicada behaviour in the fable.

The principal classical economists rationalize this image in their work. In their analysis they begin from the hypothesis of pure and perfect competition (a large number of players, although small enough to be unable to influence the market) and price flexibility (prices vary until the intersection between supply and demand in every market). These hypotheses guarantee full use of the factors of production, capital and labour. Market exchange is essentially a barter process. As a result, purchasing power equals the total product, and demand cannot limit production which depends solely on the availability of the factors of production that is, existing capital and good use of labour. In order to make work more efficient, techniques must be improved and capital intensified. Since growth is not limited by demand in this model, if instead of economizing to finance investment, we consume, we slow down future growth and the improvement of the standard of living. The origin of this way of thinking lies in Jean-Baptiste Say's famous law of markets (loi des débouchés) 'the supply creates its own demand', first laid down in his *Traité d'économie politique*, published in 1803. It was taken up in 1817 by D. Ricardo in his *Principles of Political Economy and Taxation*.

> Mr Say has however, most satisfactorily shown, that there is no amount of capital which may not be employed in a country, because demand is only limited by production. No man produces, but with a view to consume or sell, and he never sells, but with an intention to purchase some other commodity, which may be immediately useful to him, or which may contribute to future production. By producing, then, he necessarily becomes either the consumer of his own goods, or the purchaser and consumer of the goods of some other person. It is not to be supposed that he should, for any length of time, be ill-informed or the commodities which he can most advantageously produce, to attain the object which he has in view, namely, the possession of other goods; and, therefore, it is not probable that he will continually produce a commodity for which there is no demand . (p. 290)

John Stuart Mill follows the same reasoning in his *Principles of Political Economy*, published in 1848.

> Industry is limited by Capital .... (Vol. II, p. 63) Increase of capital gives increased employment to labour, without assignable bounds .... (Vol. II, p. 66) If there are hman beings capable of work, and food to feed them, they may always be employed in producing something .... This proposition is very much opposed to common doctrines. There is not an opinion more general among mankind than this, that the unproductive expenditure of the rich is necessary to the employment of the poor. Before Adam Smith, the doctrine had hardly been questioned; and even since this time, authors of the highest name and of great merit (for example, Mr Malthus, Dr Chalmers, M. de Sismondi) have contended, that if consumers were to save and convert into capital more than a limited portion of their income, and were not to devote to unproductive consumption an amount of means bearing a certain ratio to the capital of the country, the extra accumulation would be merely so much waste,

since there would be no market for the commodities which the capital so created would produce. I conceive this to be one of the many errors arising in political economy .... (Vol. II, p. 67) The limit of wealth is never deficiency of consumers, but of producers and productive power. Every addition to capital gives to labour either additional employment, or additional remuneration; enriches either the country, or the labouring class. If it finds additional hands to set to work, it increases the aggregate produce: if only the same hands, it gives them a larger share of it; and perhaps even in this case, by stimulating them to greater exertion, augments the produce itself .... (p. 68) Capital is the result of saving .... Credit is not a creation but a transfer of the means of production .... (Vol. II, p. 527) How often is an extension of credit talked of as equivalent to a creation of capital, or as if credit actually were capital. It seems strange that there should be any need to point out, that credit being only permission to use the capital of another person, the means of production cannot be increased by it, but only transferred .... (p. 527) But though credit is but a transfer of capital from hand to hand, it is generally, and naturally, a transfer to hands more competent to employ the capital efficiently in production. (p. 528)

Jean-Baptiste Say, a French Protestant, was in favour of a free market for interest bearing loans. In his *Treatise on Political Economy,* he wrote an interesting chapter on this matter, in which he points to the fact that one of the conditions for low interest rates is to respect the terms of the loan contracts and to reimburse the debts.

The ratio of the premium of insurance, which frequently forms the greater portion of what is called interest, depends on the degree of security presented to the lender; which security consists chiefly in three circumstances: (1) The safety of the mode of employment; (2) The personal ability and character of the borrower; (3) The good government of the country he happens to reside in .... (p. 301) The good government of the country, where the debtor resides, reduces the risk of the creditor, and, consequently, the premium of insurance he is obliged to demand to cover that risk. Hence it is, that the rate of interest rises, whenever the laws and their administration do not ensure the performance of engagements. It is yet more aggravated, when they excite to the violation of them; as when they authorize non-payment, or do not acknowledge the validity of bond fide contracts. (p. 303)

The resort to personal restraint against insolvent debtors has been generally considered as injurious to the borrower; but is, on the contrary, much in his favour. Loans are made more willingly, and on better terms, where the rights of the lender are best secured by law. (p. 303)

In spite of his favourable views on credit, he was opposed to borrowing for sterile consumption, however very sensible rules that he defined still apply today.

Loans are sometimes contracted, not for a productive investment, but for mere bannen consumption. Transactions of this kind should always awaken the suspicion of the lender, in as much as they engender no means of re-payment of either principal or interest. If charged upon a growing revenue, they are, at all events, an anticipation of that revenue; and if charged upon any of the sources of revenue, they afford the means of dissipating the particular source itself. If there be the security neither of revenue nor of its source, they barely place the property of one person at the wanton disposition of another. (p. 302)

In accordance with the *Poor Richard's Almanac* precepts, the classic economists considered consumer credit as being, for the most part, targeted for extravagant expenditure which was condemned as social waste. A distinction however was made between consumer durables and consumer goods, the former being preferable to the latter, since they increase the stock of goods, and therefore the wealth of the country.

For the 'classical' school, in the short term, consumer credit has a neutral effect on growth. It increases the demand for consumer goods at the expense of the demand for capital goods, since the economy is at full production due to price flexibility. As a consequence, profits and production increase in the consumer good sector and decrease in the capital equipment industry. Thus, in the long term, consumer credit has a negative effect on growth, because it slows down the formation of capital upon which increasing productivity depends. Saving, on the contrary, has also a neutral effect in the short run as it merely transfers purchasing power from consumption to investment, but in the long run it has a positive impact on the economy, as it increases the factors that can stop growth.

CONSUMPTION AND CRISIS

The classical model was not useful enough to explain the series of economic crises running through the nineteenth century. It was thus severely criticized by a group of economists who considered that a liberal economy leads to periodic crises of overproduction, due to under-consumption, particularly on the part of the working population.

R. Malthus (1766–1834) was among the first economists to attack Say's law of the markets. He explains secular stagnation and prolonged unemployment with the principle of effective demand with an overarching theory:

> While it is quite certain that an adequate passion for consumption may fully keep up the proper proportion between supply and demand, whatever may be the powers of production, it appears to be quite as certain that an inordinate passion for accumulation must inevitably lead to a supply of commodities beyond what the structure and habits of such a society will permit to be profitably consumed.... (p. 325) If, in the process of saving, all that was lost by the capitalist was gained by the labourer, the check to the progress of wealth would be but temporary, as stated by Mr Ricardo; and the consequences need to be apprehended. But if the conversion of revenue into capital pushed beyond a certain point must, by diminishing the effectual demand for produce, throw the labouring class out of employment, it is obvious that the adoption of parsimonious habits beyond a certain point, may be accompanied by the most distressing effects at first, and by a marked depression of wealth and population afterwards. It is not, of course, meant to be stated that parsimony, or even a temporary diminution of consumption, is not often in the highest degree useful, and sometimes absolutely necessary to the progress of wealth. A state may certainly be ruined by extravagance; and a diminution of the actual expenditure may not only be necessary on this account, but when the capital of a country is deficient, compared with the demand for its products, a temporary economy of consumption is required, in order to provide that supply of capital which can alone furnish the means of an increased consumption in future. All that is contended for is, that no nation can possibly grow rich by an accumulation of capital, arising from a permanent diminution of consumption; ... (p. 326) it is equally vain, with a view to the permanent increase of wealth, to continue converting revenue into capital, when there is no adequate demand for the products of such capital, as to continue encouraging marriage and the birth of children without a demand for labour and an increase of the funds for its maintenance. (p. 330)

Therefore, according to R. Malthus, stagnation occurs when people, instead of consuming, save and invest to such an extent that they have no motive for further increase of production owing to the incident fall in prices and profits. Other economists explain crises in terms of under-consumption which, they believe, derives fundamentally from an uneven distribution of wealth. Jean-Charles Léonard Simonde de Sismondi (1773–1842) develops the main ideas of this theory:

> Thus nations incur dangers that seem incompatible: they fall into ruin equally by spending too much, and by spending too little. A nation spends too much whenever it exceeds its revenue, because it cannot do so except by encroaching on its capital, and thus diminishing future production: it then does what the solitary cultivator would do if he should eat the corn which ought to be secured for seed. A nation spends too little, whenever being destitute of foreign commerce, it does not consume the excess of its production above it's exportation: for, if so, it soon comes into the condition of the solitary cultivator, who having filled all his granaries far beyond the probability of consumption, would be obliged, that he might not work in vain, partly to abandon his cultivation of the ground. (*New Principles of Political Economy*, Second Book, Chapter 6, p. 105)

However the mechanisms that regulate capitalist economies bring about under-consumption which is soon converted into an over-production crisis. The uneven distribution of income leads to excessive purchasing power, relative to consumption needs among capitalists, and excessive consumption needs relative to purchasing power among workers. A crisis of over-production thus results from the way capitalists use that share of their income which they cannot consume. They save it and endeavour to use it in production in order to increase their income even more. The investment of this sum into means of production brings excess of production over consumption and, at a certain point, the cumulative process of expansion comes to a more or less abrupt end. This theory, which was taken up by many Anglo-Saxon economists, introduces an important nuance to the preceding condemnations of consumption, as it recognizes the great importance of consumption in the economic process, if it is fairly distributed.

Sismondi has a negative enough image of credit, not because of the function it fulfils, 'which is to transmit to one the disposal of what belongs to another', but because of the use to which it is put. He does not analyze consumer credit as such, and he is not against the old bill of exchange if it is well-endorsed. However, he attacks modern bank credit, which feeds speculation bubbles and amplifies crises. He also revolts against public borrowing: 'Credit sells the work, or a share in the work of our children, and our children's children to the nth generation (…). Once the powerful have discovered this means of acquiring and taking advantage of what is not theirs, it is unlikely that they will stop.' (V. II, p. 318, 1980) If the choice were possible, he would be in favour of a State bank monopoly but, being pragmatic, he pleads for free interest rates; the only effective means of avoiding abuses.

> The efforts of many legislators to lower the rate of interest, or to fix it, or to suppress it altogether, are preposterous. The attempts at suppression and prohibition of all interest, in the name of usury, has generally been the consequence of religious prejudices, and of mad attempts to adapt the Jewish legislation to modern Europe. The effect of these laws, so opposite to the general interest, has always been either to force contractors to envelop themselves in a secrecy which they must require payment for, and may use as a snare for the unsuspiciousness of others; or else to force capitalists to employ, in other countries, that capital which they could not lend in their own neighbourhood, with the same safety and advantage. Fixing the rate of interest is foolish because the profits capitals may yield being variable and dependent on the demands of the marketplace, the charges which have to be allowed for their use must vary with these demands and profits. (*New Principles*, Fourth Book, Chapter 6, p. 295)

Karl Marx was another economist who disagreed with Say's law, but his analysis of a crisis is more complex. He deals with usury in his historical analysis of the evolution of economic systems. In his view, usury contributed to bringing down the *Ancien Régime* economies and their replacement by the capitalist mode of production. Banks and modern interest-bearing loans are at the service of the new system.

For Marx, the usury of precapitalist economies had a dual purpose.

> To that extent usury has a double effect. First, it frames up an independent moneyed wealth by the side of the merchant class. In the second place it appropriates to itself the prerequisites of labor, that is, it ruins the owners of the old requisites of production. Thus it becomes a powerful lever for the formation of the requirements of industrial capital …. (p. 716) The development of the credit system takes place as a reaction against usury …. On the whole, interest-bearing capital under the modern credit system is adapted to the conditions of the capitalist mode of production …. The usury which sucks the life out of the small producer goes hand in hand with the usury which sucks the rich

owner of large estates dry .... Under the form of interest the whole of the surplus over the necessary means of subsistence (the amount of what becomes wages later on) of the producers may here be devoured by usury (this assumes later the form of profit and ground rent), and hence it is very absurd to compare the level of this interest, which assimilates all the surplus-value with the exception of the share claimed by the state, with the level of the modern rate of interest, which gives to the interest normally no more than a part of the surplus-value ... . It is still more improper and meaningless to drag the lending of houses, etc., for individual consumption into this part of the discussion. That the working class is swindled to an enormous extent, in this way as well as in others, is an evident fact; but this is done also by the retail dealer, who sells them means of subsistence. It is a secondary exploitation, which runs parallel with the primary one taking place in the process of production itself. The distinction between selling and loaning is quite immaterial in this case and merely formal, and cannot appear as essential to any one, unless he be wholly unfamiliar with the actual condition of the problem. (Vol. 3, p. 716)

Marx's position is interesting in its ambiguity. He gives credit a modernist character, dissociating it clearly from old forms of usury. He accords little importance to consumer credit and does not distinguish it from consumption itself, seeing it as one facet of consumption, a mere technical detail.

The nineteenth century, which was to see the first concrete examples of consumer credit, thus ended in theoretical doubt as to its nature. Whereas interest-bearing loans were now perfectly acceptable for investment purposes, and for the fluidity of the economy (discount, supplier credit and so on), consumption still bore traces of ideological doubt, located somewhere between a driving force as Sismondi saw it, and Franklin's strict rejection, as seen in the *Poor Richard's Almanac*. As for consumer credit, it remained in the limbo of social and economic thought.

REFERENCES

FRANKLIN, B. *The Works of Benjamin Franklin*, (ed.) John Bigelow, Volume II New York: G.P. Putnam's Son, 1904.

HABERLER, G. *Prosperity and Depression*, London: Allen & Unwin Ltd., 1968.

LESCURE, J. *Des crises générales et périodiques de surproduction*, Paris: Domat-Montchrestien, Paris: 1932.

MALTHUS, R. *Principles of Political Economy*, New York: Augustus M. Kelley Inc. 1951.

MARX, K. *Bas Capital*, Vol. 3, London (ed.) Engels, 1909.

NUGENT, R. *Consumer Credit and Economic Stability*, New York Russell Sage Foundation, 1939.

RICARDO, D. 'On the Principles of Political Economy and Taxation' in *The Works and Correspondence of David Ricardo* Vol. 1, (ed.) P. Sraffa with the collaboration of M.H. Dobb. Cambridge at the University Press for the Royal Economic Society, 1951.

SAY, J.-B. *A Treatise on Political Economy*, Philadelphia: John Ohigg, n. 9 North Fourth Street, 1827.

SCHUMPETER, J.A. *History of economic Analysis*, London: Allen & Unwin, 1963.

SISMONDI, J.-C.L.S. de *New Principles of Political Economy,* New Brunswick and London: Transaction Publishers, Translated and annotated by Richard Hyse.

SISMONDI, J.-C.L.S. de *Etudes sur l'économie politique*, Geneva: Slatkine Reprints, 1980.

SMITH, A. *The Wealth of Nations*, London: Methuen, 1961.

STUART MILL, J. *Principles of Political Economy*, Toronto and London: University of Toronto Press and Routledge & Kegan Paul, 1977.

TAUSSIG, F.W. *Principles of Economics*, Macmillan Co., New York, 1911.

Part II
Consumer Credit in Contemporary Societies: Practice versus Dogma

Until the nineteenth century, consumer credit was seen only as the underside of society's operations. More or less forbidden but more or less practised because more or less necessary, much abused and largely dependent on other forms of credit, it developed its own shady and sporadic history. From the nineteenth century onwards, and especially in the twentieth century, it began to develop an independent existence of its own, at first based on the old models, as in France and England. But in 1850, in the United States, it took on the truly revolutionary form of hire purchase sales in order to finance home equipment for new settlers.

From then on, it became the most obvious support for, first Americans', then Europeans' improving standards of living. As an indirect effect, it helped stabilize industry in those same countries. From the sewing machine to the automobile, from the refrigerator to the television, it is impossible to disassociate Western standards of living from hire purchase sales. In this sense, consumer credit is the greatest single factor of social integration. The American example, which some Europeans consider excessive, offers a salutary lesson to those who are willing to examine it closely. For centuries, the nearest thing to consumer credit, that is the money lender, acted as a social lifebuoy for the poorest families. The United States transformed this calling into something positive. The idea of hire purchase was not to ease a difficult or even a dire present situation, but to project the consumer into the future with new domestic appliances.

The history of day-to-day life in the nineteenth century is aptly summed up by the contrast between the failure of the French *monts-de-piétés* and the success of American hire purchase sales: false public charity on one hand, acquisition of social status through possession of consumer goods, on the other. For this reason, consumer credit was legitimized earlier in the United States. As a long-standing symbol, the French legalization of credit in the *Code Civil* in 1804 stands out as the first milestone. But in order to legitimize a social practice, all aspects of it must be discussed. This must

95

be done in a democratic manner, that is by listening to all parties concerned: consumers, creditors and public authorities. The great American debate, ranging from the establishment of the Russel Sage Foundation in 1908 to the Consumer Credit Protection Act in 1968 constitutes the most extraordinary process of social legitimation of consumer credit.

The British debate prior to the Consumer Credit Act in 1974, (the 'Crowther Report', in particular) and the French discussions on the Scrivener Laws in 1978, and especially the Neiertz Act in 1989, all pale in comparison with the American example. The difficult encounter of Utopian consumerism and pragmatic professionalism nevertheless led to the first real legitimation, which was no doubt more fragile than in the United States.

The second part of this book proposes to look at the history of this legitimation by examining practices, products and regulations. Naturally, this leads us to today's niggling question: are we overindebted? The answer (or answers) to that question is obviously part of the long process of legitimation.

8 The American Way

'One aspect of the affluent consumer society that has largely gone unnoticed by sociologists is the extent to which it rests upon the institution of consumer credit.' Thus writes David Caplovitz (1969, p. 641), an American University Professor specializing in consumer credit. There could hardly be a better introduction to this chapter which looks at the way consumer credit is practised in the United States.

ORIGINS

The earliest examples of consumer credit were usually in relation to retail sales. These sales increased considerably after the conquest of the West and of the South, when the transport system throughout the whole of the United States facilitated greater mobility. For this reason, the principal creditors were traders, particularly travelling salesmen (Nugent 1939).

In the United States, as all over Europe at that time, it was common practice in agricultural areas to procure horses, carts, harnesses, furniture or seeds, paying half in cash, and the rest in the form of a bill to be reimbursed in two or three months, or after the harvest. Non-durable consumer items were usually paid for in cash, but sometimes in credit also. In this case, the credit transactions, inscribed in an Open-book, were highly informal. There were no contracts to evidence debts, nor any charge for credit service. This system was quite similar to that used by French country bakers who kept a record of their customers' debts by putting notches on identical wood batons. Customers usually paid up as soon as they came into some money. In such rural communities, credit was seen as a service to producers whose income was seasonal, and who paid their debts as soon as the harvest permitted. Traditionally there was a very low incidence of non-payment. Customers paid in order not only to avoid suspension of credit privileges, but also to keep their respectability for, in puritan America at the beginning of the nineteenth century, payment of debts was a virtue and inability to pay them a mortal sin. In this respect the system differs little from the practices of French rural society. If there is a difference it may be found in attitudes: the American farmer was a free man, a pioneer, unfettered by the semi-domestic dependency which bound the

European peasant to his creditor, the owner of the land. There was, therefore, a more liberal attitude towards credit, which was seen as no more than a tool to help run the household and farm budget.

In such a favourable environment, the development of consumer credit, in a market without banks or money lenders, was made possible by the credits that the wholesalers granted to their retail customers. The more the frontier extended westward, the more the travelling salesman became the lifeline linking the frontiers to Chicago which became the centre of this back-up trading. A vital link was thus established between the crude homes of the young families going west and business on the shores of Lake Michigan. Credit became a necessary part of the conquest of the West. To this very day, Chicago remains the largest national mail-order network as well as being home to the major specialist credit companies. The Windy City still has this role because of its history as a supplier for the settlement of the West. It is the symbolic capital of modern consumer credit, which first saw the light of day with the expanding railway and the opening up of the West.

Between 1800 and the American Civil War, credit continued to develop and diversify, although it became more difficult to recover sums lent, because the massive numbers of Europeans arriving into the country were less sensitive to social pressure, and imprisonment for non-payment of debts had been abolished. In spite of this, the practice of small loans, in the form of Open-books, spread by most suppliers of basic necessities. In the cities, where wages were paid every three or six months, employers supplied this form of credit for their employees in company shops.

When wage earners began to purchase consumer durables on credit, another method was called for: hire purchase. The idea was that the article bought became the security for the loan. The borrower contracted to make periodic payments which were considered as rent paid for the use of the article. An initial down payment was usually required and the trader remained the legal owner of the article until payment had been made in full. This system introduced considerable innovation.

The Singer Sewing Machine Company started selling its machines on hire purchase about 1850. The provision of household consumer durables of an industrial nature in return for monthly payments became an overnight success. It is worth noting that it was in relation to a machine aimed at women that our day-to-day lifestyle was changed. After 1850, the trend spread to the trade in industrial durables, particularly in the cultural domain. Books, pianos and other musical instruments were sold in this way. However, the repayment time was short and the initial down payment substantial. Businesses selling by hire purchase included the interest rates in the price of the merchandise and thus circumvented the old laws about usury which had been imported from England, but were not abolished in the United States when England abolished them.

The system which was still in its fledgling stages developed rapidly after the Civil War. It became less timorous. The payback period was extended, the down payment was reduced, and the range of products on offer was widened. Thus, toward 1870, furniture manufacturers in the large cities in the East started hire purchase sales. Such a development was spurred on by the massive urbanization between the Civil War and the 1920s. The arrival of new immigrants and population transfer from country to city were then the major factors of urban development.

To survive in this new world, families no longer depended solely on their own efforts. Each had to find a place in the highly competitive job market and sometimes it was difficult to keep up with the rising cost of living. Moreover, although there were regional and ethnic networks, family and neighbourhood links became less tight. The more urbanization continued, the more it became difficult to be able to count on such links in order to overcome exceptional situations (Hardy 1938). Throughout this phase of the emergence of the modern United States, consumer credit enabled people to alleviate some of the difficulties resulting from changes to their lifestyle or social bracket. It became the tool of a society on the move, thanks to which people were able to realize – in simple material terms – the migrant's dream.

Modern consumer credit came into being at the right time and in the right social context. Money was the only means of purchase for city-dwelling workers, producing for the market, depending on a monetary salary, yet deprived of access to commercial banks which required guarantees. Moreover, at certain periods, particularly between 1896 and the First World War, just as in the 1920s, credit benefited from good economic circumstances. Instalments are easier to pay during periods of rapid growth, low rates of interest, easy money and inflation.

In spite of its indisputable social function, credit still had a bad image. Unlike Europe, where it was condemned for ideological, essentially religious, reasons and where the lender, identified with the usurer, was stigmatized, the United States pointed the finger at the borrower. He was considered as a penniless failure. Of course, this ambiguous image merely glosses over the social pecking order reaching from the rich bourgeois to the latest arrival on the New York docks. Credit made it possible to separate current consumption from current income, and thus blurred social distinctions.

During the 1920s the climate changed. Households saved less, and to be in debt became respectable. What made this evolution possible was the generalization of hire purchase for the acquisition of automobiles. To borrow ceased to be an indication of poverty, or credulity when it was generalized in order to buy a luxury item, a car. This was the era of great credit societies, called 'captives' of their manufacturers, of which The General Motors Acceptance Corporation and The Ford Credit Company are the direct descendants. When we add General Electric Capital to the list, for the household appliance sector, we have named the three biggest world actors for the sector in recent years. This gives an idea of the impact of the 1920s on the history of consumer credit. With time, because of the items it brought within the reach of the poor, credit came to be seen as the greatest catalyst in the famous melting pot. This parallel holds one of the most fundamental keys to the American success story.

Moreover, once sale on credit has been generally established, its development leads to some positive economic results. By creating the base for a large market it facilitates mass production, and therefore an enormous reduction in unit costs. American economic vitality in the twentieth century stems from this correspondence. The immediate availability of durable goods contributes also to improve the well-being of the household. As of the 1920s, the problem facing American families was not how to procure the minimum necessary for survival but how to improve their standard of living, increase their satisfaction and security. At certain times, credit can also help to maintain buying power, particularly when the economy slows down (Hardy 1938).

Confronted with these observations, American economists quickly realized that consumer credit was an indispensable element in economic activity and saw its importance for improving the standard of living. In 1972 an official report of the National Commission on Consumer Finance 'underlines the magnitude and the importance of the consumer credit industry, both as a lubricant which oils the wheels of our great industrial machine and as the vehicle largely responsible for creating and maintaining in this country the highest standard of living in the world.'

Conscious from the beginning of the major role of consumer credit in American society, successive governments set themselves a double task: to regulate consumer credit in order to fight against the illegal market and its abuses, and to study the positive and negative economic effects. From 1920 until the present, this approach has led to a body of empirical and theoretical work of remarkable quality. The situation is completely different in Europe where few serious analyses have been done in that field and where some ideas, strongly influenced by theories of the Middle Ages, are still in vogue.

THE DEVELOPMENT OF STUDIES AND REGULATION

American mentalities differ from those of Europe, and consumer credit in America was never tainted by the same ideological prejudice. Until the mid 1970s it was the subject of many studies conducted by eminent academics and administrative bodies which mainly examined its social and economic aspects. Since then scientific interest in consumer credit has waned somewhat, but some universities still work on it and Federal Reserve banks also publish articles from time to time. However, the trend to regulation which slowly began early in the century not only continues, but has even intensified in recent years.

Before 1900, when employees asked for credit in order to face an unforeseen obstacle or to procure some necessity, it was hardly worthwhile offering small personal loans legally, as the usury restrictions were too low for these loans to be profitable. The first personal loans were made by pawnbrokers who looked more like traders giving conditional purchases than like money lenders. Personal bank loans were reserved exclusively for privileged customers. Of small amount and given at commercial rates, they were unprofitable and constituted an exception in a bourgeois world which did not yet know credit (Nugent 1939).

In such a context, the illegal market flourished. Employees in financial difficulties had no recourse other than the usurers – the famous 'loan sharks' – who granted credit but at very high interest rates. Between 1880 and 1920, loan sharks became a lucrative element of organized crime. Toward 1900, every large city had illegal finance companies operating at extremely high interest rates, and using criminal means to guarantee their repayment: assault, blackmail, slander and murder. Sometimes they used IOUs with reduced amounts on them, that is the rate of interest corresponded to the legal maximum, but the actual amount lent (in cash) was always less than the nominal sum on the IOU.

Bentham would have loved the phenomenon. The lack of suitable laws pushed serious institutions out of the market because they could not legally make a profit. The only ones who could operate in the market were those who could compensate for their lack of financial margin with their commercial margin (hire purchase traders who raised the price of the item, pawnbrokers who reduced the value of the pawn). Above all, since the demand was there, the situation led to illegal practices. The era was characterized, like the Prohibition era, by hypocrisy and over-strict regulations. As with Prohibition, local Mafias took over the vacuum created by the law. They grew rich on it at the expense of the person the law was supposed to protect.

In 1909, the moral scruples of certain States led them to authorize credit unions. This institution, a copy of the German Raiffeisen, was introduced to New England from Canada. Its purpose was to develop saving and to make loans available to its members. However, they could satisfy only a fraction of existing demand (Nugent 1939).

The first studies of consumer credit also began early in the twentieth century. Until the 1920s, they concentrated on the difficulties experienced by urban workers in adapting to the social upheaval of the end of the nineteenth century. The Russell Sage Foundation, founded in 1908 and initially concerned with the problems of borrowers victimised by lenders, undertook significant studies of consumer credit. It was the first indication of consumerism centred around credit (although the word was not coined and vulgarized until the end of the 1960s).

In 1916, as a result of the RussellSage Foundation's work, the Uniform Small Loan Law was drafted. This law had two main purposes: to increase the interest rates of small loans, in order to make them profitable enough for legal investments, and to assert the illegality of certain methods of loan recovery that until then could not be punished as they were not treated by the law, and that were currently practised by criminal organizations (Chapman and Shay 1967; Kawaja 1971; National Commission on Consumer Finance 1972).

The Uniform Small Loan Law set the ceiling for interest rates at 42 per cent per annum for loans of no more than 300 dollars. This was not a Federal law but after 1916 it was adapted and introduced into legislation by many States. In a majority of cases, it had to overcome the strong resistance of clean-living citizens and underworld money lenders – both of these pressure groups being attached to low usury rates!

In 1932, a revision of this law tightened the conditions required to be in the small loan business. The candidate had to invest 25 000 dollars in the business. The supervisory authority was entitled to examine the character and aptitude of the candidate. Finally, it had to be proven that such a new enterprise was worthwhile for the town. The principal purpose of these conditions was to reduce the destructive competition which had developed during the depression years. They marked the end of a certain liberalism of a market that became more dependent on its supervisory authorities (Kawaja 1971). More or less at the same time, many States reduced usury rates. This proved to be an error. The studies conducted by Rolf Nugent of the Russell Sage Foundation clearly show that, following this reduction, fewer small loans were granted by authorized institutions, with a simultaneous increase in the business of loan sharks.

If personal loans were thus regulated by official bodies, the same did not hold for hire purchase sales. When the lender was the seller of the item and that was usually the case, usury laws did not apply; the credit was covered by the general laws governing sales. The authorities considered that the hire purchase buyer was not destitute, ready to accept any conditions in order to receive money. In a system based on competition, like the American one, the buyer will not conclude the bargain if the conditions of sale do not suit. For these reasons the household equipment market was not suited to loan sharks, which were practically absent. Hire purchase sales became more and more widespread while new regulations continued to clean up the personal loans market. However, for hasty observers, particularly Europeans, the American market of the time was characterized by its combat against the loan sharks. No matter that the majority of loans accorded never gave rise to any problems. Hire purchase sales on a day-to-day basis, both socially integrated and integrating, do not make good press. But the free-loading loan shark does.

We find the same phenomenon 30 years later in relation to Japanese credit practices. Europe, with its clean consumer conscience, only saw the usury of the *sarakins,* blinded by them to the fact that the majority of the market was run by the *shinpans,* that is hire purchase companies which were forbidden to give personal loans and which, because of the competition, offered credit at rates very similar to those of the big banks (see below).

Although focusing on the extreme fringes of the market is certainly useful, it should not distract our attention from the essential fact; American politicians aware of the usury of the underground legislated against it. They were perfectly right to do so. But for more than 80 years they did not consider regulating hire purchase sales, precisely because such sales worked well. The first law concerning hire purchase sales did not appear until 1935 and was not generalized until the 1950s (Curran 1965).

It took many years to establish a complex legal framework, differing from one State to the next, consisting of a system of laws drawn up to deal with specific problems, abuses which had crept in, or to clarify certain relationships between lenders and borrowers. Thus, the legislation was neither Federal nor general, but relative to a particular type of institution or contract, and applicable to specific consumer categories. In the early 1960s the market was more homogeneous, but the legislation remained compartmentalized.

The Consumer Credit Protection Act (CCPA) of 1968 was the first overall Federal law protecting consumers in the domain of credit. It set up a commission, the National Commission on Consumer Finance which, after an in-depth investigation, presented its report to the President and to Congress in December 1972. This report concluded that a truly competitive consumer credit market, with adequate information on the most important points of the offer of credit, available to a public of informed consumers, backed-up by regulations eliminating the dangers of excess, both enhanced economic growth and optimized advantages for consumers. The Commission recommended that consumer protection be increased in relation to creditors options and recovery practices.

The first title of the CCPA was the Truth in Lending Act (TILA) which regulated the information furnished to the customer. The TILA designated the Federal Reserve Board as the principal authority responsible for elaborating regulations relative to consumer protection in the domain of financial services. Regulation Z, drawn up by the Board in 1969, set the norms of application of the law. Since then, the CCPA has been revised on several occasions and complemented by very thorough legislation. The main texts are: The Fair Credit Reporting Act (1970), Credit Card Amendments to Truth in Lending (1970), The Fair Credit Billing Act (1974), The Equal Credit Opportunity Act (1974) and Regulation B, Consumer Leasing Acts (1976), The Fair Debt Collection Practices Act (1977), The Electronic Fund Transfer Act (1978) and Regulation E, and the 1978 Bankruptcy Act, revised and amended in 1984.

At the end of the 1970s the regulations were loosened a little. Title VI of the Depository Institutions Deregulation and Monetary Control Act of 1980 simplified the TILA. The DIDMC Act not only reduced financial specialization and progressively eliminated the ceilings on interest rates, it also loosened the constraints which limited competition. Moreover, deregulation favoured a more active competition for deposits and the increase of funds available for consumer credit. In 1988, The Fair Credit and Charge Disclosure Act renewed regulations for credit cards.

No other country in the world has passed so much legislation so early concerning consumer credit. Some see this as the sign of a society which over-extolled the virtues of credit and is now trying to back-pedal. The reality of the matter is much simpler. Each of the laws in question takes into account ongoing policy changes in relation to credit cards, leasing, electronic transfers and so on and is each time preceded by a vast public debate of which Europeans have no idea and which shows both the democratic maturity of Americans in their daily life and the considerable importance of credit as underpinning society.

In order for such legislative work to succeed, it goes without saying that a solid opus of University-level studies should confirm the utility of this credit. Consumer credit has remained an important theme in American economic thought throughout the twentieth century, unlike Europe, where it is often neglected. But such economic thought must nevertheless be integrated into public debate if we wish to understand the reality of the phenomenon.

THE EMBLEM OF AMERICAN SOCIETY

Between 1948 and 1965, inflation in the United States was extremely low (1.7 per cent per annum on average), but consumer credits outstanding rose by 12.5 per cent per annum. Several socio-economic factors facilitated this spectacular development. Firstly, households began to catch up on the slack war years during which they purchased very few consumer durables. The birth rate also began to catch up on the war years, consequently population growth increased, and with it family needs. Moreover, young people tended to get married earlier. For all of these reasons, the demand for consumer durables increased considerably.

The economic growth and increased household disposable income affected behaviour patterns. The United States was the first country where a majority of the population disposed of an income well above subsistence level. Consumer aspirations rose and goods which had previously been considered as luxury items progressively became part of everyday life. The household wish of owning a house and living in rich suburbs (greater travel, better cinema and the introduction of television) led to an increase in demand for consumer items and social pressures to 'keep up with the Joneses'. This was the America of which the rest of the world dreamt, the modern America as depicted by Hollywood. The triumph of the industrial society, and the development of a consumer society, had a favourable effect on attitudes to consumer credit. A new generation, which had not known the Depression, arrived on the market. They lived in the present, and on credit, because they had a positive view of the future, and some insurances on which they could count to make their situation less precarious, that is unemployment benefit, retirement schemes and later, health benefits.

Before the Second World War, hire purchase, introduced by Singer and taken up by automobile and household appliances manufacturers, contributed in no small way to social integration. The same phenomenon, whereby social status was acquired more quickly along with durable goods, was to be found in this post-war period. Consumer credit, whether old fashioned hire purchase or later new style credit cards, became an important means facilitating the path of achievement which was to form the American middle class.

By the same token, the emergence of a new middle class consisting of wage earners, and the decline of the old middle class of entrepreneurs fostered a great increase in consumer credit. The entrepreneurs operated in a world of risk and uncertainty, which was subject to the ups and downs of the market. When they contracted debts it was for purposes of production rather than consumption. Only those who became very rich could afford the luxury of ostentatious consumption.

On the contrary, the new middle classes of wage earners constituted an ideal market for consumer credit. Being unable to rest their status claims on property, they were under strong social pressure to acquire the consumer goods that became the symbol of the middle-class style of life, a pressure that was experienced even by those whose incomes were relatively low. Besides, this new middle class was reasonably sure of continued employment and, consequently, of a stable, even increasing income; necessary conditions for the healthy development of a credit society (Caplowitz 1969).

New conceptions of living were being put forward. In traditional society, it was considered right to save first, in order to buy later. America reversed this model: people bought first, then saved in the form of monthly repayments. Credit enabled people to round off the income profile, since incomes tend to be smaller in early adulthood, and to reach their maximum at the age of maturity. Credit filled in the gap between the present equipment needs of the young couple and their future income. Obviously, such a scenario can only work when household incomes follow an upward trend due either to an increasing age–income profile or overall income growth, as was the case in the post-war years.

Between the second half of the 1950s and the early 1970s, consumer credit continued to expand, but at a slower rate. Marriages became less common and previously equipped households made mostly replacement purchases. Moreover, in the latter half of the 1960s, financing of the Vietnam war and new social programmes, without increased taxes until 1968, caused inflation to accelerate. Households, not used to such price increases, reacted by reducing their level of debt. This tendency was reinforced, as of 1969, by a restrictive monetary policy, which resulted in a rationing of credit. Refinancing costs of lending establishments increased spectacularly, whereas usury ceilings remained unchanged.

Credit began to pick up again towards the middle of the 1970s and continued to do so until 1990. It was helped in the 1970s by the arrival on the market of the baby boom generation who, like their parents, remained convinced that the best form of saving is paying back a loan. Firstly a mortgage loan, of course, but also loans for cars and other durable goods.

Anticipation of continuing inflationary tensions encouraged purchases on credit. Moreover, new financial products appeared on the market and the use of credit cards became generalized. It was also during this period that events caused financial deregulation and an intensification of competition.

From the end of the 1960s, in an effort to combat inflation, the Central Bank pursued restrictive monetary policies on repeated occasions. These policies caused rapid increases in interest rates on the money market. During these periods of tension the rates of remuneration of deposits, regulated by law, remained low. Then appeared the phenomenon of disintermediation. Institutions which, like savings and loans, were only allowed to lend out the resources which they collected, were confronted with a drain on deposits as savers sought more profitable investments. Thus, these institutions were forced to drastically ration credit (Gelpi 1987). In order to avoid the recurrence of these 'credit crunches', and their global economic consequences, the authorities progressively liberalized interest rates, and legalized new products allowing for remuneration of deposits at rates close to those of the money market (Wojnilower, 1980). Two new laws recorded these measures: The Depository Institutions Deregulation and Monetary Control Act in March 1980, and the Garn–Saint Germain Depository Institutions Act in December 1982.

The financial innovations and reforms of the 1980s abolished constraints limiting credit offers: (1) the withdrawal of deposits linked with the ceiling on deposit rates; and (2) the reduced profitability of financial institutions due to the ceiling on loan rates. Markets became decompartmentalized and financial institutions, as long as they stayed solvent, could always find funding although sometimes at a high cost. Moreover, some establishments extended their field of lending activities. Thus, deregulation reduced specialization and intensified competition. Monetary control was no longer based on credit rationing, but on the dissuasive effect that high interest rates could exercise on the demand. Until 1986, this had little effect on consumer credit, since interest payments were still tax deductible.

Therefore, consumer credit continued to progress rapidly during the 1980s, apart from the period of economic recession from 1980 to 1982, although in a different socio-economic environment from that of the 1970s. It was favoured not only by the intensification of financial competition and the development of the use of credit cards, but also by a decrease of lending rates from the temporary highs of the early 1980s. The growth of credit continued in the second half of the 1980s, thanks to home equity loans which, by doing away with the distinction between consumer and mortgage credit, allowed for longer repayment periods and enabled people to equip their homes with the mortgage guarantee. Above all, home equity loans enabled people to continue to benefit from the fiscal advantages attached to property loans.

However, in an indebted society, circumstances can change: late repayments due to divorce, loss of work, overindebtedness caused by bad budgeting. The incidence of these phenomenona has hardly increased, since the families who went deepest into debt had high incomes and realisable assets which, if needs be, enabled them to reimburse their debts.

CONSUMER CREDIT, GROWTH AND ECONOMIC FLUCTUATIONS

Apart from a few individual cases which are always dramatic and apparently inevitable, the important thing for society is to ascertain whether consumer credit is an economically healthy practice. The question has long been raised by numerous American academics who very quickly pointed out its stimulating effect on growth.

In the early 1950s, American economists travelling in Europe remarked on the fact that consumer credit was almost totally non-existent. Groups of European industrialists visiting the United States on productivity missions arrived at the same conclusion. Experts claim that this partly explained the recognized differences in standards of living between the two continents. It is a fact that hire purchase sales help improve living conditions by fostering the birth and development of new mass consumer industries, thereby creating millions of new jobs, cheaper production costs and better quality durable goods. Consumer credit also helped raise the standard of living by encouraging wage earners to work harder in order to get more pay. A French group even went so far as to say:

> 'enjoying personal credit and using it, the American workman finds in his obligations the necessary stimulant to improve his position as much as possible' (Phelps 1954).

A few years later, in 1965, The Board of Governors of the Federal Reserve System underlined:

> Consumer credit is thus an important means of financing the flow of goods and services into final consumption and is a factor influencing the level of economic activity. Over long periods of generally rising activity the extension of credit to purchasers of consumer goods has supplemented current purchasing power, and this has tended to stimulate

production and employment. But substantial increases in consumer purchasing power through the extension of credit in periods of high economic activity are appropriate only when the terms on which credit is extended are prudent, the growth of such credit does not contribute excessively to monetary expansion, and when the new purchasing power is matched by an increase in the supply of goods at relatively stable prices. (Chapman and Shay 1967, p. 3)

If we think about it, these general advantages seem to be the consolidation of flexible consumerism available to households: greater flexibility in planning for expenditures and the idea of budgeting family durables and life-style. A simple example comes to mind: it was no longer necessary, as in the early days of the industrial revolution, to choose between having children while still young or equipping the home first. Goods could now be bought as needed without reference to the liquidity of the moment. Besides, it is sometimes preferable to incur debts rather than sell financial assets. Such were the lessons drawn by American economists and sociologists observing the situation, lessons which were both very simple and very innovative for family budgeting. Not to mention the historic fact that hire purchase sales enabled the least privileged families to accede to consumer society and thus to gradually lay the basis for a higher social status.

Consumer credit was never considered as a necessary evil in America, unlike Europe where, even official bodies have compared it to prostitution! At certain times, however, its rapid expansion gave rise to serious worries. It was feared that it might become an amplifying factor in economic cycles. It was thought that it might favour overspending in boom periods and intensify recessions, since families with debts would be forced to over-restrict consumption in order to meet their debts. American economists have left an abundance of literature on the subject. Beginning with the Depression in the 1930s, they show that consumer credit had a negligible role to play both in the initial crash and in its later evolution. But the development of the slump had a major impact on the credit market.

The Depression, which began in 1929 and continued until 1936, was international, striking particularly the United States and Germany. It had many causes: the exhaustion of viable investment opportunities following a period of over-rapid growth; insufficient increase in incomes in relation to productivity increase leading to under-consumption; stock market speculation and so on (Lewis 1963). The crisis began with the Wall Street crash of October 1929, putting an end to more than two years of wild stock market speculation. By the end of 1926, the four dominant economics, the United States, Great Britain, France and Germany had returned to the gold standard. The Central Banks therefore had to maintain sufficient gold reserves to be able to respect the convertibility commitment of their fiat money to fixed parities (Gelpi 1982). However, this extremely constraining system rested on a very fragile base because the International monetary exchanges were in fact unstable, as competition on financial markets increased international short-term loans that were then immobilized in long-term investments or used for stock market speculation.

Germany had to borrow massively in order to pay war reparations and to finance its investments. This forced the country to maintain high interest rates in order to attract foreign capital. The British pound was still a key currency, but the economic power and gold reserves of Great Britain were insufficient to enable the pound to play this role. The situation further deteriorated when, after the Poincaré stabilization in July 1926, floating capital left London for Paris. France maintained a restrictive monetary policy, in spite of this inflow of capital, then, in May 1927, France added to the difficulties of the Bank of England by exchanging its pound reserves for gold.

During the summer of 1927, the American Federal Reserve System lowered its interest rates in order to help Great Britain. Without meaning to do so, it gave the starting signal to the stock market speculation which coincided with the first signs of weakness in the economy (Yeager 1976). Being financed by credit to as much as four fifths, speculation fed on rising stock prices, and no longer had any connection with the evolution of dividends. The funds which formed the base of the pyramid of credit came, in part, from overseas. The monetary authorities did not wish, of course, to favour stock market speculation but, disposing of abundant gold and silver reserves, neither did they wish to worsen the problems of the economy, particularly in the domain of agriculture. Their relatively accomodating policy delayed the Wall Street crash. The crash nevertheless came when a tougher economic policy in the principal European countries interrupted the flow of capital to the United States. On 6 August, 1929, the Federal Reserve System raised its discount rate to 6 per cent, but this had no effect on stock market prices. However, the rise in European interest rates in September caused a withdrawal of foreign funds from the United States and a reduction in credit available to brokers. With a lack of credit to continue buying, prices dropped and the same mechanism which had amplified rising prices now brought them toppling down (Gelpi 1982).

The Wall Street crash put an end to movements of international capital (Morsel 1977), caused lack of confidence, highlighted the weaknesses of economies and started the deflationary spiral. In the United States, consumer prices fell by 24 per cent between 1929 and 1933; in the same period the GNP in constant dollars was reduced by 30 per cent and did not return to its 1929 level for another ten years. The unemployment rate of 3.2 per cent in 1929 rose to 25 per cent of the economically active population in 1933. With the decrease of nominal national income which, in four years fell by 53 per cent, the repayment of debts contracted during the euphoric growth years became such a burdensome commitment that many debtors were unable to meet their payments. Between the end of 1929 and 1933, more than 5000 banks went bankrupt, hit by massive withdrawals of deposits, depreciation of securities in portfolio and the insolvency of their customers. This threatened the banking system and caused large-scale monetary destruction there by feeding deflation. The reduction of nominal wages, as of 1930, further increased the trend.

The majority of studies devoted to the cyclical behaviour of consumer credit show its low impact on the internal logic of the Depression. On the contrary, the consequences of the slump on the evolution of consumer credit proved formidable. The turnaround in the curve tracing the development of the market coincides exactly with the stock market crash of October 1929. Financial establishments were overcome by the lack of deposits and this led to a brutal reduction in the provision of credit. Afterwards, faced with growing unemployment and falling wages, the sector became mainly depressed due to repayment difficulties which were frequently accompanied by seizure of goods, particularly in the automobile and furniture domains. Uncertainty and fear of the future weighed heavily on consumers; between December 1929 and December 1933 consumer credit dropped by 50 per cent, while its relative share of available household incomes dropped from 4.25 per cent to 3.5 per cent. Demand collapsed. Delays caused by lack of repayment multiplied. In short, a social crisis of the first order developed, brought on by the economic crisis, the burden being borne by the weakest households, not so much because they were in debt, but because they lost their source of income.

In 1955, less dramatic events give an equally illustrative example of the way in which consumer credit is often confused with other things: consumer credits outstanding rose by almost 20 per cent. The result was that the authorities considered taking measures of control and promoted a conference for 1956. The results of its deliberations were published in several volumes (Board of Governors of the Federal Reserve Banks, 1957). The great success of this conference affords an idea of the importance of the subject in the United States. By obliging the different actors and schools of thought to express themselves, the conference reflected national awareness of the social and economic utility of consumer credit. Practically devoid of philosophical questionings, the conference was characterized by its pragmatism. Some experts feared that a large increase in consumer credit would lead to over-production of automobiles and other durable goods, which would necessarily be followed by a tightening of these sectors which would then be passed on to the rest of the economy. They wondered whether it may be wiser to organize a more reasonable increase in credit, thereby bringing it more into line with an orderly growth in the economy. To this end they discussed the idea of implementing specific measures in monetary policy in order to reach that target.

In the end, their fears were not borne out by the facts: in spite of a great and continued increase in credit, at no time during the period did debts prove excessive. In some cases, households could choose between purchasing a service and purchasing the goods which performed the service, that is buying a washing machine or sending clothes to the laundry. Substituting the purchase of the item at credit for the repeated purchase of the service does not necessarily increase the expenditure of the household and does not reduce its capacity to take on further debts. What determines repayment capacity, therefore the viability of a loan at a given income level, is both the cost of the debt itself, and the future evolution of income. Of course, to engage the future income in order to satisfy present needs only works well if income grows or at least does not fall in real terms. It may grow in an overall manner (that is including the reduced cost of the debt, a phenomenon which was familiar in the inflationary economies of Europe at the time, but less true of the United States) or individually, through prospects of salary increases which mark the pathway of *achievement*.

Societies whose members live on credit need growth and, most important of all, prospects of employment. However, both of these may be endangered. It is at such times, when the economic situation deteriorates, that the consequences of the optimistic plans of the previous period can be seen. All studies are agreed that recessions have a deadlier effect on repayments which become more difficult than on new credit which becomes more rare. Thus, consumer credit may increase the intensity of a business cycle, but it is never the driving force behind such economic downturns.

The United States is both the oldest and most highly developed modern consumer credit market in the world. Consequently, Americans have greater social awareness of credit. It is there that the greatest number and often the best studies of the subject have been conducted. For all of these reasons, the United States affords the best overview of credit available. Credit professionals look to the United States for innovative ideas. In both Europe and Japan, everything from hire purchase sales to the varying uses of revolving credit, including scoring techniques and methods of recovery, all such innovations have been imported from the United States.

Consumer associations and public authorities also look to the United States. The very concept of consumerism is American. American consumerism could teach a thing or two about positivism and practicality to its European devotees, who sometimes get carried away with the Utopian enthusiasm of the beginner. Consequently, all too often, they see the United States as a model to avoid. All the bad connotations of America, which can be summed up in two words that is too much, are to be found in the famous household debt rate (between 17 per cent and 20 per cent of available income in recent years) which is cheerfully blamed for a wealth of evils, a plethora of sins! Woe betide us the day we reach the American level, seems to be the tacit refrain of European consumer authorities and associations. As if it were a demon to be avoided! At the same time, the same people do all in their power to import the lessons of American consumerism! A fine example of the love–hate relationship which binds the Old and the New World.

However, without naiveté or prejudice, we can say that the debt rate of American households indicates, above all else, the great spread of consumer credit throughout all the social classes, unlike Europe where it is more class related. Secondly it shows the major role of petty, everyday credit as a force of social integration and consensus building. What Europeans are prone to consider as a fault in the economic system, is in fact the sign of a modern day open society. The low paid labourer in Houston or Phoenix, who is today negotiating a loan to buy his first mobile home, is living proof of the validity of the system. Whether we look at its social role or its economic function, consumer credit constitutes one of the driving forces in the American success story.

THE CASE OF JAPAN

It is easy to see why we deal with Japan just after the United States, since Japan combines a particular historic tradition with an extremely high level of American influence. Of course there is a great difference between Japanese and Euro-American civilization, with respect to the moral foundations of consumer credit. On the one hand biblical dogma continues to a greater or lesser degree to influence certain judgements, while on the other, and this is true for all of the Asian world, usury never gave rise to philosophical or theological debate. For instance, in the Brahminical tradition, lending at interest, which Dante relegated to the seventh circle of his *Inferno*, is considered as one of the seven legitimate means of increasing one's wealth. The Golden Age of Chinese Buddhism, during the Tang dynasty, between the seventh and tenth centuries, corresponds to the appearance of *monts-de-piétés* run by monasteries. These institutions continued to develop without any social opprobrium until the begining of the twentieth century (Malamoud 1988).

This favourable ideological climate explains the very early appearance of the first forms of consumer credit in Japan. Only slightly after the Tang period in China, the first pawnshops, the *tsuchikura*, appeared during the Nara period in the eleventh century. The pawn usually consisted of rice, tools or clothes, in return for a short-term advance. With the sixteenth century, these shops were complemented by mutual associations, generally run by temples under the name of *mujin*. They lent for longer periods than the *tsuchikura*, financing personal equipment, or better, professional equipment for artisans. In the ninteenth century, these *mujins* formed the associational basis for the majority of mutual banks which are still so prominent in Japan (Yajima *et al.* 1992).

Another very old form of lending was peddling from boats, the *wanbune*. They sold their merchandise of porcelain, lacquerware, tatamis or mosquito nets in return for seasonal repayment schemes based on rice harvests.

Thus, by the end of the nineteenth century, the two major forms of consumer credit already existed in the Japanese consciousness, that is on the one hand, the personal loans of the *mujin* and the *tsuchikura*, and on the other, the loans to buy *wanbune*'s goods. This distinction, which is probably the most fundamental distinction of the Japanese market, still exists today, although numerous recent projects wish to abolish it. It lies at the root of the present day organization of credit professionals. The personal loan comes under the jurisdiction of the Ministry for Finance, while the object loans come under that of the Ministry for Industry and Trade, the famous MITI. The establishments, and the products which they offer to their customers, remain strictly listed in each category.

All innovation in the sector is therefore chanelled toward one or other of the two ministries. This situation has continued since the earliest manifestations of consumer credit in its modern form. This was the case in 1901, when Singer introduced their sewing machines on the Japanese market, with a system very close to hire purchase. It was also the case when, in 1928 and 1930, Ford and General Motors created financing societies based on the American model in order to boost their sales. All of these endeavours came under the category of establishments regulated by the MITI, in other words, the category of *shinpans* (literally credit sales).

The American influence was also felt a little later in the private loans sector under the Ministry for Finance. In 1953 a new law created the *sarakin*, an abbreviation for *salaryman kinyu*, 'wage earner financing'. This system replaced the old '*kori-kashi*' (high-interest) system which dated from the Meiji era, at the end of the nineteenth century. It had given rise to a multitude of small local lending offices operating without any real controls (Cobbi 1988). The new *sarakin* system was modelled directly on the American practice of debt consolidation, as it existed in the United States at the time. The idea was to introduce a more moral aspect into the profession by fixing a usury ceiling of 109.5 per cent! (Yajima *et al.* 1992).

At the same time, the *shinpans* continued to develop and expand in all the directions which the American model suggested, that is automobile and household appliance financing, even credit cards, from the end of the 1950s, particularly in department stores, with variable rates depending on the refinancing conditions, but never in excess of 30 per cent, and very generally situated a few points above the discount rate. Favoured by their good public image, and by their social utility linked to domestic equipment financing which they made easier, the *shinpans* developed rapidly, and acquired a preponderant position with, on average a 43 per cent share of the market from the 1960s on. They rank just behind all the mutual banks, with an average share of 48 per cent. Two *shinpans*, Nippon Shinpan and Orient Finance, dominate the category with 20 per cent of the total market. Both were found between the wars.

It is nevertheless the phenomenon of the *sarakin*, with only a 7 per cent share of the market, which most concerns both Japanese authorities and consumers. With the growth period of the 1960s, and the scope allowed them to practise serious usury, *sarakin* have flourished. In 1983 there were as many as 97 000. The *sarakins* are often ruled by the underworld, the famous *yakusa*. The great majority of them distribute cash loans for a very short period, to meet all sorts of debts, even the most inadmissible, particularly gambling debts. With such a vocation, the methods of recovery can only be detestable! A large opinion campaign, based in particular on the increasing rate of suicides due to the *sarakins* (5 per cent of Japanese suicides in 1982, according to Cobbi 1988) resulted in a progressive plan to revise the maximum legal rate, and in a series of bans relating to methods of recovery. Today the *sarakin* sector is growing rapidly. The number of firms is decreasing while their methods are becoming more respectable, and although their rates are still apparently high (since 1991 the maximum has been 40 per cent), it should be borne in mind that the amounts are small and short-term. Some *sarakins*, particularly the four big ones, Takefuji, Acom, Promise and Lake, accounting for more than half the category, now offer a quality service.

The famous *yenshops*, blending proximity and maximal computerization, offer lines of revolving credit accessible through automatic cash distributors, at rates comparable to those of the big department stores' credit cards.

Thus, only a few years behind the United States, Japan has gone through its own transition towards high-tech and moral consumer credit. The household debt rate is just over 20 per cent of household income (in 1990); comparable to that of the United States. In contrast with the high media coverage of the real excesses due to the more marginal *sarakins*, this rate, which is one of the highest in the world, is perfectly compatible with a high savings rate, also among the highest in the world (16 per cent in 1992), giving an indication of the high degree of evolution of Japanese society.

REFERENCES

Books

BOARD OF GOVERNORS OF THE FEDERAL RESERVE SYSTEM, *Consumer Instalment Credit*, Six Vols., National Bureau of Economic Research, Washington, 1957.

BUERGER, A.A. '*Revolving Credit and Credit Cards*' in N.C. DURHAM, *Consumer Credit Reform, Law and Contemporary Problems*, Revue de Economic Politique, Paris, fall 1968.

CHAPMAN J.M. and Associates, *Commercial Banks and Consumer Instalment Credit*, Washington NBER, 1940.

CHAPMAN, J.M. and R.P. SHAY, *The Consumers Finance Industry: Its Costs and Regulation*, Columbia University Press, New York and London, 1967.

COBBI, J. 'Une forme nouvelle de suicide pour dette au Japon, le problème des "sarakin",' in C. Malamoud, *Lien de vie, noeud mortel, les reprsentations de la dette en Chine, au Japon et dans le monde indien*, Paris: Ecole des Hautes études en sciences sociales, 1988.

CURRAN, B.A. *Trends in Consumer Credit Legislation*, University of Chicago Press, 1965.

FOSTER, W.T. *Loan Sharks and their Victims*, New York Public Affairs Pamphlets, 1945.

GELPI, R.M. 'Mécanismes de la création monétaire et régulations économiques', PhD thesis, Université de Paris-Dauphine, 1982.

HABERLER, G. *Consumer Instalment Credit and Economic Fluctuations*, Washington NBER, 1942.

HARDY, C.O. *Consumer Credit and Its Uses*, NY: Prentice-Hall, 1938.

KAWAJA, M. *The Regulation of the Consumer Finance Industry*, Columbia University, 1971.

KISSELGOFF, A. *Factors Affecting the Demand for Consumer Instalment Sales Credit*, NY: NBER, Technical Paper 7, 1952.

KLEIN, P.A. *The Cyclical Timing of Consumer Credit, 1920–67*, NY: NBER, 1971.

LEWIS, W.A. *Economic Survey 1919–1939*, London: George Allen & Unwin Ltd., 1963.

MALAMOUD, C. (ed.), *Lien de vie, noeud mortel, les représentations de la dette en Chine, au Japon et dans le monde indien*, Paris: Ecole des Hautes études en sciences sociales, 1988.

MALCOLM, W.D. and J.J. Jhr. COURTIN, 'The New Federal Attack on the Loan Shark Problem', in N.C. DURHAM, *Consumer Credit Reform*, Revue d'Economic Politique, Paris fall, 1968.

MANDELL, L. *Credit card use in the United States*, University of Michigan: Institute for social research, 1972.

MANDELL, L. *The Credit Card Industry: a History*, Boston: Twayne Publishers, 1990.

MOORE G. and P.A. KLEIN, *The Quality of Consumer Instalment Credit*, NY: NBER, 1967.

MORS, W.P. *Consumer Credit Charges*, Washington NBER, 1965.

MORSEL, H. 'La grande crise du monde capitaliste', in P. LEON, (ed.), *Histoire économique et sociale du Monde* Vol. 5, Paris: Armand Colin, 1977.

NATIONAL COMMISSION ON CONSUMER FINANCE, *Consumer Credit in the United States*, 1972.

NUGENT, R. *Consumer Credit and Economic stability*, NY: Russell Sage Foundation, 1939.

PHELPS, C.W. *Instalment Sales Financing: Its Services to the Dealer*, Baltimore: Commercial Credit Company, 1953.

PHELPS, C.W. *Financing the Instalment Purchases of the American Family*, Baltimore: Commercial Credit Company, 1954.

PLUMMER, W.C. and R.A. YOUNG, *Sales Finance Companies and Their Credit Practices*, Washington NBER, 1940.

SELIGMAN, E.R.A. *Etude économique de la vente à tempérament*, Librairie des Sciences Politiques et Sociales, Rarcel Rivière, Paris, 1930.

SMITH, P.F. *Consumer Credit Costs: 1949–1959*, NBER, Princeton University Press, 1964.

VADON, R. *La vente à crédit des biens de consommation durables: ses incidences économiques*, PhD thesis, Université de Lyon, 1959.

YEAGER, L.B. *International Monetary Relations: theory, history and policy*, New York: Harper and Row, 1976.

Articles

'*Consumer Credit in the American Economy-Vigor of Youth or Middle Age Spread*', Federal Reserve Bank of Philadelphia, Business Review, July 1965.

'*Consumer Credit, 1960–80*', Survey of Current Business, February 1981.

AVERY, ELLIEHAUSEN, CANNER, '*Survey of Consumer Finances, 1983*', Federal Reserve Bulletin, September 1984.

AVERY, ELLIEHAUSEN, CANNER, '*Survey of Consumer Finances, 1983*': A Second Report, Federal Reserve Bulletin, December 1984.

AVERY, ELLIEHAUSEN, KENNICKELL, 'Changes in Consumer Installment Debt: Evidence from the 1983 and 1986 Surveys of Consumer Finances', Federal Reserve Bulletin, October 1987.

CANNER, G.B. and A.W. CIRNAK, '*Recent Developments in Credit Card Holding and Use Patterns Among U.S. Families*', *Journal of Retail Banking*, Autumn 1985.

CANNER, G.B. 'Consumer Use of Credit Cards: Evidence From Recent Surveys', *Board of Governors of the Federal Reserve System Working Paper*, 1987.

CAPLOVITZ, D. '*Consumer Credit in the Affluent Society*,' *Law and Contemporary Problems*, Vol. 33, no. 4, pp. 641–55, 1969.

CHRISTELOW, D.B. 'Converging Household Debt Ratios of Four Industrial Countries', FRBNY, *Quarterly Review*, Winter 1987–8.

GELPI, R.M. 'El Estats Units i l'economia mundial: evolucions estructurals, politiques conjunturals', Societat Catalana d'Economia, *Anuari*, Vol. 6, Barcelona, 1987 (typed French version).

LUCKETT, C.A. 'The Growth of Consumer Debt', *Federal Reserve Bulletin*, June 1985.

LUCKETT, C.A. 'Personal Bankruptcies', *Federal Reserve Bulletin*, September 1988.

TAPSCOTT, T.R. 'Consumer Installment Credit, 1980–85', *Survey of Current Business*, August 1985.

WOJNILOWER, A.M. 'The Central Role of Credit Crunches in Recent Financial History', *Brookings Papers on Economic Activity*, 2: Washington DC: The Brookings Institution, 1980.

YAJIMA, Y., Y. SHINODA, C. ICHIKAWA and Y. HONJO, '*The origin and development of consumer credit in Japan*', Consumer Credit Industry Association, Consumer Credit Research Institute, Japan, Tokyo: 1992.

9 European Ways

New countries develop new techniques, whereas old countries adapt traditions to suit the times. The history of consumer credit in the United States is almost entirely free of historic influences, whereas in Europe, it still suffers from a sort of mental hangover, the result of centuries of bans and taboo. Practices derive from and are explained by age-old traditions. For this reason, this chapter, which is devoted to Europe, is mainly concerned with France and Great Britain, since they represent the two mentalities which diverged in the sixteenth century, that is Reformist and Catholic.

In order to understand the phenomenon we need to look back to the classical period. Pawnbroking, as practised by the *monts-de-piétés* is, in fact, the ancestor of consumer credit. Pious offerings from the faithful enabled Catholic countries to establish philanthropic organizations to fight against money lenders, who took advantage of the severe Church bans on money lending to impose conditions which were sometimes disastrous for the borrower. As for Protestant countries, they preferred to open the door to free market practice. This simple observation can still serve to explain many contemporary divergences.

THE FRENCH *MONTS-DE-PIÉTÉS*, 'MY AUNT'

The first French *mont-de-piété* was established in Avignon in 1577. At the time, the countship of Venaissin was under the dominion of the Papacy, and the *mont-de-piété* was highly influenced by the Florentine model. In 1607, Bartholomé Masurel opened a free loan office in Lille, and in 1637 Théophraste Renaudot opened a pawn office in Paris, lending at a rate of 3 per cent, which was soon closed by order of Parliament, because it was considered that credit would have a disastrous effect on commercial morality. In 1684, the *monts-de-piétés* at Angers was opened on the strength of charitable contributions. The same holds true of Marseilles in 1688. These dates herald the first period of credit development.

Not long after the opening of Masurel's establishment, the government of the Spanish Netherlands encouraged the opening of *monts-de-piétés* in the Flanders region. These latter offices were of a dual nature: they were highly privileged offices, invested with the exclusive right of the pawnbroker, while also functioning as veritable financial institutions which issued perpetual loans in order to get the funds necessary for the lending service. The creator of the service, the engineer Wenceslas Cobergher, designed it so that only very poor borrowers could get loans free of interest (Claveau 1876).

In France, the edict of February 1626, aimed at institutionalizing *monts-de-piétés*, had gone unheeded. It was not until 1777 that Louis XVI created the Paris *mont-de-piété* by letter patent, 'to ease the subjects of the king in their domestic affairs and to help traders avoid the shame and inconvenience of seizures of property.' In its first year the Paris office made 128 000 loans, in spite of the severe selection criteria, which gives an idea of the need of the population for such a service. During the period of the Revolution, all *monts-de-piété* were closed down, and pawnbrokers were declared legal, but this was short-lived: Regnault de Saint-Jean d'Angély, in an attempt to 'fight against the lending cave which accepted children's pallets', convinced the *Directoire* to reintroduce the stipulation making it obligatory to have a *Conseil d'Etat* authorization in order to open a *mont-de-piété*. The principal office, in Paris, was established by order of Napoleon I. Coming close on the heels of the *Code Civil*, the decree instituting the office modernized the Italian concept of the *monts-de-piétés*. Its innovative nature is borne out by the fact that a few years later the Milan office was established along the same lines. Exit the old Franciscan idea embodied by Florence; for nearly a century the '*mont de Napoleon*' was to be the state of the art. It became the prototype for all modernizing states throughout Southern Europe. In Milan it was adopted as the name of the most famous street in the city, reputed for its luxury (*sic*): the via Monte Napoleone.

A more general law, passed on 6 February 1804, was elaborated to prevent usury. It granted the exclusive right of pawnbroking to certain authorized institutions. It stipulated that lending shops could only be established in the service of the poor and with government authorization, and that any such institution which had not received authorization should cease to lend on security and should go into liquidation. In Paris, as in all other cities boasting *mont-de-piété*, the office monopolized the pawnbroking activities, at least in theory. It was however bound to give its profits to the Welfare Services (Caisse de l'Administration Générale de l'Assistance Publique).

The law passed on 24 June 1851 to regulate other *monts-de-piétés* was less strict. It stipulated that they should pay their excess takings to hospital funds, but only when the establishment's funds were sufficient to enable it to cover its overheads, and to lend at 5 per cent. Some lending offices for example in Metz, Avignon and Nancy, joined up with savings banks (Raiga 1912).

For the general public, charity, social assistance and poverty were the norm, and as the proverb says: 'Never lend to the poor'. It is often poor and modestly well-off people who need to borrow, usually to fulfil a specific and immediate need. The *mont-de-piété* was established to remedy this situation. An unemployed labourer; an artisan crippled by an industrial accident or a slack season; a trader whose debts exceed his resources or who needs a small sum – not available from a bank – to close an advantageous deal; a wage-earner whose savings have been exhausted by illness or other unforeseen circumstances; (Raiga 1912) all examples taken from files of the *monts-de-piétés*. For the moment, credit was mainly a specifically moral assistance for ordinary people going through a temporary crisis, and who have no securities other than their tools, their furniture, their jewels, their linen, their old clothes which – in the expression of the time, they 'nailed' – the image being taken from the storing technique most commonly used in *monts-de-piétés*. The image also gave expression to the sense of dispossession experienced by those using the service.

They had the other option of going to the local money lender who, although the rates were higher, had the advantage of not requiring any security. The process of getting a loan was something of a social Calvary. We only have to think of Balzac, whose work abounds with descriptions where credit denotes shame. The famous portrait of Gobseck condenses all the images from history, into one character.

Imagine vividly that pale, wan visage, to which I wish the Academy would allow me to apply the word moon-faced; it looked like tarnished silver. My usurer's hair was flat, carefully combed, and sandy-gray in color. The features of his face, impassible as that of Talleyrand, had apparently been cast in iron. His little eyes, yellow as those of a weasel, had scarcely any lashes and seemed to fear the light; but the peak of an old cap protected them. His pointed nose was so pockmarked about the tip that you might have compared it to a gimlet. He had the thin lips of those little old men and alchemists painted by Rembrandt or Metzu. The man spoke low, in a gentle voice, and was never angry. His age was a problem: it was impossible to say whether he was old before his time, or whether he so spared his youth that it lasted him forever.

All things in his room were clean and shabby, resembling, from the green cover of the desk to this bedside carpet, the frigid sanctum of old maids who spend their days in rubbing their furniture. In winter, the embers on his hearth, buried beneath a head of ashes, smoked, but never blazed. His actions, from the hour of rising to his evening fits of coughing, were subjected to the regularity of clock-work. He was in some respects an automaton, whom sleep wound up. If you touch a beetle crossing a piece of paper, it will stop and feign to be dead; just so this man would interrupt his speech if a carriage passed, in order not to force his voice. Initiating Fontenelle, he economized the vital movement and concentrated all human sentiments upon the I. Consequently, his life flowed on without producing more noise than the sand of an ancient hour-glass. Occasionally, his victims made great outcries, and were furious; after which a dead silence fell, as in kitchens after a duck's neck is wrung.... (p. 8) The man and his house resembled each other, like the rock and its barnacle.... (p. 8) Later, when I managed his affairs, I discovered that when we first knew each other he was sixty-six years old. He was born about 1740, in the suburbs of Antwerp, of a Dutchman and a Jewess.... (p. 10) I sometimes asked myself to what sex he belonged. If all usurers resemble him, I believe they form a neutral species. Was he faithful to the religion of his mother, and did he look upon all Christians as his prey? Had he made himself a Catholic, a Mohammedan, a Brahman, a Lutheran? I never knew his religious opinions, but he seemed to me more indifferent than sceptical. (p. 12)

'This man transmuted to gold' (p. 12), Balzac adds in his extraordinary portrait which condenses metaphorically all the stereotypes of usury. Even today, this secret, pale and spiteful character constitutes the ghost image which still haunts modern forms of consumer credit.

Nothing escapes Balzac's pen, not the famous Gobseck, not the *monts-de-piétés*, 'that queen of usury who casts her nets at the corners of the streets to strangle every misery and never misses one', nor Cérizet, a small-time money lender in *Les Petits Bourgeois*, whose portrait sums up the ambiguity of the phenomenon.

Above the door of a horrible entry hung a swing lamp on which 'Beds' were announced.... (p. 122) Cérizet had two rooms, one on the ground floor and one on the entresol, up to which he had a private staircase; the upper room had a window on a horrible paved court-yard from which rose mephitic odours.... But charmed his 'customers'; he spoke their language. Cadenet, his two shopmen, and Cérizet lived surrounded by the utmost misery, but preserved the indifference of a mute among the heirs of the deceased, of old sergeants of the Guard amid the killed; they no more groaned when their listened to cries of hunger or despair

than surgeons groan on hearing their patients in the hospital .... (p. 125)
Cérizet never made a mistake, nor did his poor debtors; they told each
other no lies, neither as to capital nor interest. On many occasions,
Cérizet, who was, after all, a man of the people, had rectified one week
the involuntary mistake of a previous reckoning to the advantage of the
wretched creatures who had not discovered it. So he was regarded as a
dog, but an honest dog; in the midst of that city of woes his word was
sacred .... (p. 127) Short loans at high interest, as practised by Cérizet,
is not, take it all round, so cruel a system as that of the Mont-de-Piété.
(Balzac 1898, p. 127)

Coming from Balzac the comment is of major importance. It indicates
quite simply that institutionalized money lending, as practised by the
monts-de-piétés, under the guise of a good Christian conscience, did not
necessarily achieve the charitable aims for which the institution was
founded, and that perhaps the local money lender, reviled by all, offered a
service more in line with the needs of the people.

On Sunday morning, when accounts were made up, Cérizet was abused;
still more was he cursed on Saturday, when borrowers had to work hard
to find the sum lent and the interest on it. Still, he was Providence, he
was God, from Tuesday to Friday every week. (p. 124)

Apart from the destitute and those reduced to a permanent state of financial embarrassment, the *monts-de-piétés* provided a much needed service
for a widespread clientele of traders and small industrialists (Claveau
1876). At the time, small bank loans were a rarity, despite the liberalization which was introduced during the period of the French Revolution.
There were two reasons for this: loans were usually given on a guarantee
of mortgage, which was difficult to obtain. Consequently they were not
very attractive; but most of all, borrowing and lending were frowned upon
(Bigo 1947). A hangover from the days of the Counter-Reformation, people borrowed secretly, which of course left the way open for all sorts of
abuse. Balzac gave voice to the accompanying cliches. The very expression '*ma tante*' (my aunt) comes from the famous anecdote concerning the
Prince of Joinville who, having pledged his watch at the *monts-de-piétés*,
claimed to have forgotten it at his aunt's.

   The solid reputation of the *monts-de-piétés* attracted a faithful clientele
in search of sound investments. This clientele was made up, for the most
part, of the *petite bourgeoisie*. In the interests of security, and in order to
provide a minimum return on these investments, the *monts-de-piétés* were

obliged to diversify the distribution of their credit to a more reliable clientele. This paradoxical situation merely highlights the fact that credit establishments with a purely social calling could not possibly develop while simultaneously trying to make a profit. They were caught between their initial social vocation on the one hand, and the requirements of their investors on the other. Many venerable institutions invested in this manner, among them the *Comédie Française* (French National Theatre) which, dating from the famous 1812 decree which Napoleon signed by the light of Moscow in flames, had a 20 per cent share in the Paris *mont-de-piété*.

With astonishing rapidity all classes of society came to frequent the *monts-de-piétés*, pawning furniture and even borrowing on the strength of securities. In the second-half of the century there were 45 *monts-de-piétés* in France. They are recognized as having had some major shortcomings: unwieldy formalities, expensive credit, insufficient loans and the famous sale of pawn tickets.

The deposit of an item at the *mont-de-piété* in return for a loan was known as pledging the item. The evaluation of the item was the first stage in the operation. Once the pawner's right to pawn the item had been established, the pawnbroker issued a receipt known as a pawnticket. The clauses of the contract were written on the pawnticket, a description of the item pawned and the amount of money lent. The pawnticket, which gave the pawner the right to the amount of money marked on it, was then kept by the pawner as a title to the item. The pawner returned the ticket in exchange for the item when he redeemed the item, that is when he returned the capital sum lent to him, as well as the interest costs of the operation. Of course the period of time during which an object could be redeemed was stipulated by the clause indicating the duration of the loan, which generally did not exceed one year. After an extension period of up to three months and on the approval of a judge, unredeemed items were put up for sale to the public. However, up until the moment of sale the pawner retained the right to redeem the item, or even to renew the pledge by paying the interest and costs (Claveau 1876). As a measure of caution, the statutes of most *monts-de-piétés* prescribed that only four-fifths of the intrinsic value of jewels or gold or silver items should be lent, and only two-thirds of the value of other items. The items were evaluated by auctioneers or other specialists.

In 1875, an administrative survey of a sample of nine *monts-de-piétés*, including those of Paris, Bordeaux and Marseille, showed interest rates of 9 per cent and over, with costs of funding between 3 per cent and 4 per cent. Furthermore, although 95 per cent of items pledged were in fact redeemed within the allotted time, three-quarters of the loans did not cover their own costs. But the *monts-de-piétés* were profitable. It follows from this that the profits were made on the large loans, which paid the same rates and thereby subsidised smaller loans (Claveau 1876).

Last though not the least of the paradoxes of this institution with a social vocation, the systematic under-valuation of objects pledged often resulted in the loan being insufficient. Hence the appearance, alongside the *monts-de-piétés*, of ticket merchants. These were private money lenders who lent money illegally in return for the pawnticket, but at a rate of 10 per cent *per month*. If the interest was not paid up regularly, the money lender owned the ticket after three months. All he had to do then was pay back the loan, the interest and costs, and thus acquire the grossly under-valued pledge!

So much for the double-edged intentions prevailing over the Napoleonic revamping of the *monts-de-piétés*: consumer credit was banned with one hand, while the other instituted false charity. Naturally, the small time money lender of Balzac's universe took over the market! By closing their eyes to the real needs of the time, the legislators were bound to fail in their social intentions, and to restrict credit in an unhealthy and outmoded system. 'Ma tante' was nothing but a hypocrite and everyone knew it. Unfortunately, the deservedly bad reputation of the system only served to increased the moral ostracism applied to credit. There is a salutary lesson to be learned from establishing a parallel between the French authorities' blinkered defence of the *monts-de-piétés* monopoly and the collective memory of the abuses of the 'ma tante' system.

THE ENGLISH PAWNBROKER, 'MY UNCLE'

Although the French expression 'ma tante', is linked with the Napoleonic decree which led to the spread of *monts-de-piétés*, the English expression 'my uncle', is older and more universal. The English expression contains the same social irony, crediting the money obtained by the family to the 'uncle', though the expression is used for all forms of money lenders. The expression first appeared in Flanders in the middle of the seventeenth century, spreading to the surrounding areas, including France, but it found its home in the English 'my uncle'. Later, in the nineteenth century, the myth of the 'American uncle' – who made a fortune in the New World and then discovered an heir in the homeland – also came from England. These two uncles could serve as a base for a history of European mentalities, the expressions give voice to the ambiguous role of money and credit in the collective unconscious, both vice and virtue, the best and the worst.

The history of consumer credit in England provides a perfect example of these attitudes.

From the time of the earliest Elizabethan liberalism, lending against a pledge was a private industry and not a state monopoly. As in most countries, it was frowned upon: borrowing money was admitting poverty. Indeed, the majority of transactions were conducted within the working classes. In the eighteenth century, this kind of borrowing was so widespread that numerous moralists condemned and stigmatized it. Daniel Defoe estimated that the majority of London families owed two to three times their annual income 'so that we can say that they eat the calf while it is still in the cow's belly'. In fact, at this time, the pawnbroker's shop was a sort of bank for the poor. The methods of collecting debts were rudimentary and often brutal. The debtors' prison was the ultimate threat, and so horrible was the prospect that there were charitable institutions which specialized in paying the debts of those imprisoned there. At the end of the eighteenth century, about 700 releases from custody were negotiated per year in the London area alone. Like Balzac in France, Dickens gives the best descriptions of these 'uncles' who provided a local service, which was sometimes downright usurious, and sometimes in line with what was to become the American 'money shop', a sort of bank that was open to all.

The early appearance of capitalism in Great Britain separated the house from the place of work. The needs of the family were no longer satisfied by domestic production, but by market purchases using currency. Insufficient means or an unforeseen expenditure forced households to borrow, sometimes with disastrous effects on domestic finances, sometimes enabling the family to come a little closer to the standard of living of the middle classes.

The pawnbroker's shop, frequented mostly by women, was an essentially urban phenomenon, which expanded massively between 1850 and the First World War. They sprang up especially in London and in other big industrial centres like Lancashire, Liverpool and Manchester. Warwickshire affords an informative example: in 1870, there was one pawnbroker for every 2656 inhabitants, a ratio roughly equal to that in present day countries with the greatest number of banks (Tebbutt 1984).

The *modus operandi* of pawnbrokers in the cities was different from those operating elsewhere. In working-class boroughs and suburbs there was strong social pressure on pawners to redeem the items pledged. The majority of pawnbrokers dealt each week with a regular working-class clientele. Loans did not exceed £10. Loans of sums in excess of £10 were not regulated by the laws applying to pawnbroking, but by those applying to usury. Later, such loans were to be regulated by the Money-lenders acts of 1900 and 1927.

More substantial pledges were accepted in the business areas of the big cities. These city pawnbrokers accepted valuable items and had large sums at their disposal. Dealing with an occasional clientele from the middle classes, they were closer to modern day banks than other pawnbrokers.

Strict regulations governed loans on pledge: a law passed in 1784 stipulated that for loans of less than two guineas the maximum annual interest rate was 20 per cent, and 15 per cent for larger sums. Interest rates on loans of more than £10 were freely negotiated by the parties involved. In practice therefore, the rates paid were distinctly higher than the annual rate of 20 per cent. In 1872, the interest rate on loans of less than £2 rose to 25 per cent per annum, and to 20 per cent for greater sums. Costs were deducted from the loan, and interest was paid when the object was redeemed or the contract renewed. Up until that time, the maximum period in which to redeem a pledge was 15 months. In 1872 it was then shortened to one year and seven days.

British legislation, with true pragmatism, recognized the tension between the desire for respectability of the pawnbrokers with a rich clientele, and those of the poorer quarters. The former were very strict about what they took on pledge, whereas the latter were much more lax, even accepting children's clothes as surety. For them, clothes amounted to more than a quarter of all objects pledged. It was even known for linen maids to take out a loan on the laundry given them to wash. Apprentices, household staff and day labourers sometimes pawned the objects committed to their care. This was particularly true of staff working with jewels and precious metals. Conversely, sometimes the pawnbroker used and damaged pawned clothes! Naturally, stolen goods were also pawned. In short, the whole spectrum of working-class society had recourse to pawnshops – (Tebbutt 1984).

The earliest laws, dating to 1603, were meant to prevent criminal behaviour; later they would have more social preoccupations. A law passed in 1757 attempted to define the obligations relating to pawnbroking. Symbolically enough, the law was a part of legislation relating to fraud and games of chance in public places! In 1800 came the *Pawnbrokers Act*, which was revised in 1872 (Crowther Report 1971).

The liberal, *laissez-faire* philosophy of the nineteenth century distinguished between pawnbroking, which was regulated by law, and money lending which was not. In 1839, loans of more than £10 were no longer regulated by usury laws, which were entirely abolished in 1854. From then on, money lenders were free to act as they wished, and their middle-class clientele was more than able to look after their own interests by taking full advantage of competition.

Small-time pawnbrokers, on the contrary, were protected by law, as it was considered that they had the important social function of helping the working poor who had an irregular income. Naturally, pawnbroking was subject to certain legal constraints, but in return the lenders were guaranteed a cosy interest rate, in order to avoid abuse of the system. We can see this in the Pawnbrokers Act of 1900 which, in counterbalance to a strict system of agreements and controls designed to protect the borrower, allowed for high interest rates, particularly on small operations.

The customer received between two-thirds and three-quarters of the market value of the item pawned, the item being evaluated correctly. It was on their regular customers that the pawnbrokers made their profit, and they therefore looked after them by giving them decent conditions. Mathematically, however, the interest rates on small very short term loans went as high as 1000 per cent, sometimes even 2000 per cent. Philanthropists, socialists and economists regularly objected to this state of affairs. The newspapers took up the question and brought it before the public eye. A long campaign was conducted against pawnbroking, as practised in England (London, 1894), and the law protecting it was described as a national disgrace. The usurious British 'my uncle' was compared to the charitable French 'ma tante', little realizing that behind the appearances of the Napoleonic laws reigned the greatest hypocrisy, in so far as the social vocation of the *monts-de-piétés* was ignored both in official practice, and in the consequences deriving therefrom.

Nevertheless, attempts to establish *monts-de-piétés* in Britain failed. The capital sum needed to launch them would have been at a high interest rate, and they could never have shown a profit. At no time did the campaign receive government support, be it Whig or Tory. The bureaucracy of the *monts-de-piétés* was off-putting: the more personal contact of the pawnbroker was preferred. The high moral tone of the time was also accompanied by a highly pragmatic vision of the role of 'my uncle'.

Firmly established in the British tradition, the pawnbroker was a major figure in the social upheaval caused by the Industrial Revolution. The development of the pawnbroker, beginning in the eighteenth century and expanding in the nineteenth, corresponds to the first suburbs being filled with new arrivals from the country. It was at this time that Dickens wrote *Hard Times*. His famous portrait of the 'banker to the poor' falls somewhere between the classic usurer and a financial services office adapted to its milieu. British legislators had a perfect comprehension of the essential role of the pawnbroker as a social lubricant. The pawnbroker was not, as Utopians always like to affirm, the cause of the hardness of the times; he was merely a consequence of them. In the final analysis, when regulated by some common sense laws to prevent abuse of the system, 'my uncle', not to give too much importance to theoretical interest rates, was a much better social mediator than 'ma tante', which was floundering in the quicksands of its own noble principles.

THE ARRIVAL OF CONSUMER CREDIT

Credit sale of necessary items was legalized in 1572 and became as widespread as pawnbroking, until the second-half of the nineteenth century, when instalment credit developed along totally different lines to those followed by pawnbroking. In 1881, the Providence Clothing Company offered easy payment terms. Customers found it preferable to buy a new garment on credit rather than to pay interest in order to redeem a worn one. This represented a fundamental change in the day-to-day lives of the British working classes. From 1890, pawnbrokers were progressively replaced by credit sales. The idea of the pawnbroker as a lifesaver in difficult situations gave way to the idea of instalment sale as an instrument to improve the way of living.

It was also during the nineteenth century that a new practice, hire purchase, appeared in the market. Initially the idea came from the French practice of renting luxury furniture with an option of buying. It was applied mainly to pianos, sewing machines and household furniture and was open to a well-off, low-risk clientele. Originally this sale technique was used by piano manufacturers and by the Singer Sewing Machine Company, among others. Until the end of the 1870s, people referred to the 'two year system' (sewing machines), the 'three year system' (pianos) and the hire system (furniture). The expression 'hire purchase' was a blanket term. Legally speaking, many of these contracts established by the manufacturers were, in law, conditional sale agreements, since the 'hirer' had to complete payment of the full price before taking legal possession (Crowther Report 1971).

Hire purchase was aimed at a cultured and well-to-do clientele who borrowed to improve their standard of living. There was practically no risk for lender or borrower. For this reason it was distinguished from money lending, and did not come to be regulated by law in Britain until 1938.

Traditionally, money lenders lent to members of good families who had fallen on hard times. They used bills of sale as security for loans. A bill of sale is a document by which the property in goods is transferred from one person to another, the grantor of the bill remaining in possession.

The 1878 Bill of Sale Act protected lenders from sale of guarantee goods to a third party prior to seizure. In cases of bankruptcy, these goods could not be reclaimed by the receiver. They became the property of the creditor who held the bill of sale. In 1882, the law was amended to protect the borrower from illegal seizures of personal property. The new law set out in precise detail the conditions governing the issuing of bills of sale, their domain of application and their register in the royal courts of justice. These laws were further completed by the Moneylenders Act in 1900, which was later revised in 1927. This law covered the different facets of money lending, including consent and contracts.

As in the United States, the development of car and motorcycle production after the First World War favoured the expansion of the hire purchase system, and the appearance of specialized financing companies. They financed not only the purchase of cars but also the stocks of dealers, since sales showed marked seasonal variations. This special link between household credit and supplier credit, which still constitutes the base of car sales today, characterized the beginnings of such sales in England.

It was at this time that the principal finance houses were founded: The Forward Trust, founded in 1928 to finance car purchases; The Mercantile Credit Company which grew in 1939 out of the merger of The Bankers Commercial Security which financed the purchase of pianos, The Mercantile Union Guarantee Corporation, which specialized in financing cars, and The Equipment Trust Company which funded household appliances. Also the United Dominions Trust which was initially American, but became an English limited liability company in 1923. Pre-existing financing houses such as the North Central Wagon and Finance Company added financing of hire purchase sales to their list of services (Drury 1982).

The report of the Crowther Committee estimated that in 1891 there were one million hire purchase contracts in Britain and about 21 million in 1921. These figures indicate the extraordinary impact of the product. Whereas the pawnbroker had helped the first generation of the Industrial Revolution to survive from day-to-day, hire purchase sales took up where they left off, by helping households to equip themselves with durable goods. The future, rather than the past, came to be the daily preoccupation.

The development of hire purchase between the wars can be explained in terms of its being a driving force behind the mass sale of consumer items, and incidentally by the fact that it did not come under the dominion of the Moneylenders Act. The Crowther Report confirms the exclusion of hire purchase sales from the Moneylenders Act: 'There can be little doubt that this by-passing of the Money Lenders Act has been in the interests of consumers as a class, since otherwise, the great extension of credit to ordinary households, and the higher material standards of living based upon it, would not have been possible' (p. 44)

In fact, the rise in the standard of living helped bring about new types of loans, which were no longer intended to ensure subsistence or to provide in case of accident, but to help finance the purchase of consumer durables. Little by little, today's consumer credit began to take shape, as a result of increased household incomes. Households became aware of the possibilities deriving from a desire for durables. As money lenders went into decline, loans offered by traders, banks and financing companies increased spectacularly.

As a consequence of this credit boom, laws were enacted to regulate hire purchase sales. The first, The Hire Purchase Act, was introduced in 1938 after a great public debate which underlined both the incontestable social utility of consumer credit, and the need to protect customers. This law made it impossible – except by bringing the case before the courts – to take back the good once a third of the price had been paid, a small but important step toward credit pure and simple.

The shortages and restrictions of the war years halted the expansion of hire purchase sales. After the Second World War, faced with the consequences of general measures to regulate the economy, credit companies were also confronted, for the first time, with numerous regulatory constraints relating to their business. It was during this period that sales were definitively distinguished from financing loans.

During the period immediately after the war, finance companies suffered from policies aimed at curbing the expansion of consumer credit, which was considered as part responsible for the high inflation of the time. Between 1952 and 1958, the Board of Trade modified the legislation relative to financing companies more than 22 times. This was the first time that the British public authorities had been seized by such regulatory fervour. Their attitude to credit had always been characterized by a great liberal pragmatism, which suited both British society and the economy. Restrictions on raising capital above a certain ceiling slowed the growth of existing financing companies. Paradoxically this fostered the establishment of a great number of smaller companies which spread rapidly, and ran counter to the government's attempts to squeeze the credit industry.

From 1952 onwards, the authorities also imposed conditions on the granting of instalment credit: a down payment of one third and a maximum repayment period of 18 months. These conditions were changed eight times up until October 1958. In April 1957, a Commission presided over by Lord Radcliffe had been set up to study the functioning of the monetary system and of credit, in order to propose improvements. After a long and detailed study the Commission declared itself opposed to regulatory control of credit as part of a monetary policy and following the publication of the Radcliffe Report in August 1959 all controls were abolished.

In spite of the regulatory constraints, the post-war years were a period of great expansion. This phenomenon was obviously helped by a radical change in the prevailing attitude to credit. Moral prohibitions disappeared and people of all classes whether deeply involved in economic mechanisms, or in the domestic domain, recognized the necessity of consumer credit and its advantages in terms of social evolution and activity.

As far back as the nineteenth century, pawnbrokers had come to be recognized as having a role to play in managing poverty, seen first of all as a necessary evil and later as a lubricant in the economic machine. During the 1930s, retailer credit was unanimously seen as an instrument of survival for the unemployed. Later, some began to see hire purchase as a form of enforced saving and therefore salutary. The last remaining reservations disappeared after the Second World War. The motto became 'take the waiting out of wanting'. From then on, consumer protection became the principal concern. In this context, the work of the Molony Committee, set up in 1959, provided the basis for the Hire Purchase Act in 1965, ushering in a new period for the consumer credit sector.

Later, in 1968, the Committee presided over by Lord Crowther examined the chaotic situation of the legislation, and gave a detailed analysis of the impact of consumer credit on British society: there was no link with inflation, nor did it have any negative influence on saving, no effect on the cyclical character of the economy and very few negative consequences socially. The report finishes its analysis with these words: 'Our main conclusion is that on balance consumer credit is beneficial, since it makes a useful contribution to the living standards and the economic and social well-being of the majority of the British people' (p. 141). It later adds: 'To sum up, we believe that the first principle of social policy should be to treat the users of consumer credit as adults, who are fully capable of managing their own financial affairs, and not to restrict their freedom of access to it in order to protect the relatively small minority who get into difficulties' (p. 153). Published in March 1971 the report led to the passing of the Consumer Credit Act on 31 July 1974. This act which, as its name indicates, covers the whole spectrum of consumer credit, is both extensive and complex. It established a framework to regulate all consumer loans of less than £15 000. The act covers everything from professional licences to the system of granting credits, from calculation of interest rates to documentation and advertising available to consumers, as well as arbitration contentions and procedures. It took more than ten years for the complete implementation of this law.

The act is the culmination of intense legislative work encompassing the extraordinary richness of the British market. Around traditional hire purchase sales a variety of different forms of credit had sprung up, ranging from simple sales promotion by a distributor to the consolidation of household debts by means of a mortgage (second mortgage loan), from bank cards to customer cards from local shops, from payment administration to pure offers of credit, from discount on a purchase to interest-earning value days ... a vast and complex panorama.

Great Britain – with its hardsell marketing and powerfully established actors; banks, retailers, financial houses and also credit bureaus – is often seen as a counter example by French consumer credit moralists. In this respect, Britain is a sort of United States within easy reach of Europe, but without the attractions of the frontier. The role of consumer credit as a force in social integration was just as strong in Britain, though at different periods, but with the same techniques and the same legislative balance based on broad economic liberalism, counterbalanced by the strong influence of consumer protection movements. This protection covers essentials such as the morality of the offer and the right to privacy; it does not go into fine details of each form of credit, but leaves the market to decide such things, and puts abuses in the hands of the courts. In this sense Great Britain is an example, and the Crowther Report an important step in the history of European consumer credit.

THE FRENCH WAY

Throughout the nineteenth century consumer credit in France continued to be confined essentially to the *monts-de-piétés*. The number of workers paid by the week rose in the second half of the century but the numbers were still low. Besides borrowing money against pledged objects, people also had recourse to a book at the grocer's, the unpaid debt ('ardoise') at the inn and the double notch at the baker's, not to mention the numerous Cérizets (small-time money lenders) in working-class areas. The rest of the population still received the majority of their income in a few yearly payments. The sums received in this way were quite sizeable. A part of this money would be put aside for day-to-day expenses, the rest was for expensive outlays. Moreover, household equipment remained rudimentary and unsophisticated. It had, however, a long lifespan and thus formed part of the many legacy. Savings for household equipment were therefore passed on from the previous generation.

In this social climate, characterized by rural lifestyles, private loans continued to be stigmatized. Public opinion, for the majority, condemned borrowing money, considering that credit ruined small farmers who fell victim to a bad harvest, forcing them to, in the popular expression, 'trade oats for hay' and also that wealthy young men by means of borrowing squandered their inheritance even before their fathers died. By the same token, credit makes bankrupt the artisan trying to become industrialist, or the trader whose wife has an inmoderate taste for luxury things. Inherit, scrimp and scrape and save – such was the motto of French society. Even as late as 1934, when the British were debating the Hire Purchase Act, a French professor of economics, Baudin, in his book entitled *Le Crédit*, launched an attack on consumer credit in no uncertain terms:

> Credit has caused an increase in the cyclical upturn movement, but credit is not made only by banks, in the wake of national or international operations. We see it springing up on all sides in the form of consumer loans. What could be more tempting than to acquire right away the much-coveted automobile by committing oneself to paying out an apparently modest sum for a certain number of months to come? Mr M.H. Hausser has pointed out that people who are greedy for bargain rate luxuries are easily persuaded of the soundness of the bargain, the more the payment date recedes into the future. The producer, on the other hand, has everything to gain: he increases the immediate demand and guarantees a future demand, since a car sold is as good as a guarantee of future repairs services. Moreover, he is careful to calculate repayment annuities in such a way as to more than cover interest rates. Everyone is happy and it is easy to see that this procedure may sometimes be useful. Martin Saint-Léon has observed that 'it is better to eat on credit than to die of starvation'. In this context, the *monts-de-piété* provide an important public service. But, except in cases of necessity where the very existence of the individual is at stake, consumer credit has serious drawbacks. The extremely fragile increase in demand, which the producer has created, leads him to increase production beyond the average buying power of the consumer during the period of prosperity. When a crisis comes along, not only will the producer no longer be able to count on promised annuities, but the demand will plummet catastrophically from the artificial heights to which it had unwisely been allowed to rise. The consumer, for his part, who is living off his future income and who has become used to an artificially high standard of living, will have to cease to satisfy his need for luxury items, a need which was created in the first place by credit sale. He will

thus have to settle for a more modest standard of living more in line with his real earnings (...). Consumer credit, being non-productive, does not create the income like production credit which enables the borrower in the future to free himself from his obligations. The development of consumer credit was facilitated in the United States by laws which allow mortgaging and right of repossession on movable property (...). The French have always been hostile to this kind of procedure, firstly by virtue of their natural prudence, and secondly because of the law which states that 'with regard to movables, possession amounts to title', thus precluding any seizure by the seller. The French have remained true to the motto in village shops in days of yore: 'he who sells for cash grows rich, he who sells for credit grows poor'. Dufayel was an isolated case for a long time. It is only since the war that a small number of companies have followed his example, particularly Parisian department stores and automobile producers. These operations are financed by a few specialised banks. Consumer credit has developed in France mainly as something shameful, shopkeepers using it as an arm against the competition or not daring to refuse it to a certain reliable clientele'. (pp. 201–204)

Today the text would be considered typically French. But it is also typical of a conservative, individualistic and rural France, a petit-bourgeois and conservative France, which was closed to American practices. A France that still believed in the old formulas, including the hypocrisy of 'ma tante', preferring to stagnate with cash rather than to grow with credit. In spite of this ideologically unfavourable soil, what was to become modern consumer credit took its first shaky steps in the second-half of the nineteenth century.

In 1856, Crépin, the son of a farmer, opened a furniture shop on the Boulevard Barbès in Paris. Prior to that he had had numerous other jobs, particularly peddling jewels on credit. In 1865, he decided to establish a system whereby he sold furniture by subscription. To qualify for the vouchers, the customer had to pay a quarter of the value of the item and the rest in monthly payments. Later, Crépin asked other traders to accept his vouchers. He set them up and took a percentage on the sales, as well as interest and the responsibility for collecting payments.

Dufayel had a similar sort of profile. He came from the Vendée to Paris to make his fortune in trade. He worked for and later became Crépin's associate, bringing a new dimension to the business. On the rue Christiani, near Barbès-Rochechouart, he built the Palais de la Nouveauté, a department store specializing in furniture and household equipment. He could sell more cheaply than others because he bought in bulk and encouraged sales by a system of credit which he improved. He became his own banker, as well as that of the shops who worked with him, among them the Samaritaine, owned by Ernest Cognacq, which owed a lot of its turnover to Dufayel. He recruited door-to-door sales teams offering his vouchers, as well as house-to-house debt collectors. He covered the walls of Paris with advertising posters. His methods made it easier for affiliated traders to increase their sales (Drancourt 1961; Durand 1966).

In 1913, some of his staff left to found La Semeuse. Then when Dufayel opened up a clothing department in competition with La Samaritaine, Cognacq put an end to their dealings and transferred his business to La Semeuse, which proceeded to expand rapidly (Drancourt 1961). Until the early 1960s it continued to do quite well but, faced with new credit techniques, it was unable to revamp its outdated image.

The successes of Dufayel and Cognacq are obviously based on a mass market. They realized that they could serve this market only by offering modest wage earners a means of payment which would enable them to buy goods which, if paid for in cash, would be beyond their means. This idea, which gained acceptance during the first half of the twentieth century, became more general, along with other products, after the Second World War. What is interesting in the subscription system is how it compares with the American hire purchase system. As with the latter, subscriptions were monthly, sometimes even weekly; similarly, sales were often made door-to-door, usually with some confusion between sales and payment; and like the hire purchase system, because they facilitated household equipment, they became a considerable factor of social integration. Like immigrants arriving on the new continent, new arrivals from the French provinces flooded Paris and Cognacq cared for them. The only difference between the two systems was that hire purchase came from the producer, whereas the subscription system bolstered the sales of the distributor. Hence their opposing characteristics, hiring out an item as opposed to facilitating consumption. Later this distinction would result in different nuances in the minds of legislators, not to speak of trust in America and Britain or lack of it in France.

Around 1900, many Parisian and provincial department stores were operating this system of sales by subscription. Their sales staff were to be seen pacing out their catchment area, catalogue in hand. *Dames de France* was the great specialist: a city centre store, it flooded its 'hinterland' with items for wedding trousseaus and vouchers. Households were faithful to one store and the sales staff discreet, thus business passed from one generation to the next. This remained true almost up until the day when the carpark of the hypermarket took over from the door-to-door sales staff. Even small shops were known to group together in order to have sufficient capital to enable them to offer subscription sales.

However, it was not until just after the First World War that car consumer credit made its first timid inroads, in conjunction with the widespread distribution of the automobile. It was also during this period that the first specialized finance companies appeared. The SOVAC (Company for credit sales of automobiles) was founded by Citroën in 1919 in association with the Lazard Bank, who quickly bought it out and went on to expand its activities to include household electrical appliances and real estate. The DIAC (Industrial Distribution of Automobiles through Credit) was founded on Renault's initiative in 1924 and in 1928 Peugeot founded DIN (National Industrial Distribution). The very term 'distribution' in both DIAC and DIN is an indicator of their vocation to support industry. By 1939, a quarter of all vehicles purchased were financed on credit. During the same period, Thomson and some other large producers, along with their bankers, founded the CREG (Gas and Electric Credit) aimed at facilitating household durables.

This first generation of finance companies, particularly the 'captive companies' of the car industry, have remained essentially unchanged from the period between the two world wars, forming since then the essential base of the sector. Obviously, their continued success is dependent on the exclusive contract linking the dealer to the producer, as well as on common practices of transferring the margin between the price of the vehicle and the cost of the loan. If, in the future, the ties become less exclusive as many suspect, or if real prices are more rigorously put into practice even in promotions, then these companies may well suffer.

In the household equipment sector, however, exclusivity of franchise did not survive the 1960s and prices are more transparent, to the buyer's advantage. In this sector, sales continued to increase right through the post-war boom years ('les trente glorieuses') and beyond.

The Cofica (Company for Financing Industry, Commerce and Agriculture) founded on 8 May 1945 (the day the Second World War ended), was followed by many other financing companies, the most important among them being the Sofinco, Cofinoga and Cetelem. The Sofinco (Industrial and Commercial Financing Company) was founded by the Furniture Federation in 1950, on the intiative of what was to become the Suez group and, above all, Cetelem, as one of the group that later became the Compagnie Bancaire. In 1953, the founding fathers of Cetelem followed the example of the Americans. As a result of a study trip sponsored by the Federation of Electrical Industries (which was one of the capital holders of the company), they opted for a radical innovation, abolishing bills of exchange, introducing mass management, direct involvement in commerce and establishing a policy of development of customer loyalty. Cetelem's confirmed success stems from these initial innovations and subsequent transformations. Today, due to its constant modification of its products in line with social change, Cetelem is at the forefront of European finance companies. Its very name symbolizes success. Originally, Cetelem was a contracted form of 'crédit à l'électroménager' (credit for electrical appliances), today it sees itself as providing 'crédit à l'équipment des ménages' (credit for household equipment).

This change corresponds exactly to transformations in French society. Wage earners have become the greater part of the population; they receive a monthly wage packet which is not substantial enough to allow them to make major purchases for cash. New products are constantly appearing on the market, stimulating demand, and thereby improving the standard of living of the majority of people. Also, the life expectancy of these new goods rarely exceeds ten years, thus households no longer inherit such items from the preceding generation, but buy them for themselves. In 1960 some considered this to be a mere nuance, in fact it is a complete change. The demographic boom, public support for home-buying, full employment and unprecedented prosperity fuelled the demand for consumer durables, decreasing their relative cost. The pace of life changed; time became more precious and women's expectations changed considerably.

In France, as elsewhere, following the example of the United States, modern consumer credit formed the link between more extensive need and greater diversity of product. It expanded because a large part of production and exchange now revolves around the satisfaction of needs for durable good. Consumer credit took over the role, once played by the dowry without being reserved for the lucky few, of democratizing the well-being of the population.

Naturally, it could only develop under favourable conditions and where society had attained a certain level of wealth. It goes hand in hand with prosperity and contributes to its maintainence when societies which aim at increasing the well-being of the greatest number of people, make the necessary productive efforts to achieve that goal. In this respect, the greater the number of households above the level of strict subsistence, the greater the number of buyers on credit. In 1966, Henri Durand highlighted the situation: 'usury is the contemporary of misery and penury; consumer credit is the contemporary of industrial abundance'. Its development in France after the 1950s took place in a favourable economic framework of rapid growth, contributing to the improvement of post-war standard of living as indicated by the increase in the number of cars and a greater comfort within the home.

However, many of the old prejudices still had firm roots and a new hostility appeared in some political circles. In the early 1960s, many people still disapproved of credit purchases, considering that people who borrowed could only be either poverty-stricken or spendthrift. One part of public opinion saw credit as a sort of American disease, a means of hoodwinking the gullible, a game in which the banks were the only winners. For moralists, credit was still something to be ashamed of. It drove people to live beyond their means, spending on superfluous and ostentatious commodities. It was more 'virtuous' to save 'before' rather than to pay back 'after'. This was the period when Elsa Triolet's novel '*Roses à Credit*' was such a great success, the heroine dying because she had too well fulfiled her dreams of equiping her house (1959). Much in the same spirit, Jacques Tati, the comic actor, poked fun in 'Mon Oncle' (surely with no conscious pun on the pawnbroker, 'my uncle', intended) at the inhuman modernism of a society geared to household robots.

Lastly, for some of the Left – with Baudrillart as its main representative and over-eloquent apologist – credit was a sort of tax levied on poverty by monopolistic financial institutions. According to this analysis, wage earners need recourse to credit because they are poorly paid. Thus they compensate for the income, which they have been deprived of, by relying on future income. This renders them powerless: they no longer dare make claims or go on strike because they live in fear of losing their jobs. Continuing on a Leninist dialectic, Baudrillart claims that credit corrupts the upper layer of the proletariat by insidiously imbuing it with the rules of the capitalist system. By having to ensure the monthly payments on their washing machines, they are familiarized with the ground rules of budget management, and thus become inculcated with the spirit of the market economy. What better illustration of the social integration accomplished by consumer credit than Baudrillart's response to the current practice all around him!

In spite of these attitudes, private loans have continued to increase over the last 30 years, though they still lag behind the United States and Great Britain. Economic conditions had been unfavourable to a ban on credit, necessity and an inherent distrust have been reconciled through constraining legislation. In this respect, France has finally outstripped other industrialized countries and has become a reference for European regulations.

Access to the profession is regulated by the law passed on 14 June 1941. Only financial institutions can offer consumer credit. In 1954, the Conseil National du Crédit (National Council for Credit) fixed the duration and maximum value of hire purchase credit. This law, which was supposed to protect the consumer and help regulate the distribution of credit, was repealed in 1979. The law of 28 December 1966, relative to usury, to money loans, certain forms of door-to-door canvassing and advertising, determined the interest rate ceiling at precisely double the rate of first category bonds. Rates in excess of this were considered usurious. The law also regulated canvassing and advertising relative to consumer loans not linked to goods or services.

The criterion governing the maximum interest rates was redefined by the Neiertz Law on 31 December 1989. This law states that 'a loan is usurious when its global effective rate, at the time when the loan is agreed, exceeds by more than one third the average effective rate practised over the previous quarter by credit institutions for loans of the same type involving similar risks.' Because it follows market movements and relates directly to observable reality, defining different kinds of loans, this law represents a distinct improvement. Obviously, a usurious rate on a property loan over 20 years does not bear comparison with a six month loan to buy a new television.

The Scrivener law (10 January 1978) 'relative to information and protection of consumers in the domain of certain credit operations' and the Neiertz laws (23 June 1989 and 31 December 1989) constitute the essential body of legislation relative to consumer credit today. These laws establish the general conditions of credit operations. In particular, they stipulate conditions relative to advertising of the cost of credit, terms of contracts, a cooling off period, the relationship between the loan agreement and the sale agreement with the seller, the execution of the contract of credit (early repayment partial or total, abolition of penalties for early settlement or repayment, penalties for late payment, default of the borrower, the role of the courts, and so on ...), as well as the means of renewing permanent accounts which some prefer to call 'renewable credit', in order to avoid the negative connotations associated with permanent repayments. Whereas the people who coined the expression in 1965 did so because they saw only the positive connotations of permanent credit! The Belgians, being more technically minded, prefer 'crédit rotatif', a direct translation of the American 'revolving credit'. The Neiertz Law, dating from 31 December 1989, also deals with 'the prevention and regulation of difficulties related to overindebtedness of private individuals and families' (see Chapter 10).

The Computer Technology and Freedom Act, passed on 6 January 1978, deals, among other matters, with credit files which can have a direct effect on the granting and recovering of consumer credit. Together with the above-mentioned laws, this act ensures that the French consumer is one of the best protected in the world. This is not to say that everything is for the best in the best of all possible worlds. In spite of the important progress made in defining usury, in order to approach healthy market practices the sector is over-regulated and the public authorities intend to go even further, particularly in relation to overindebtedness. Such an action would inevitably have the perverse effect of excluding customers from the market, thus going against the very idea of helping people to become more socially integrated. We only have to think of the illusory good intentions of the *monts-de-piétés*.

The most positive aspect of the new legislation seems to be the long-term awareness it has given rise to. In spite of the archaic and often mediocre media coverage and the fact that most credit professionals are too sensitive to detail and tend to look at the short-term, the public image of consumer credit has been modernized and acclimatized. Modernized, by the simple fact that consumer credit is in the public domain: the previously sacrosanct rule of the professionals 'to live happily you must live in secret' – an inheritance from the days of the money lenders – has today been abandoned by all the credit establishments which are no longer ashamed to advertise. Acclimatized, insofar as the number of households having access to credit for consumer durables has increased enormously. Fifty years after the Russell Sage Foundation in the United States and 20 years after the Crowther Report in Great Britain, France now seems to have finally shaken off the guilt so long associated with credit.

THE REST OF EUROPE

In 1985, Cetelem exported its know-how to Italy in the form of consumer credit divested of the old constraints. In the same year, the President of the Italian Association of Financial Establishments delivered a speech to his European colleagues in defence of the bill of exchange, the famous *cambiale*, presented as the ideal type of guarantee for consumer loans. It would be an insult to the companies which then led the Italian market, Compass or Banca d'America e d'Italia, to associate them with this rearguard battle and, obviously, the state of the Italian market cannot be summed up in this 1985 event, but it cannot be ignored either.

Mediterranean Europe on the whole was just a few years behind France in the evolution of consumer credit, and similar to France in its psychological reserves inherited from the Counter-Reformation, as in its regulatory practices born from the adaptation of the Napoleonic Code. There was the same modernization of the *monts-de-piétés* in the nineteenth century, with the same failure as in France, due to the conflict between the hypocritical social vocation and the necessity of replenishing funds. By the end of the century, the illusion had been shattered all over: *monts-de-piétés* would never be the instrument of modernization.

As in France distributors experimented with credit systems. In 1929, Fiat created its own finance company on the Anglo-Saxon model, though trying to rationalize the chain of bills. However, the climate of disapproval was so widespread that nothing succeeded until the 1950s. The next two decades saw the founding of the first independent finance companies, like Compass in Italy (part of the Mediobanca group), or Finamersa in Spain (part of the Hispano-Americano group), and the first credit cards issued by department stores (Galerias Preciados in Spain). Demand increased with economic growth and the social advances of the 1960s and the 1970s. It was favoured by the rising of the number of people having a bank account, particularly in Spain. This development was also enhanced by the modernization of the financial sector, the best examples being the Spanish savings banks, for the banking activities, and Findomestic, the Italian subsidiary of Cetelem, for consumer credit. In Spain, as in Italy, the demand corresponds clearly to the sociological development of families. When, in 1960, the public group, Mediobanca, founded Compass on the initiative of the Federation of Manufacturers of household appliances, the principal argument delivered to the political world was that of 'freeing the housewife': to mass production, assisted by credit without bills, corresponds a new kind of family, often with two incomes, and a rising standard of living, due to the acquisition of consumer durables. The *transicion*, changed Spain from a tradition-bound, often closed society still functioning as it did in the last century, to a twentieth-century Western society, and owes much to the availability of consumer credit. If credit is not permitted within a legal framework then it finds all sorts of other means of operating, though with the disadvantage of having no regulatory structures. With its post-dated cheques and rental companies which blithely step around official bans on hire purchase sales, Portugal gives the best example of a legislature who was unable to face up to changes in society.

The countries of Northern Europe offer a more fruitful history of consumer credit. Greatly influenced by the different varieties of Protestantism, they all, to a greater or lesser degree, practised loans on interest from early times, thus tempering the biblical disapproval. However, the model of bourgeois society being developed during the classical era, the archetype of which is to be found in the black-costumed portraits of the Dutch school, quickly rejected consumerism as being harmful and ostentatious. It was this mentality of the bulwark which favoured the merchant economy, approving of saving and disapproving of personal expenditure. This bourgeoisie remained ignorant of what was going on under the cloak of respectability, in the pawnshops of the suburbs and villages, unlike the British who were aware of these transactions, tolerated them and regulated them.

The German response aimed at greater virtue. The first savings banks appeared at the end of the eighteenth century and quickly became a model for all of Europe, beginning with the Scandinavian countries, then France, followed by the Mediterranean countries. The idea was to create a 'poor man's bank', thereby avoiding recourse to the money lender. The savings banks were philanthropic institutions run by volunteers from the upper and middle classes. Their aim was not to lend money at a low rate, like the *monts-de-piétés*, but to do away with poverty entirely by showing the advantages of thrift. The basic idea was to provide ordinary people with a convenient and safe place where they could put their savings when things were going well. They would then be able to face difficult times without falling into the hands of the usurers, and without becoming paupers. They encouraged servants, workers, artisans, sailors and farmers to start a saving fund which would be a sort of saving for retirement as well as an insurance in case of accident.

The same can be said, more or less, for the great German mutualist movement, which also became a model for the whole world. Born in the mid-nineteenth century, it had two basic forms: the agricultural mutual, the *Raiffeisen*, founded in 1850 by Friedrich Wilhelm Raiffeisen, mayor of a Rhineland village, and the urban mutual, the *Schulze-Delitzsch*, founded in 1860 by the Prussian deputy, Hermann Schulze, mayor of Delitzsch. The austere Raiffesein wanted to improve the situation of the agricultural world which had greatly suffered as a result of industrialization. To this end he founded buying co-operatives, which granted loans and accepted savings deposits. The co-operatives born from Schulze's inspiration, the *Volksbanken*, were aimed more at artisans and traders. They combined mutuality of credit and security while defending the ideal of individual liberalism. Both of these institutions aimed at making credit more available in order to help people overcome downturns in business cycles and to increase economic expansion. They had no real role in consumer credit. The important thing, as in the case of the savings banks, was their great popular success and their early spread to the lower classes of society. A large part of the German and Scandinavian model rests on this mutual form of banking.

At the end of the nineteenth century helped along by urbanization, the demand for consumer credit began to grow as families moved and had to equip themselves. As in France, some shops offered credit slips through their network of brokers. Seizing their opportunity, the mutual societies joined in the game, developing what was to become one of the characteristics of German banking, the simultaneous management of credit and savings for households.

If the present day level of personal debt in Germany is the highest in Europe (19 per cent of available income), this is because the level of household equipment and the standard of living are among the highest and also thanks to the mastery of family budgeting which the *Sparkassen* and the banks have achieved. They have integrated savings and credit into the global management of accounts, based mainly on the mortgage related to house acquisition. Acting as ongoing partners of households, they have also discovered the beautiful marketing prose so admired by the Americans of the 1960s.

The role of the mortgage in consumer credit, which is common to both the German and the Anglo-Saxon markets, may well constitute one of the touchstones of their differences. In Britain and the United States, it appears in the form of a second mortgage or a home equity loan, as a consolidation of a more expensive debt giving fiscal advantage; the household reduces its debt-burden by increasing the term, using a mortgage as collateral of the loan. Moreover, the interest is tax-deductible. In Germany, savings banks and banks 'fill in', with consumer credit, the part of the mortgage that has been freed by repayments on the property loan. By this means the capital released may be used for household durables or reducing overall indebtedness. Must we conclude from this that the German method is inherently better? If we wish to show that a high level of debt is not a danger to the society which engendered it, but is on the contrary, fecund for its standard of living and its social consensus, the answer is certainly yes. If, on the other hand, we are looking for a recipe which we can copy elsewhere ... then caution should prevail. The conditions surrounding the growth of a consumer credit market are, above all, historical, arising from a web of history and regulations, which is the mirror of social evolution. This is particularly true of the other characteristic of German-influenced markets, the correlation between powerful networks of credit intermediaries and so-called positive debt files.

It was between the wars, exactly as in France or Great Britain, that the first companies specializing in hire purchase sales appeared. They were usually linked to a manufacturer and became a factor in the promotion of his products. The most famous is the first German bank specializing in consumer credit, the KKB (Kunden Krediet Bank, which became the Citibank after its incorporation into the American group). Originally, in 1920, it was set up to finance bicycle production in East Prussia. It has come a long way from the bicycles of Köningsberg to one of the finest balance sheets of any retail bank, skilfully balancing credits and deposits.

The KKB is a unique example. In the 1950s, the number of specialized finance companies increased but they never succeeded, as elsewhere, in acquiring a dominant position on the market. They remained small and marginal, or like the linked finance houses of the car builders, completely devoted to managing the promotion of the products of the core companies. This is due, to a great degree, to the success of savings banks.

This framework does not take into account the new clientele not yet integrated into the banking system. Germans from abroad; refugees from the downfall of the Third Reich; immigrants to the economic miracle, particularly Turks; and finally the inhabitants of the *fünf neue Länder* since the reunification. This clientele is less well-informed, less settled, therefore more 'dangerous' in terms of banking risks, but the desire to become integrated, therefore to equip themselves exists. The solution is the credit broker, an independent intermediary agent, whose main job is to manage and recover credit. The intermediaries compensate for the lack of network of the specialist financial institutions and for the lack of '*savoir-faire*' of this risky clientele.

As a counter balance to these peripheral market developments – which are nevertheless natural and necessary in terms of society – these countries have designed a sort of fortification against abuse of the system. This is the obligatory debt file, managed by bodies related to professional associations. Called the *Schufa* in Germany, the ZEK in Switzerland and the BKR in Holland, these files are 'positive' in the sense that they record the totality of credits distributed to an individual and follow their progress. Unlike the 'negative' files of countries like France which only contain 'bad folders', that is those debts which have reached a stage of late payment that makes recovery difficult (Huls, 1992).

In fact, the positive files are not a very useful check for the majority of the customers who take credits secured with a mortgage from savings banks, or are regular customers of a bank, this connection being by itself the best measure of risk. However, they tend to be 'too useful' for other clientele because they pervert the role of credit intermediaries who find the best possible information enabling them to consolidate and even over-consolidate debts. This is what the Swiss professionals, with their fine sense for an image, call the 'hot potato': customers are solicited by competitor firms, to repay old credits with new increased advances. This sort of race lasts until the client/horse cannot find any more brokers to bet on him! In order not to burn their hands with the 'hot potato', specialist establishments protect themselves as well as they can, deliberately forgetting to record the delays of their bad customers, hoping by this means to pass them on, or alternatively by indicating difficulties where none exist for their best customers in order to keep away the competition. As a paraphrase of the old principle, a bad client drives away the good. And too much protection protects nothing at all.

THE EUROPEAN DIMENSION

For a long time, consumer credit remained a purely domestic activity, linked to national manufacturers of durable goods, and incorporated into a more or less modern legal and technical system of repayment. The fact that Great Britain passed its first laws concerning loans to individuals as early as the nineteenth century, whereas Italy only did so in 1992 on a Directive from Brussels, concerning advertising of credit operations, gives an idea of the time lag between these two countries. Britain being traditionally the most advanced country in matters of credit, and Italy the most deeply marked by the old bans. And although there is little difference today between their products and techniques, it is still worth remembering that at the very moment when all of Britain was debating the Crowther Report, the Fanfani government established a draft bill regulating credit practices. What is interesting about this project is that it was in direct response to a much publicized suicide as the result of abusive recovery on the part of a local loan shop. A law was called for immediately. The text of the law was inspired almost word for word by an earlier law concerning prostitution! However, the law was never enacted.

Car manufacturers were the first to wish to expand beyond their national territories. The Treaty of Rome opened the frontiers for them and, naturally, to help their sales, they hoped to find in these new markets similar credit practices to those they already knew. The movement began in the early 1960s with European manufacturers or their importers making local agreements (for example Ford with Cofica in France and Compass in Italy). Then, in the 1970s, they developed their own financial structures, 'captive' companies which they soon federated into large parabanking groups. The most highly advanced manufacturers in this domain are Renault, Fiat and Volkswagen.

The second impetus to federate European markets came, funnily enough, from across the Atlantic. With new products such as the credit card, and a marketing system based entirely on accessibility (the money shop as opposed to the traditional bank), consumer credit became the spearhead of American banking in Europe. From the middle of the 1960s, it was already operative in Great Britain, in Germany (with the extension of services to the American troops) and in Italy where the Bank of America, founded at the beginning of the century by the famous Giannini, reopened its subsidiary, the Banca d'America e d'Italia. The most enterprising of all, and the one whose effort proved to be most long-lasting, is still Citicorp. Their policy of acquiring local companies enabled them to be present today in all Western European countries, centring around their German flagship, the former KKB.

The most recent initiatives came from the European companies themselves. The movement was begun by Barclays in Italy and grew to its present proportions when Cetelem established Findomestic in 1984. Thanks to its avant-garde techniques this company revolutionized the Italian market and now occupies the premier position. Today, the movement still continues with a few French and British companies; Cetelem and Lombard Group (National Westminster) deserve particular attention. All these initiatives indicate an eventual unification of the European market, both in terms of its actors, and its products and services. This evolution has concerned credit professionals ever since the signing of the Treaty of Rome.

In 1959, on the initiative of the German Walter Kaminski (the founder of the KKB), two associations saw the opportunity: Eurofinas and the Amstel Club. The Amstel Club had a company in each country (UDT in Great Britain, Sovac in France, IDM in the Netherlands, Compass in Italy and KKB in Germany). Its principal aims were the exchange of local and the know-how follow-up of major credit subscribers, particularly in the car sector. However, because of non-competition between national markets, it disappeared just after Citicorp bought out KKB. Eurofinas grouped together national associations into a European federation whose role is to discuss the legal and political orientations of the profession. Obviously, its role expands as Brussels influence increases. In this respect, the decision taken at the Milan summit of June 1985, to create the single European market, with all of its consequences in the services sector, is of major importance. Consumer credit, being sensitive to public opinion, thus becomes one of the major subjects of European regulation.

Consumer protection and advertising of conditions of credit form the basis of the first Directive on the subject, issued on 22 December 1986, followed by another Directive on 22 February 1990, relating to the calculation of annual global effective rates. The prudential aspects, in the broadest sense of banking, and its free operation in the whole of the unified market, are the subject of the second Directive on banking coordination, issued on 15 December 1989. Elsewhere, consumer credit while not at the heart of the matter is indirectly affected by other considerations (for example protection of personal data). With regard to consumer protection, the wind blows from the North, that is from countries where private loans have greatest economic impact and social consequences. The strength and age of consumer associations there offer some sort of balance to the high level of household debt. Brussels increased centralized guidance of national legislation has sometimes led to problems arising from the imposition of regulations. Regulations which were conceived and adapted for a specific social, economic and legal context are sometimes imposed into another, very different, context. Among the dangers of the current European legislation, is the eternal temptation to try to regulate everything in detail, particularly if the principle of subsidiarity is not respected. And, among the stakes in the process, is the hope, on the part of market actors, for an increased recognition of the positive role of consumer credit.

REFERENCES

Books

ARNAUD, L. 'Le marché bancaire des particuliers', *Banque*, July and September 1983.

ASHTON, T.S. *Economic History of England in the 18th century*, London: Methuen & Co Ltd, 1964.

BALZAC, H. *Les Petits Bourgeoise* (*The middle classes*), London: J.M. Dent and Co.; New York: The Macmillan company, 1898.

BALZAC, H. *Gobseck* (*and other stories*) , Boston: Roberts Brothers, 1896.

Banque de France, *Bulletin* May 1992.

BAUDIN, L. *Le crédit*, Paris: Aubier, 1934.

BAUDRILLARD, J. *La société de consommation*, Paris: Denoël, 1970.

BIGO, R. *Les banques françaises au cours du XIXᵉ siècle*, Paris: Sirey, 1947.

BOLEAT, M. *National Housing Finance Systems, a Comparative Study*, London: Croom Helm, 1985.

CAMERON, R. and V.I. BOUYKIN, *International banking 1870–1914*, Osford: Oxford University Press, 1991.

CHEMINEAU, L. (ed.), *L'argent invisible, l'ère des flux électroniques*, Paris: Autrement, 1987.

CLAVEAU, M.O. Ministère de l'Intérieur, *Situation administrative et financière des* monts-de-piété, Rapport et documents présentés à M. de Marcère au nom du Conseil des inspecteurs généraux des établissements de bienfaisance par M.O. Claveau, Paris: Imprimerie Nationale, 1876.

Commission Bancaire, *Le financement de la consommation. Atouts et enjeux d'une spécialisation*, Rapport annuel, Paris, 1991.

Conseil National du Crédit, *Crédit à la consommation et à l'équipement des ménages*, May 1987.

CROWTHER, Lord, (Chairman), *Consumer credit*, report of the Committee, London: Her Majesty's Stationery Office, March 1971.

DIAMOND, A.L. *Commercial and Consumer credit: an introduction*, London: Butterworths, 1982.

DRANCOURT, M. *Une force inconnue: le crédit*, Paris: Hachette, 1961.

DRURY, A.C. *Finance Houses: Their Development and Role in the Modern Society*, London: Waterlow Publishers, 1982.

Dupont Paul *La question du prêt sur gages: recueil d'articles*, Paris, 1896.

DURAND, H. *L'abondance à crédit*, Paris: Le Seuil, 1966.

Economie Géographie, 'Le crédit à la consommation', No. 223, March 1985.

FERRONNIERE, J. and CHILLAZ, E. de *Les opérations de banque*, Paris: Dalloz, 1980.

FORD, J. *The Indebted Society: Credit and Default in the 1980s*, London: Routledge, 1988.

GOMEZ, F. 'La vente à crédit aux particuliers', *Banque*, June, July, September 1985.

HEYMANN, G. *La vente à crédit dans le commerce de détail: ses aspects juridiques*, Paris: Centre d'Etudes du Commerce.

HEYMANN, P. and P. CLEMENT (eds), *De la 4CV à la vidéo, 1953–1983 ces trente années qui ont changé notre vie*, Paris: Communica, 1983.

HILL SMITH, A.G.L. *Consumer credit, Law and Practice*, London: Sweet & Maxwell, 1985.

HULS, N. (ed.), *Overindebtedness of Consumers in the EC Member States: Facts and Search for solutions*, Leyden, Netherlands: Leyden Institute for Law and Public Policy, September 1982.

MAYO, O.G. *Consumer Credit Control*, London: Gower Press, 1971.

MEADE, J.E. *Consumer's Credits and Unemployment*, London: Oxford University Press, 1938.

MINKES, A.L. 'The Decline of Pawnbroking', *Economica*, February 1953.

MOLONY, J. Committee on Consumer Protection, Her Majesty's Stationery Office, London: 1962.

MOSCGETTO, B. and PLAGNOL, A. *Le crédit à la consommation*, Paris: 'Que sais-je?', P.U.F., 1973.

PECHA, J. and P. SICSIC, 'Développement du crédit à la consommation et économie réelle', *Revue d'économie financière*, Nos 5 and 6.

PETIT-DUTAILLIS, G. 'De Richard Lenoir à Stavisky', *Banque* No. 418, June 1982.

MESLIER, P. *Tout à crédit*, Paris: Le livre de Poche, 1967.

PINET, H. *Ventes à crédit*, Paris: Sirey, 1961.

RADCLIFFE, *Report of the Committee on the Working of the Monetary System*, Her Majesty's Stationery Office, London, 1959.

RAIGA, E. *Le mont-de-piété de Paris*, Paris: Sirey, 1912.

Revue d'Economie Financière, No. 18.

TEBBUTT, M. *Making Ends Meet, Pawnbroking and Working Class Credit*, London: Methuen, 1984.

TRIOLET, E. *Roses à Crédit*, Paris: Gallimard, 1972.

ULLMO, Y. 'Endettement et surendettement des ménages', *Les Notes Bleues*, No. 581, 1992.

VERHOOSEL, G. *Le financement des ventes à tempérament*, Paris: Institut international d'études bancaires, 1955.

10 Are We Overindebted?

In the course of the twentieth century consumer credit has been progressively emancipated from the ideologies and beliefs which, over the millennia, placed a stigma on borrowing at interest. Attitudes have changed and credit has become part of everyday life. It may be seen to foster growth and promote social integration, both of which, in return, give credit ability to the sector. However, this relatively privileged status is now at risk, as a new cloud began to cast its shadow over credit at the end of the 1980s: overindebtedness. The effects of overindebtedness may be twofold: economic and social. Some perceive consumer credit as having pernicious consequences within the economy, and on private individuals, who are its main victims.

THE ECONOMIC FACTS

The anxiety of the authorities at the over-indebtedness of the French does not stem solely from the fear of seeing further layers of society for example young adults and the economically fragile succumb to the bitter-sweet pill of credit. In fact, the increasing power of credit is dangerous because, from numerous points of view, it threatens the fundamental equilibriums of the nation ... The increase in credit threatens the stability of the franc, no less .... The truth is, however, that some specialists do not believe that private borrowing can have such an effect on the franc, since it amounts to only 5.9% of the overall credit of the economy. Nevertheless, others claim that the franc is experiencing inflationary credit, having had difficulty overcoming the inflation in costs. But, in a domain where confidence is a primordial factor, the government, whatever its colour, cannot afford to allow any doubt to persist. (CNAF, 1989, p. 2)

Credit poses a threat to the franc, not just because it swells the monetary aggregates, but also because it increases the deficit of foreign trade. As long as credit was related essentially to housing and accommodation, it provided work for the building industry, which is 80% French. But VCRs, hi fis, household appliances and furniture stand every chance of being Japanese, German or Italian, therefore imported. This is inopportune, to say the least, particularly at a time when the government is using every means in its power to restore the balance of trade.

(CNAF, 1989, p. 3)

This purely economic justification for anti-credit attitudes may seem naïve and based on archetypes dating from the last century. It is nevertheless a view shared by a large number of important people who, because of their poor economic awareness, are all the more willing to admit the need for intervention on a social level.

Recent years in France have by no means confirmed the inflationary risk associated with an increase in consumer credit. On the contrary, years showing a strong growth in consumer credit correspond with those showing a downward inflationary trend, as illustrated in Table 10.1. The falling inflation rates were mainly the result of extremely moderate growth in private sector real wages and the huge rise of social charges in wages. Until recently this last factor helped finance the increase of public expenditure and therefore avoid an increase in the budgetary deficit. Without the efforts made by wage earners in terms of wages and taxes, inflation would never have been reduced no matter how tight consumer credit policy had been. Of course, if costs go up sharply or the productivity capacity are fully utilized then, the inflationary pressures will be fuelled by easy credit. However, the mere impact of consumer credit will be marginal and never the leading factor.

The objection that consumer credit indirectly threatens the national currency, through increasing imports, is also unfounded. The foreign exchange rate is mainly a function of the flow of capital. This, in turn, is influenced by interest rates and expectations, that is confidence in the future exchange rate. Overheating of the economy may diminish this confidence, and in that respect, consumer credit may have some small influence. As for the balance of goods and services, this depends, in part,

Table 10.1   Year on Year Inflationary Change 1981–91 (%)

	1981	1982	1983	1984	1985	1986	1987	1988	1989	1990	1991
Consumer credit	14.0	25.7	10.1	15.8	21.5	39.3	32.8	23.8	22.4	5.6	−2.4
Price index for private consumption	13.9	11.5	9.7	7.7	5.8	2.7	3.2	2.7	3.5	3.0	3.1

Sources: Banque de France and OECD, 1993.

on the competitiveness of the economy in question, that is on variations in production costs, and the degree to which production corresponds to demand. The problem is not to curb consumer credit, but to increase competitiveness. A high rate of consumer credit is perfectly compatible with a balance of payments surplus. Japan, with a debt rate of more than 20 per cent of available family incomes, is a case in point. Ranking higher than both the United States and Germany, it consistently shows a positive balance of trade. The same held true for Germany before reunification.

It has also been said that consumer credit is at least partly responsible for the recent recession. According to this theory, when people are heavily in debt and monetary policy becomes tighter, they reduce their consumer expenditure. This causes a reduction in the demand and thus a drop in economic activity. Moreover, the amount of non-performing loans increase and this affects the solvency of the financial system. This was the subject of serious study in the United States after the great depression of the 1930s. These studies concluded that consumer credit had only a negligible role to play in bringing about the crisis. The depression itself, however, had a very damaging effect on the personal loans market. What about the recession that hurt some industrialized countries at the beginning of the 1990s? It started in the United States and Great Britain, and later affected France where it worsened imbalances created by structural factors.

THE AMERICAN RECESSION

In 1983, the United States entered a period of relatively high growth (about 3 per cent per annum on average). This trend lasted until the end of the decade and was only slightly inflationary. However, two major imbalances appeared and grew: the current account deficits and its matching accommodation of a huge foreign debt and also budgetary deficits on a scale not seen since 1945.

The economic recovery of the first half of the 1980s was helped by the Economic Recovery Tax Act (ERTA) in 1981. This law rolled back marginal personal tax rates, offered new tax breaks to savers and investors, and in doing so, encouraged expansion in the building sector. ERTA extended the investment tax credit to more short-term assets, allowed firms to use the accelerated cost recovery system for depreciating capital and allowed 'safe harbor leasing' so that companies could take advantage of tax credit even if they had no taxable income. The act also made major changes in the treatment of rented housing: it reduced the taxation of capital gains, accelerated depreciation write-offs and provided incentives for the expanded use of real state tax shelters that allow individuals to shelter earned income with 'passive' real state losses. These changes substantially increased investor return on rented housing (Akhtar and Harris, 1992; Gabriel, 1987).

In the course of this cycle, financial deregulation continued and competition intensified, thus leading to increased weakening of financial establishments (Gelpi, 1987). It was easy for builders and buyers of property to find loans to finance their operations. The new financial environment also facilitated greater corporate debt, and the financing of the wave of mergers and acquisitions which took place during the period. Insofar as interest is tax-deductible and dividends taxable, companies opted for credit instead of equity financing.

Toward the end of the 1980s, numerous factors were introduced which, while aiming to correct these excesses, simultaneously reduced economic growth. In 1986, the Tax Reform Act did away with several of the fiscal advantages made available to the construction sector by the ERTA law. This immediately put an end to speculatory fever. Then, some regions, particularly in the North East and South West, found that the supply of buildings surpassed the demand. Prices plummeted, the value of assets dropped, and a large number of debtors became insolvent. The first symptoms of this crisis coincided with the October 1987 stock market crash, which put a halt to the financial speculation developing around the mergers and acquisitions.

The monetary authorities were aware of the growing fragility of financial establishments and, confronted with the crisis of savings banks, they imposed more strict prudential and control regulations. They fixed high ratios for equity capital and demanded that requests for loans from already heavily indebted companies be examined with greater rigour. Banks operating with a low level of equity capital, and those with a considerable number of doubtful assets, could no longer find the capital necessary to maintain the growth of their activities. The result was a decline in credit that helped to precipitate the downturn of the business cycle.

Alongside these recessionary factors we must also rank the reduced military budget and Japanese competition, as well as, from the summer of 1990, a crisis in consumer confidence, brought about by the fear of a war with Iraq. The recession coincided with the Gulf War. It was not very severe and was short-lived, but was followed by a period of slow growth. The economy started to pick up in 1993, after nearly three years of particularly low real interest rates. This enabled the financial institutions to reconstitute their margins and thus to be able to relaunch loans to the economy.

All these factors are very far removed from consumer credit, which played no role in the reversal of the cycle. Furthermore, in direct contradiction with the popularly held image, the ratio of debt service payment to income remained relatively low in the years preceding the turning point. True, the ratio of consumer credit outstanding debt to disposable income of families rose from 15 per cent in 1981 to 21 per cent in 1988 while that of mortgage credit rose from 47 per cent to 50 per cent. However, this growth was concentrated among high-income families, with financial assets portfolios (Kennickell and Schack-Marquez, 1991). Moreover, debt servicing which determines liquidity constraints and influences consumer's default rates, increased, though less rapidly (Paquette, 1986). This was particularly true of consumer instalment credit. Although interest rates were higher than in previous cycles until 1986, because of tax deductibility, it was the repayment of the principal which burdened household budgets. However, longer maturities lightened these repayments while they increased credit outstanding.

Until 1986, extensions of most types of consumer loans relative to income did not exceed the levels reached in the previous cycle. The average maturity of new car loans issued by finance companies increased from 38 months in 1975, to 51 months in 1986, and from 29 to 43 months for used car loans. Interest amounted to 31 per cent of debt service payments in 1975, and to 45 per cent in 1986. This was because of the increased rates and extended maturities, being tax deductible, this made the service payments all the cheaper. In 1986, the tax deductibility of interest payments on consumer credit was abolished. The impact of this measure, however, was reduced due to the lower growth of new consumer loans to the benefit of home equity loans – revolving credit backed by a mortgage guarantee – the interest on which still remained tax deductible.

Surveys conducted in 1990 and 1991 by the University of Michigan at the request of the Federal Reserve show that 85 per cent of households had one or several loans. Of these 86 per cent of them met their scheduled debt payment obligations; about 14 per cent of those surveyed reported falling behind on at least one of their payments, but only 3 per cent were having serious problems. Half of these cases were considered becoming overextended, the other half to have suffered a life accident (divorce, health problems, less work or loss of work). The study nevertheless indicates that a substantial proportion of households facing debt payment problems do not really have serious problems, just day-to-day problems which can be solved in a short period of time. And let us not forget that this survey was conducted during a recessionary period (Canner and Luckett, 1991).

Personal Bankruptcies and Credit Bureaux

These observations are corroborated by the cycle of payments past due observed throughout the 1980s, which hardly differed from those observed previously. Nonetheless, the number of personal bankruptcies shows an exceptional growth: 311 000 in 1982, a recession year, and 617 000 in 1989, after seven years of uninterrupted growth! But bankruptcies pose an indirect threat to the whole system by punishing borrowers who respect their commitments, since they have to pay higher interest rates and are subjected to more rigorous criteria of selection. Thus, recent decreases in interest rates were not fully implemented for certain types of credit, for example revolving credit, because of the increased bankruptcy rate and the additional risk it generates.

This increase in the number of personal bankruptcies could be interpreted as indicating an unprecedented level of indebtedness in American households. This is the traditional analysis of European observers, who are often hostile to credit. Unfortunately the analysis is inaccurate because it is too superficial. Consumer credit today is one of the most disputed aspects of trade, being presented either as virtuous therapy or as a social and economic heresy.

Studies conducted by the Federal Reserve System suggest an explanation which is all the more useful in that it is exemplary. The steep increase in the number of bankruptcies, during the expansion phase which began in 1983, corresponds to a change in attitudes occasioned by law reforms. Federal law, which had remained unchanged since 1898, was completely overhauled in 1978, and further modified in 1984 (Luckett, C.A., September 1988). The Bankruptcy Act, which came into effect on 1 October 1979, offered greater protection to individuals seeking to file a bankruptcy petition. The reforms aimed at creating favourable conditions which would allow the bankrupt to 'make a new start', the famous 'fresh start' of the consumer associations. The legislators considered that the individual could merit a non-punitive bankruptcy for two reasons: either because of one or several life changes (illness, unemployment, divorce, partial or total loss of income and so on), or because he had been pushed into overindebtedness by financial institutions; in either case, deserving of a chance of making a new start in life.

Thus, the 1978 law enabled a private individual in a critical financial situation to file a bankruptcy petition in accordance with the standards laid down in chapter 7, or those in chapter 13 of the Act. In cases of 'pure' bankruptcy, as described in chapter 7, the petition is generally granted, except if it can be proved that the candidate has behaved dishonestly or fraudulently. The bankrupt is exempted from all his past debts, with a few exceptions (in particular he remains liable for any dues he may have accumulated in income or customs taxes). From the moment he files his petition, no action can be taken against him in order to collect unpaid debts. Once bankruptcy has been declared, his non-exempt goods are liquidated and the sum used to pay creditors (Luckett, 1988).

One of the purposes of the 1978 reform was to increase the number and the value of goods exempt from seizure, in order to enable the bankrupt to make a fresh start from a good base. There is a federal list of exempt goods and another list drawn up by each State. The bankrupt is free to choose either the federal system or that of his own State, except if State laws forbid him to choose the federal system. The list of exempt goods and their values, varies considerably from one State to another. It usually includes: the residence of the bankrupt up to a certain value ($50 000 in Massachusetts under the 1978 law); about 75 per cent of the salary in numerous States; a vehicle up to a certain value; personal possessions (clothes, furniture, electrical items, books, musical instruments and so on); jewels up to a certain value; financial assets up to a certain value; tools or professional instruments; life insurance policies; health insurance allowances or unemployment benefit and so on etc. In short, a certain minimal level of equipment, which many Europeans, even from the middle classes, would envy. This illustrates greater awareness of the link between social status and household equipment which guides the American model. It also highlights the relativity which must be introduced into any comparison of the two sides of the Atlantic.

In general, a person will choose the 'pure' bankruptcy when all he has left are exempt goods. His creditors will get nothing, or very little, and will have no means of legal redress. On the other hand, a minimum of six years must elapse between two 'pure' bankruptcies. However, a 'pure' bankruptcy may be followed by one or several plans of adjustment, that is bankruptcies as described in chapter 13 of the Bankruptcy Act. Finally, if a person is declared bankrupt, this fact is recorded in the individual's credit report for six years.

An individual experiencing financial difficulties may opt for an adjustment plan for the debt, again as described in chapter 13 of the Bankruptcy Act. This consists of coming to an arrangement with the creditors, under the supervision of the bankruptcy judge. The debtor undertakes to pay his debts from future earnings, with the assistance of a repayment schedule adapted to his means (exoneration of part of the debt, often ranging from 60 per cent to 80 per cent, extended repayment period and so on). In this case there is no seizure of goods. The creditor loses all rights of legal redress, at least insofar as the debtor respects the repayment schedule. Neither can the creditor accumulate interest or late payment penalties. The bankruptcy court, through the intermediary of the trustee, checks that payments are made in accordance with the adjustment plan. The administrative costs, payable by the debtor, amount to between 10 per cent and 17 per cent of the sums reimbursed.

An adjustment plan may not be followed by a 'pure' bankruptcy. This ban holds for six years, except if, in the meantime, the debtor pays off at least 70 per cent of the debt. A chapter 13 type bankruptcy may, however, be very rapidly followed by one or several bankruptcies of the same type. Such bankruptcies will be recorded in the debtor's credit report for ten years.

In practice, the implementation of the 1978 Act gave rise to numerous abuses, as courts were not always sufficiently rigorous in checking the honesty and good faith of debtors. Thus the 1984 amendments granted judges the power to refuse the protection of bankruptcy to a debtor, if it appeared that he had substantially abused the system. However, since the law was favourable to the debtor, and since the number of applications makes it difficult to check them all rigorously, abuses of the system can be curbed only by the self-imposed discipline of consumers. To encourage some level of social responsibility, a sufficiently strong sanction needs to be introduced to discourage private individuals from having recourse to the system except in cases of extreme necessity. The fact that the bankruptcy is recorded in the user's credit report and the importance of this report in American life constitutes two moderating influences. This brings us to the omnipresent system of the credit bureaux.

American credit bureaux are private organizations which collect data, and from these data they can chart the credit history of an individual (past and present loans, punctuality of repayments, incidents, bankruptcies and so on). They also collect numerous data concerning the individual's private and professional life, particularly any police or criminal record. However, they do not have access to records of bank accounts. Between them, the largest (Equifax, TRW, Trans Union) have files on hundreds of millions of consumers. The earliest credit reports date back to 1900. From 1920 on, they became generalized and all were computerized in 1965. Most credit bureaux are members of the Associated Credit Bureaux which organizes and facilitates the exchange of information between its members. Their activities are regulated by the Fair Credit Reporting Act of 1970.

The data collected by the credit bureaux play an essential role in American life. Not only will the data contained in an individual's credit report have a deciding role to play in the granting of any future loans, but they are also of major importance in gauging an individual's respectability. If one or more bankruptcy appears on the file, the sanctions are not measured purely in financial terms, as the bankrupt will often end up finding an organization which will grant a new loan. Indeed, the bankrupts market constitutes an interesting sector for certain establishments because it promises higher rates and protection against further bankruptcies. As ever, that which is intended to be a protection against certain forms of consumer intemperance is rapidly transformed by practices which are sometimes located at the extreme fringes of the market! More important, a bankrupt will have problems finding new accommodation, joining a sports club, enroling children in a private school and, of course, renewing credit cards. Moreover, the individual's work life may be seriously affected, prospects of promotion blighted and honesty called into question. However, the latest public surveys indicate that the social stigma attached to bankruptcy has been somewhat modified, and that it is no longer seen as a disgrace to file for bankruptcy.

In spite of the traditional climate against personal bankruptcy and the universal rating of households by credit bureaux, the new law caused, and continues to cause, a considerable number of bankruptcies. Has a breach been formed in the balance of the American system by accepting too many bankruptcies? The American authorities are directing present efforts at moderating some of the details of the Bankruptcy Act, rather than putting a squeeze on, or reducing the so-called overindebtedness of individuals.

If Europe is to take any lesson from recent developments in the matter of consumer credit in the United States, it may be one of caution in legislating for consumer protection.

THE CASE OF GREAT BRITAIN AND FRANCE

The latest economic turnaround in Great Britain coincided with that of the United States, though its recession was more serious and longer lasting. The first phase of the cycle began in 1983 and continued until 1989, being dominated by the growth in private domestic demand. Consumption was fed by the increase in real earnings, by reduced taxes and more easily available loans, due to the deregulation of the financial system.

Liberalization had a great effect on the real state market. Before 1980 mortgage loans were administered by building societies operating on a rationed market where interest rates were lower than those available on the free markets. Loans were not expensive but, on the other hand, applicants had to queue up to get them. In 1980 deposit control was abolished and banks entered the increasingly competitive market; the queues disappeared and interest rates became the same as those on other credit markets.

The ease of getting a mortgage loan, together with the different measures adopted to foster housing triggered a formidable speculative bubble in the sector. The bubble was shared by the whole population as the 1980s legislation of the 'right to buy' facilitated subsidized sales to tenants of public sector housing. Moreover, public spending on building new or restoring old public housing was reduced. The rental market began to shrink and young people were forced to acquire their first home earlier. The interest on mortgage loans was tax deductible (up to a ceiling of a £30 000 loan), and capital gains on property sales were not taxed if the dwelling had been occupied for at least one year. Thus, 1.3 million tenants became owners between 1980 and 1989. As a consequence of all these measures, and the speculative bubble they caused, rising property prices outstripped inflation.

Encouraged by optimistic forecasts, many households paid off their original mortgage loans after six or seven years, only to take out another larger loan which enabled them to move into a bigger home. The increasing demand caused prices to rise and the anticipated continuation of this rise caused people to buy even sooner! Households which had gone into debt to purchase their home became further indebted in order to equip it, particularly by mortgaging their capital gains. This enabled them to acquire further loans through the developing second mortgage loan system. As the value of their assets increased, they became richer, but also more vulnerable to increasing interest rates and loss of income. Saving rates showed a brutal drop and, as in any euphoric period, stock market activity was largely financed by loans.

The downturn in the economic cycle began in 1989, as a result of restrictive measures in monetary policy, taken in order to reduce growing tensions in prices and costs. The prime rate rose from 7.5 per cent in May 1988 to 15 per cent in October 1988, then maintained high levels for one year. This increase took its toll on household debt servicing, as it did on industry, and brought about a noticeable reduction of new expenditure susceptible to interest rates, particularly within the property and car sectors. The resulting drop in property prices and increases in debt servicing led to budgeting problems and a great increase in delayed payments. A large number of mortgaged properties were then repossessed, which further intensified the drop in prices. All of this – the slowing down of the economy, sluggishness on the stock exchange, and England going into general recession – was largely as a result of the desire to become home-owners, and falling for the pleasures of speculation.

In October 1990, just as the economy was going into recession and the Gulf conflict was causing a crisis in confidence, Great Britain joined the EMS (European Monetary System), while choosing an overvalued exchange rate in an effort to fight inflationary tensions! This led to a further drop in demand and a new increase in interest rates, further worsening the already heavy debts of industry.

Between early 1984 and mid-1990, the British economy had created three million jobs; between the end of 1990 and the end of 1992, a million had disappeared. The recession then transformed a large number of hitherto happily indebted households into overindebted ones. They became overindebted because of a property dream which collapsed, since the majority of British mortgage loans were at variable interest rates.

Significantly, consumer loans, which are often considered more unrestrained than property loans, had no role in causing the crisis. The increase of these loans in previous years were in no way unreasonable and they even decreased once the recession had started. The bubble which fed the illusions of British households was largely based on mortgages, and the socially disastrous spectacle of whole streets 'for sale', following repossession, has very little to do with consumer credit. However, as in other examples of recession, the risks involved in consumer loans increased greatly since the rise of the mortgage loan service first affected repayments on credit cards and then car loans! All studies are agreed on this: households with financial difficulties will continue to make repayments on the home as long as they can, at the expense of other loans. Thus, in the beginning, the property crisis in Great Britain was to be felt in the form of an increased risk for consumer credit. Which only goes to show that this type of credit is always the scapegoat for social and economic phenomena on which it has little or no influence, neither as a cause nor as a remedy.

In France, the recession was two years behind Great Britain, but it was preceded by a great increase in unemployment. It was the result of a trend which began after the second energy crisis and accelerated in the latter half of the 1980s. During this period the economy was riven by two opposed forces. On the one hand, preparations for the Single European Market and economic globalization increased competition. On the other hand, the tax burden reached one of the highest levels of the great industrialized countries. All other things being equal, this reduced competitiveness. In spite of this, the slow increase in salaries and the moderating effect it had on cost enabled French products to remain competitive for a while. However, at the beginning of the 1990s, the European economy began to slow up considerably. French companies, confronted with high social contributions, a strong franc and astronomic real interest rates, were sorely hit by international competition. At the same time, the speculative bubble which, as in other countries, had developed in the property sector, burst. Companies reduced their investments which had become too expensive, and laid off workers in order to increase competitiveness. The symbolic threshold of three million unemployed was reached in the very same quarter as the downturn in early 1993, and poverty, which had practically disappeared since the 1960s, reappeared in France, as it did in the rest of Europe.

From the end of 1992 onwards, this economic climate generated a distinct decrease in household consumption. This was further compounded by an increase in social charges on wages. The result was a reduction in the level of household debts and the expansion of precautionary savings. Consumer credit cannot be accused of having any responsibility in these phenomena; nor is it accused, in contrast with what happened on previous occasions. This seems to prove that the collective mind has learned how to better analyze economic problems, after the veritable catharsis provoked three years earlier by the debate surrounding the Neiertz Law on overindebtedness. The public seems to have become acclimatized to the idea that consumer credit is an instrument which poses no great threat to either public morals or to the equilibrium of society.

The French recession, which began at the end of 1992, is not, however, without effect on the budgeting of indebted households. As a result of unemployment, in particular, and the loss of rights to unemployment benefit, the number of cases appealing to the Departmental Commissions for overindebtedness has increased considerably.

OVERINDEBTEDNESS AS A SYMPTOM

A study conducted by the CREDOC in 1992, before the recession set in, showed that the French are very attached to the idea of credit. Studies conducted in other industrialized countries show the same results. But, although everyone is willing to admit that it would be very difficult to live in today's world without credit, it can also be very difficult to live with it.

There are many different reasons why some households have difficulties in meeting their payments. Some stem from personal behaviour: poor family budgeting; unbridled consumerism or social problems such as gambling, drug taking, alcoholism and so on. But, above all else, it is family break-up in the form of divorce or separation which is responsible for a sudden imbalance which results in overindebtedness. A loan, which a couple could easily handle in the context of self-actualization, or achievement as the

Americans would have it, becomes an impossible burden after the couple has separated. Firstly, because fixed costs often increase (two households instead of one) and secondly because outstanding loans, the symbols of a happier past, often become the objects of emotional wrenching. Nearly a half of the 600 000 files of overindebtedness in France stem from family restructuring of this type.

A quarter of overindebtedness arise from households where the income is too low; where they cannot 'make ends meet'. Cases of real poverty account for 8 per cent, while small earnings or unemployment benefit account for 16 per cent. Some people, when they take out a loan, overestimate their resources or underestimate the full amount of the repayments. It is the role of the financial establishments to inform potential borrowers so that they realise the limits of their own budgets. In order to do so, however, the loan candidate must enter into this 'dialogue' and abstain from providing false data concerning income.

Similarly, some households try to 'live beyond their means'. Such people have always existed, but they make up only a small fraction of risky loans. Over-consumers have long been considered as going hand in hand with consumer society, which constantly develops new temptations. Serious British studies (Berthoud and Kempson, 1992) show that the problem is really very small, consisting for the most part of well-to-do, usually young households, who manage to find the means to solve any problems that may arise. In this context (which were frowned upon by French financial establishments), numerous applications filed for overindebtedness just after the Neiertz Law was passed. Many were filed by relatively well-to-do people who hoped that the Departmental Commissions would give them a way out of repaying their loans. A certain 'beat the system' Press actively encouraged readers to take such steps, suggesting that they had nothing to lose, and everything to gain. From one point of view we can see that it is the old anti-credit morality on the march again, although on the other it is nothing less than incitement to fraud – and it was heeded by a certain portion of the population, notable among them were civil servants or young executives, eager to make a quick buck by any means at their disposal! It would be hard to find a better mixture of social and philosophical hypocrisy. Fortunately, such excessive behaviour did not last long. But let us note the extreme fragility of the balance involved in consumer credit.

Some of the most painful causes of true overindebtedness are of an economic nature. They may be permanent or temporary. Poverty or insufficient income belong in the first category, while unemployment or illness (when there is no health insurance, as is sometimes the case in the United

States) make up the second category. Thus, periods of crisis or recession contribute massively to the risk of overindebtedness. At such times, the bodies set up to deal with the problem, such as the laws for private bankruptcy in the United States or the Neiertz Commissions in France, fulfil their true social vocation. At other times, the same bodies may be confronted with, or even cause, a total lack of responsibility on the part of the public. Such an attitude is disastrous, both economically and socially.

Changes in the conditions governing loan granting, or loan management, may also have an effect on overindebtedness. Deregulation of financial institutions, when it causes a great increase in competition, may encourage the credit institutions to take all sorts of risks in order to win a share of the market, or quite simply to maintain their position. Loans which are too easily available may thus lead to an abnormal increase in credit. Some households are tempted by this and take out more and more loans in order to meet their repayments. We have seen it time and again in recent years, either in the form of mortgage consolidation of typical consumer debts, as in Great Britain and the United States, or in France in the form of an irresponsible wave emanating from commercial banks. Some lending techniques also increase the risk of overindebtedness: increasing monthly repayments, as it was widely practised in property loans, because it relied on inflationary salary increases, are still, today, one of the causes of imbalances in family budgets because, in fact, salaries increased at a slower rate.

Finally, when the very laws governing overindebtedness are too lax they can cause a sort of overindebtedness on the part of irresponsible individuals ('big spenders' of all sorts) who find a means to avoid paying their debts by really becoming overindebted. The laws can also arouse the interest of 'fraudsters', as seen in the United States when the Bankruptcy Act was reviewed and in France as soon as the Neiertz Law came into effect.

Although the psycho-sociological nature of the phenomenon makes it extremely difficult to define, American, and more recent French, studies indicate that credit which is made available too easily, or promoted too actively through the media, produces a diminished desire to repay on the part of more economically fragile customers. The day-to-day experience of the Neiertz Departmental Commissions is revealing in this respect: in a large number of cases (excluding life accidents), the profile of the overindebted, whether we view them from a socio-occupational angle or in terms of available income after fixed costs have been paid, differs little from that of the majority of borrowers who continue to make their repayments to term. A deeper examination of the phenomenon, through further quality studies, reveals that the feeling of being overindebted comes as a result of a sudden lack of will-power. In other words, at a given moment, people give up. Let there be no misunderstanding on this point. We are not denying the socially necessary role of institutions like the French Departmental Commissions when it comes to life accidents or, with depressing frequency, problems of total poverty (in which cases electricity, local taxes or children's meals are more important than consumer credit). Rather, we are pointing out an attitude which is typified by a loss of ability to deal with day-to-day budget difficulties. This attitude pertains in some households, and too much regulatory laxity increases its frequency. When it comes to family budgeting, if the safety net is too reliable it can produce a kind of psychological reassurance in certain sectors of the population. Since family budgeting is at the heart of social integration, we may well wonder whether, except in cases of life accidents, the effect of too much consumer protection is not more perverse than beneficial.

That apart, there is a great temptation, when problems of overindebtedness arise, to lay the blame at the doors of the credit establishments; sure scapegoats in this type of situation. Naturally, the creditors should be held responsible, as should the debtors, but creditors cannot, on their own, provide an answer to problems, the causes of which are not connected to them, any more than are the solutions. Moreover, when seen in the context of great economic balances, household overindebtedness seems to be a myth, useful to hide political and social flaws. However, it is obvious that it constitutes a social problem which worsens in times of crisis. Thanks to the regulations which exclude certain forms of abuse, and thanks, in particular, to the good management techniques of credit – overindebtedness is only fractional in terms of the number of loans. When it does appear, it is more often than not the consequence of an unfortunate event outside the domain of credit (divorce, unemployment, illness), rather than a social sin. In this respect, overindebtedness is more in the order of a symptom than a disease in itself.

Contrary to a popularly held belief, credit institutions do not earn money by managing their defaulted accounts. They lose money. Such losses can sometimes even pose a threat to their very existence, especially if they are specialists, and small to medium in size. It is therefore very much in their own interest to be selective in granting loans, by using modern credit scoring techniques, by consulting credit registers, and by conducting rigorous budget studies of their customers. The proportion of credits refused depends naturally on the type of credit in question: it is about 15 per cent for hire-purchase domestic appliances, and can rise to 50 per cent and even higher for personal loans. This gives an indication of the extreme vigilance of specialist institutions, and of their awareness that their own interest lies in a customer who makes his repayments, and who never feels overindebted.

In the event of an accident, they also know how to find a solution for most of their customers. A part of their financial margin is used to cover such risks. It is very small, ranging between 1.5 per cent and 3 per cent in France, and a little higher in Great Britain and the United States. This is an indication of the small size of the overindebtedness phenomenon, both socially and economically. Consumer credit is still one of the greatest instruments of social integration. In order for it to function economically, the institutions controlling it must follow the laws of the market. In other words, profitability and solvency. Credit institutions are not charitable organizations. They cannot take responsibility for 'all the misery in the world'. In spite of their productivity efforts, the margins within which they work are very narrow and becoming narrower. It is a common error to think that consumer credit could become a substitute for public assistance. This old reflex of the *monts-de-piétés* still lives on today in the attitude of certain alternative economies, as in the example of the recent 'Banking for people' movement, which proposed a sort of neo-mutuality, comparable to a credit 'social security'!

When overindebtedness occurs as the result of economic policies which were unable to curb either unemployment or a depression, then the only real solution is to put the economy back on the road to growth. Everything else is either social illusion or poor political faith. It is a poor doctor who treats only the symptoms.

REFERENCES

AKHTAR M.A. and E.S. HARRIS, 'The Supply-Side Consequences of U.S. Fiscal Policy in the 1980s', *FRB of New York*, Vol. 17, No. 1, Spring 1992.

ANOSIKE, B.O. *How to Declare your Personal Bankruptcy without a Lawyer,* New York: Do-it-Yourself Legal Publishers, 1983.

BIS, Annual Reports.

BERTHOUD R. and E. KEMPSON, *Credit and Debt: the PSI Report*, London: Policy Studies Institute, 1992.

BROWNE L.E. and E.S. ROSENGREN, 'Real State and the Credit Crunch: An Overview', *New England Economic Review*, FRB of Boston, November–December 1992.

CANNER, G.B. and C.A. LUCKET, 'Home Equity Lending', *Federal Reserve Bulletin*, May 1989.

CANNER, G.B. and C.A. LUCKET, 'Payment of Household Debts', *Federal Reserve Bulletin*, April 1991.

CANNER, G.B. and C.A. LUCKET 'Developments in the Pricing of Credit Card Services', *Federal Reserve Bulletin*, September 1992.

CASE, K.E. 'The Real State Cycle and the Economy: Consequences of the Massachussets Boom of 1984–87', *New England Economic Review*, FRB of Boston, September–October 1991.

CHRISTELOW, D.B. *Converging Household Debt Ratios of Four Industrial Countries*, FRBNY, Vol. 12, No. 4. Winter, 1987–88.

CNAF, 'Consommer et s'endetter' (consuming and setting into debt), *Informations sociales*, No. 2–3, 1989.

J.O. COOK and R. WOOL, *All you need to know about banks*, New York: Bantam Books, 1984.

CREDOC, 'Les Français et le crédit en janvier 1992', *Banque Stratégie*, No. 84, May 1992.

DEFOURNY, P. 'La loi Neiertz:un premier bilan', *La revue du financier*, No. 87, July–August 1992.

European Community Commission: *Economic Papers, Country Studies, The United Kingdom*, July 1990 and March 1991, Brussels.

EUGENI, F. 'Consumer debt and home equity borrowing', *Economic Perspectives*, FRB of Chicago, March 1993.

FORD, J. *The indebted Society: credit and default in the 1980's*, London: Routledge, 1988.

GABRIEL, S.A. 'Housing and Mortgage Markets: The Post-1982 Expansion', *Federal Reserve Bulletin*, December 1987.

GELPI, R.M. *Els Estats Units i l'economia mundial: evolucions estructurals, politiques conjunturals*, Societat Catalana d'Economia: *Anuari*, Vol. 6, Barcelona, 1987.

HOÖRMANN, G. (ed.), *Consumer Credit and Consumer Insolvency*, RFA: Bremen, 1986.

HULS, N. (ed.), *Overindebtedness of Consumers in the EC Member States: Facts and Search for Solutions*, Leyden Institute for Law and Public Policy, Netherlands: Leyden, September 1982.

JOHNSON, 'The Bank Credit "Crumble" ', FRBNY, *Quarterly Review*, Vol. 16, No. 2, Summer 1991.

KENNICKELL A. and SHACK-MARQUEZ, J. 'Changes in Family Finances from 1983 to 1989: Evidence from the Survey of Consumer Finances', *Federal Reserve Bulletin*, January 1991.

LUCKETT, C.A. 'Personal Bankruptcies', *Federal Reserve Bulletin*, September 1988.

MORNET, F. *Justice et recouvrement de l'impayé*, Paris: Documentation française, 1980.

McNEES, S.K. 'The 1990–91 Recession in Historical Perspective', *New England Economic Review*, FRB of Boston, January–February 1992.

OECD, Economic Studies: *United States*, Paris, several years.

OECD, Economic Studies: *Great Britain*, Paris, several years.

OECD, 'Private indebtedness', *Financial Market Trends*, October 1992.

PAQUETTE, 'Estimating Household Debt Service Payments', Federal Reserve Bank of New York, *Quarterly review*, Volume 11, No. 2, Summer 1986.

PEEK, J. and E.S. ROSENGREN, 'The Capital Crunch in New England', *New England Economic Review*, FRB of Boston, May–June 1992.

POLLAN, S.M. *How to Borrow Money*, New York: Simon & Schuster, Inc., 1983.
RAVIER, M. *Le crédit mode d'emploi*, Paris: Nathan, 1984.
REIFNER, U. and J. FORD, *Banking for People*, Berlin and New York: Walter de Gruyter, 1992.
SPIRE, A. (ed.), *L'argent, pour une réhabilitation morale*, Paris: Autrement No. 132, 1992.

Conclusion

Consumer credit, or its equivalent, has always been a central preoccupation of society: from ancient times, when it was one of the signs of the transition from the traditional clan system of gifts and barter to the first forms of urbanization, right up to modern times, and its role in Western industrial society as a corollary of the material well-being of households. Hence its importance in social and economic history, hence also its role in the history of ideas. Curiously enough, where there ought to be a concomitance between theory and practice, the subject has given rise to a millennary controversy. There seems to be a sort of social schizophrenia whereby the day-to-day indispensable practices of collective life are accepted on the one hand, while being condemned on the other, in the name of philosophical ideals. There can hardly be a more deep-rooted and widely accepted example of such a prejudice.

It is only in recent years that a slow process of legitimation has begun to take place, with public discussions organized around the drawing up of laws to regulate the sector. The process began in the United States where, thanks to the mobilization of the different parties concerned, ideas, arguments, counter arguments and pleas were produced against a backdrop of in-depth university research, thus bringing the legitimation to its conclusion. Nor does this mean that there are no longer any problems, but that American society treats them in an objective fashion, freed of the guilt complex which still dictates positions everywhere else.

The American experience is central to the history of consumer credit. From the sewing machines of the frontier to the ubiquitous credit bureaux, from loan sharks to the abuses of personal bankruptcy, from the invention of hire purchase to the advent of credit cards, there is no better reference than this immense and multifarious market. To realize the truth of this statement we only have to look at the way European professionals periodically return to sources in the United States. We only have to look at the way the detractors of credit, also European, seize upon what they see as market excesses in order to build up a negative image. Consumer credit in America is therefore both an inspiration as regards the services it offers, and a scarecrow in the domain of consumerism. This double image constitutes the latest incarnation of the ideological arguments which have always clouded reality.

Each significant step in the history of credit, or of consumer credit in particular, has been in relation to a centre of economic progress. What was

169

true for the Code of Hammurabi was true for the ecclesiastical records of Catalonia during the Visigoth period, for the scholastic arrangements of Saint Antonin of Florence, or for Bentham's struggle against the fixed ceilings of usury – and remains true today for the social legitimation which characterizes the United States.

Techniques and products have advanced considerably faster and more radically in the United States than in the rest of the world. For centuries, consumer credit amounted to no more than bridging loans: the main idea was that of necessity, of getting over a difficult period, in a word, bridging. The market, being officially more or less obscure was therefore widely abused (it was Bentham who introduced the 'therefore'). The result was the double failure of the pawnbroking system in England, with its social role as lifesaver, and the French *mont-de-piété*, with its notion of charity.

In contrast with this consolidation of the past, the United States offered to build the future, equipping the household by means of hire purchase sales. The central idea changed from that of getting over a momentary budgetary difficulty to ensuring comfort and social status through equipping the household. However, the car is the greatest example of this change in attitude. Consumer credit then became the business of the salesperson, builder or distributor. The market terms and trade jargon spoke of 'captives' (associated with a builder, usually in the car industry) and private agents (associated with a distributor, usually a department store). What had previously been reserved for times of family financial difficulties became progressively a reasonable means of purchasing goods, developing along with the idea of a monthly salary: good household budgeting evolved in relation to the monthly salary and monthly instalments on major family purchases. The old social model of family equipping through inheritance was replaced by that of personal acquisition. As a corollary of this, credit became commonplace among young couples, precisely the people who need to equip themselves for life.

Then, from the 1960s onwards, family equipping became more diversified: the importance of a sewing machine in a log cabin or of a car in the post-war period ceased to have their social status but more the answer to a need. Consumption fragmented into different needs, not all of which were material: interior decor, travel, culture, education, even health. This development became more and more perceptible, and was reflected by a profound change in credit. Hire purchase sales were perfectly suited to a certain specific domain. Different forms of personal loans and credit cards corresponded better to new ways of being and consuming. Family budgeting ceased to be a crutch for getting over difficult periods, and became the symbol of the freedom and independence of the household.

This trend was to accelerate. The periodic lamentations heard over the years about declining consumption are really, once we take into account the effects of the economic situation, only the signs of a stubborn refusal to see new life trends. Yesterday's status symbols were the car and the stainless steel kitchen, today's are travel and sport; culture, pure and simple, is already beginning to emerge as tomorrow's status symbol. Consumer credit, with its more varied and adaptable forms, seems ready to embrace the future.

These new forms have specific consequences: the development of the personal loan, in its broadest sense (be it a credit card or traditional durables), is directly related to the technique of credit scoring, which sums up the household's ability to repay a loan. The fact that the central element in this scoring system is stability (of employment, of bank account and of residence), is an indication of the prudence of credit professionals and of the social role of consumer credit.

Secondly, personal loans correspond to the arrival of banks in this market. The French example at the end of the 1980s is a good illustration of the great innocence of newcomers in the matter of risk evaluation. Be that as it may, the progressive trend from credit, associated with the purchase of a specific object, therefore in the majority of cases negotiated at the point of sale, to a more generic credit, based on the internal equilibrium of family budgeting, is one of the best indicators of the degree of advancement of the market. The more of this generic credit there is, the more credit is integrated in all classes of society, the greater its legitimation. In this respect, the United States, Germany and Benelux lead the way with less than 10 per cent of credit granted at the point of sale, against about a quarter in France and England and a third in Italy.

The usefulness of consumer credit resides in its ability to integrate families, to finance their equipping and give them social status. In a word, self-actualization. This was exactly the conclusion of the reports of the official American and British authorities, particularly the noteworthy *Crowther Report* in 1971: credit is one of the greatest promoters of social mobility. Even in the old days of bridging loans, it constituted a safety net in the event of unforeseen accidents. Hire purchase sales then transformed it to equip households. Thanks to this, millions of newly urbanized families were able to acquire a minimum of life comfort from the outset. Then came a veritable life fulfilment as the well-being of what was called consumer society developed and, as a corollary, the techniques and products of credit, now also called consumer credit.

In the 1920s the automobile and domestic appliance industries gave shape to the phenomenon. From 1950 onwards, all of society was enjoying the results. Sociologists define achievement, itself so intimately related to the notion of good family budgeting, as being the prime American model. Corresponding with the concept of achievement, is the trend of society towards the middle classes, a sort of generalized achievement, based on consumption and its financing. People speak today of the obvious link between the level of economic development and democracy. The same consideration could be applied going from the micro to macro: the level of family economic development, which is generously facilitated by credit, is the best indication of a balanced society.

This adaptation of credit is the result of a process which is characterized by its slowness and much backtracking. One of the interesting things to come to the fore, in this historical review of consumer credit, is the fact that its social utility is constantly scapegoated as soon as society, for one reason or another, enters a period of difficulty. The Biblical bans came into being at a time of brutal change in society, just as the condemnations of the Church Fathers were born out of the decadence of the Empire. More recently, each cyclical recession sees moralists raise their voices to proclaim the old anti-credit refrain. In periods of inflation, it is condemned; when deflation comes, it is expected to perform miracles! In both cases, without a shadow of a doubt, and leaving aside the modesty shown by those who practise it on a day-to-day basis: it is not credit that sets consumption in motion, rather, it is consumption that calls credit into being.

In the Middle Ages, the plague was reason enough to have the local usurers hanged. In recent years it has become fashionable to point the finger at the credit crunch as one of the major causes of unemployment. As soon as society experiences a crisis of any kind, credit is blamed: it is so much easier to focus on the symptom, and blame it for all the vices of the world.... Moreover, trotting out the old prejudices is an apparently enriching exercise, insofar as it is basically reassuring. Each new occasion brings a flood of stereotypes which, of course, are modified with time. Saint Basil's viper has given way to today's overindebtors. But the fundamental image remains poor, even loathsome. This is particularly true of Europe, as if the repeated echoes of Church excommunications were still resounding down through the ages. This very nearly pernicious reputation is particularly reserved for establishments specializing in credit, whereas banks are spared, due to their other products although, paradoxically, they generally have the lion's share of the consumer credit market!

What we have is a strange love–hate relationship, a constant battle between a prejudicial image and a totally different reality! In fact, this image is inherited from two philosophical currents which give it its negative connotations. The first derives from the Biblical tradition. It concerns credit itself, as soon as it engenders interest. The second concerns consumption seen as destruction, in accordance with the principles put forward by *Goodman Richard*.

At the end of the 1960s, the favourite activity of the advertising department of the biggest French consumer credit company consisted of avoiding the word 'crédit'. They spoke instead of financing, of loans, staggered payments, easy repayment terms, and so on. Moreover, great care was taken to use blank envelopes in correspondence, in order to avoid tarnishing the reputation of the client by association with a credit company! This attitude continued until a new marketing department realized that it is always better to use real words than insincere rhetoric.

Over 30 years the term 'crédit' has entered into daily usage, almost regaining its etymological meaning of 'credere', to believe (in the future). The old bans are no more than reminders, a sort of tunic of Nessus which is commonly associated with credit: credit is expensive. There has been a rush of recent legislation about 'publishing interest rates', all in the same tone: under the pretext of financial clarity, interest rates which appear unreal to the ordinary man must be made public. The result is that even professionals have begun to 'socially downgrade' the status of their job.

The basic problem, in terms of the public image of credit, lies in the fact that it is difficult to understand that money is bought and paid for with money. Which of course means that those offering credit must market their product almost exclusively in terms of the object financed. The only really positive progress in the debate is that today people distrust free credit as something which is likely to be misleading, in the context of open competition, or to hide some other manipulation. This constitutes a total overthrow of biblical commandments.

The second negative image concerns consumption itself. Most dictionaries define 'consume' as 'to destroy by wasting'. Ever since Benjamin Franklin, a large part of European awareness focuses around the idea of destruction rather than usage. The word 'consumption' is nevertheless traditionally retained by most economic aggregates. And, for many thinkers, it is this aggregate which characterizes the recent history of Western society, the so-called consumer society.

Today, criticism has begun to re-emerge from the collective subconscious: on the one hand, though limited, there is the fundamentalism of the rejection of the golden calf, while on the other, there is the much more widespread avoidance of exclusion. These trends can only be intensified by the present crisis which, beyond cyclical depression, has an effect on social equilibrium through the development of unemployment. It is nonetheless true that the material well-being resulting from consumer society has not, with few exceptions, been called into question. Its distribution, as well as some of its more extravagant forms, has been.

This is why French professionals now prefer to speak of home equipment credit. But the niceness of their terminology comes back on them in an insidious manner: in a world where the basic counter-power of everyday life is made up of 'consumer' associations, and where family equipping is more and more a matter of budgeting and associated products, such as credit cards, they are obviously suspected of manipulation. They themselves do not realize that in the unlikely event of their formula becoming more acceptable than that of 'consumer credit', it would trap them into market practices which are today disappearing.

This fear of the negative connotations of the word 'consumption' is like that attached to the word 'credit' 30 years ago. The sense of the term is just as limited and just as indicative of old, ill-received guilt feelings and thereby reveals precisely what it sets out to hide. The more consumer credit tries to disguise itself, as in the days of the bans on money lending, the more it awakens the old demons; and the more it presents itself in simple everyday terms, the greater the chance that it will be taken quite simply for what it is: a tool at the disposal of household budgets.

Indeed, if there is a danger, a new danger in relation to the public image of consumer credit, it is in relation to the social exclusion of which it might become a symbol. This, in turn, relates to the notion of family equipment. Following on the excess of overindebtedness – one of the main symptoms of the recession for families – comes insufficiency: if unemployment persists, the future horizon may well hold a sort of dual society. Then, it is pretty much sure that a sort of credit support system would come into being (much like the present day income support system). This update of the right to credit is being worked out by the most active consumer associations of Northern Europe, under the heading 'Banking for people' (the social role of credit being pushed to its limits by institutions of a neo-mutualist type). This is one of the current subjects of reflection for the American administration, in the form of 'politically correct' ratios, obliging lenders to exclude no minority. Here again, consumer credit, or rather its image, could become the scapegoat of a social situation with which it has nothing or little to do.

The Americans, with their sense of the concrete, have found the appropriate term: the credit crunch. Extended to the techniques for studying personal loans it would arise, not from the lack of liquidity of the lender but from the insolvency of some of their potential borrowers.

Of course the prime vocation of consumer credit is social integration, but it is certainly not a charitable institution. The regulations governing it have always aimed at avoiding abuse of the system. In the Code of Hammurabi, the protection of the faulty debtor who had become the slave of his creditor was central to the debate. Most other ancient laws concerned the maximum legal rate of interest. In contemporary legislation, (which is sometimes born on the fringe of the market, as in the case of the 1957 Belgian law concerning loading rates or the 1978 French law concerning information available to the borrower) the most important thing is usually the definition and the advertising of interest rates, often the regulatory ceiling, the formalities of contracts, consideration time available to the consumer, responsibility of the parties, particularly the salesperson, as well as the details of the contract (redemption before due date, late payment allowance, role of the courts and so on).

The trend in recent years, particularly in the United States, but also in France, has been to legislate in the domain of recovery; firstly to avoid abuse (Japan leads the field in this respect), secondly to offer the consumer a certain means of withdrawal on the pretext of overindebtedness. In France there are the Neiertz Commissions, and personal bankruptcy in the United States. Here, in an insidious manner, the notion of assistance makes its appearance. It operates on two levels: it makes the lenders bear the costs of a social situation for which they are little or not at all responsible. This means that they assist some of their customers at the expense of others who pay for this in higher rates. For borrowers, there is the danger of a certain irresponsibility, not to mention downright dishonesty.

In such a socially sensitive sector as consumer credit, it would seem that the most recent French and American laws have reached a limit. They have unquestionably introduced more humane solutions to a certain number of cases of objective overindebtedness, while treating the different creditors in a more equitable fashion (although those of a public status retain privileges which are curious to say the least, in a domain which is so close to social work). On the other hand, they may well have shaken an essential psycho-sociological balance, that of individual responsibility in social integration. This seems to be indicated by certain attitudes of facility on the part of households since personal bankruptcy was reviewed in the United States and its French equivalent introduced by Véronique Neiertz. Against that, American credit bureaux have started to evoke the idea of generalized rating of families, along the lines of the rating system used for companies, which we know from experience to have a remarkably energizing and moralizing effect, in spite of a few minor inconveniences. On the one hand, a sort of social discouragement is actively promoted, while the statistical evaluation of achievement is encouraged on the other. Consumer credit has not yet finished measuring the state of health of society.

We must be prudent in this type of observation: we are, of necessity, looking at the long-term. It is nevertheless striking that the questions arising in an analysis of consumer credit should be of such a social nature. In the 1920s, they focused around industrial distribution, and around monetary equilibrium during 'les trente glorieuses'. In the last 20 years, the questions have revolved around social problems.

The long public debate which marked the first two phases led to the economic legitimation of consumer credit; consequently, the principal actors were recognized, therefore given greater responsibility. Let us be optimistic, as this stroll through history teaches us to be. Present day questioning will be fruitful if it leads to greater household responsibility in relation to their future in society. The time is no longer very far away when the head of the household will, with reason, be able to be considered the entrepreneur of the basic social cell. Consumer credit, among many other products and services, will have had its own role to play in this process.

Appendix 1

THE IMAGE OF CREDIT IN PROVERBS

Taken from the *Dictionnaire de proverbs et dictons* – les usuels du Robert, Paris: Le Robert, 1993 and from *Proverbes et dictons catalans*, collected by H. Guiter, edited by R. Monel, 1969.

Borrowing is the firstborn of poverty. (African)
A bad loan is like a broken mirror. (American)
Debts are the scissors of friendship. (Arab)
Lending fosters hatred. (Arab)
He who weds in debt pays interest with his children. (Arab)
He who seeks payment of an old debt seeks a new argument. (Catalan)
Borrowing begets repayment. (Catalan)
In an indebted household the harvest has no effect. (Catalan)
He who buys more than he can afford must later sell all. (Catalan)
He who takes charge of debts takes charge of misery. (Catalan)
A hundred thoughts never paid a debt. (Catalan)
What is bought on credit costs dearly. (Catalan)
He who owes, and pays, grows rich. (Catalan)
He who pays what he owes amasses wealth for his inheritors. (Catalan)
He who pays has credit. (Catalan)
No year is good for an indebted farmer. (Catalan)
Interest is a dangerous animal. (Catalan)
He who borrows to build must sell to repay. (Catalan)
He who borrows and pays his debts lives on his wealth. (Catalan)
Pay what you owe and you will know what you have. (Catalan)
Even Lent is short for the debtor. (Catalan)
Credit banishes custom. (Chinese)
Shame fades passes, but debts remain. (Chinese)
Ten francs of tears does not pay ten centimes of debts. (Corsican)
Payment today, credit tomorrow. (Creole)
Long suffering never paid a debt. (Dutch)
He who pays with another's money is buying trouble. (English)
Better to give a shilling than lend a pound. (English)
Speak not of my debts, unless you wish to pay them. (English)
Lend to a friend, and lose both money and friend. (English)
He who lends to a friend loses both or gains both. (French)
A borrower is always a friend, a debtor an enemy. (French)
    Variations:
        A borrower is always kin, a debtor a whoreson.
        A borrower is always an angel, a debtor a devil.
Lending money loses memory. (French)
He who lends a needle without a pledge cannot sew. (French)
A loan is not an advance. (French)

The borrower cannot choose. (French)
He who owes, owns nothing. (French)
 Older variation :
 He who has a hundred and owes a hundred, has nothing.
Bad debtors make bad lenders. (French)
A hundred pounds of melancholy never paid a sou of debts. (French)
He who owes asks for more. (French)
Better old debts than a new melon. (French)
He who pays his debts grows rich. (French)
 Older variation :
 He who pays his debts acquires much.
What is good to borrow is good to return. (French) '
Better buy than borrow. (French)
He who leaves a blacksmith must pay for old horseshoes. (French)
Better old debts than old bitterness. (Gaelic)
Regrets never paid debts. (German)
Three things enter a house without knocking : debts, old age
 and death. (German)
Better master of a sou than slave of two. (Greek)
Even an old loan is not a gift. (Hungarian)
Debt is the worst poverty. (Indian)
Credit is dead, bad debtors killed it. (Italian)
There is no such thing as a good loan. (Jewish)
Pay your debts before you become a lender. (Jewish)
A thousand thoughts never paid a single debt. (Jewish)
Old debts are never paid, new debts grow old. (Latin-American)
To borrow – a friend, to pay back – an enemy. (Lithuanian)
Debts make thieves. (Madagascan)
The debtors door is always watched by a fierce dog. (Madagascan)
Debts are husbands to men. (Persian)
Of these four things we have more than we think: sins, debts,
 years and enemies. (Persian)
Better die of hunger than live in debt. (Persian)
Neither owe to the rich nor lend to the poor. (Portuguese)
The greatest virtue of a debtor is to pay his debts. (Russian)
Who drinks on credit is twice drunk. (Serbo-Croate)
Borrowed money disappears laughing and returns crying. (Turkish)
A thousand tears never paid a debt. (Turkish)

Appendix 2

Table A.2   Consumer credit in the principal industrialized countries 1992–5

	Consumer credit outstanding				Rate of growth (%)			Consumer credit outstanding/ disposable income of households (%)			
	1992	1993	1994	1995	1992/3	1993/4	1994/5	1992	1993	1994	1995
SPAIN (billions of pesetas)	5 004	5 368	5 408	5756	7.3	0.7	6.4	12.2	12.1	11.8	–
UNITED STATES (billions of $)	802	864	989	1132	7.7	14.5	14.4	17.8	18.0	19.7	21.3
FRANCE (billions of FF)	378	383	394	409	1.3	2.8	3.8	7.8	7.7	7.7	7.6
ITALY (billions of lira)	34 588	32 513	32 712	36 132	–6.0	3.7	7.2	3.0	2.9	3.0	2.8
JAPAN* (billions of yen)	71 538	74 105	74 911	74 800	3.6	1.1	–0.1	23.2	23.4	ˆ23.2	22.7
NETHERLANDS (billions of florins)	20	20.5	21.4	22.1	2.5	4.3	3.8	5.7	5.8	5.8	–
WEST GERMANY (billions of deutschmark)	324	346	363	371	6.5	5.1	2.0	16.1	16.5	16.9	16.6
UNITED KINGDOM (bilions of £)	53.5	53.3	58	65	–0.4	8.9	12.0	12.3	11.6	12.3	–

*excluding loans for housing; *Source:* International Department of Cetelem, 1997.

Appendix 3

Table A.3 Consumer credit margins

Net commission	12.6
Net refunding cost	−4.4
Financial margin	8.2
Overheads	−3.6
Cost of risk	−0.9
Miscellaneous	−0.3
Profit before taxes	3.4

(production margins as a % of average outstanding consumer credit for a French group specialising in consumer credit, end 1997)

Index